Islamic Finance

Law, Economics, and Practice

This book provides an overview of the practice of Islamic finance and the historical roots that define its modes of operation. The focus of the book is analytical and forward-looking. It shows that Islamic finance exists primarily today as a form of rent-seeking legal arbitrage. An alternative that emphasizes substance rather than form would serve religious and moral objectives better, through mutual and similar financial practices.

Mahmoud A. El-Gamal is Professor of Economics and Statistics at Rice University, where he holds the endowed Chair in Islamic Economics, Finance, and Management. Prior to joining Rice in 1998, he had been an associate professor of Economics at the University of Wisconsin at Madison and an assistant professor of Economics at California Institute of Technology and the University of Rochester. He has also served in the Middle East Department of the International Monetary Fund (1995–6) and as the first Scholar in Residence on Islamic Finance at the U.S. Department of the Treasury in 2004. He has published extensively in the areas of econometrics, finance, experimental economics, and Islamic law and finance.

Islamic Finance

Law, Economics, and Practice

Mahmoud A. El-Gamal

Rice University

CAMBRIDGE
UNIVERSITY PRESS

CAMBRIDGE UNIVERSITY PRESS
Cambridge, New York, Melbourne, Madrid, Cape Town, Singapore, São Paulo

Cambridge University Press
32 Avenue of the Americas, New York, NY 10013-2473, USA

www.cambridge.org
Information on this title: www.cambridge.org/9780521864145

First published 2006

Printed in the United States of America

A catalog record for this publication is available from the British Library.

Library of Congress Cataloging in Publication Data

El-Gamal, Mahmoud A., 1963–
Islamic finance : law, economics, and practice / Mahmoud A. El-Gamal.
p.   cm.
Includes bibliographical references and index.
ISBN 0-521-86414-3 (hardback)
1. Banking law (Islamic law).   2. Business enterprises – Finance – Law and legislation –
Islamic countries.   3. Securities.   4. Finance – Religious aspects – Islam.   5. Economics –
Religious aspects – Islam.   I. Title.
KBP940.E45   2006
332.0917'67–dc22   2006005127

ISBN-13   978-0-521-86414-5 hardback
ISBN-10   0-521-86414-3 hardback

To
Father
& Mother,
who taught me
that religious forms
should continually serve
their central moral substance

Contents

List of Illustrations

Preface

In recent years, financial activities conducted under the banner of "Islamic finance" have grown significantly in volume and scope, attracting significant attention worldwide. Numerous books and articles have been published on the topic over the past few decades. Their genres have ranged from highly religious treatises on Islamic law and worldview to highly practical surveys of the latest Islamic financial products to reach the market. Why, one must ask, should one read – let alone write – another book on the subject?

This book provides a qualitative overview of the practice of Islamic finance and the historical roots that have defined its modes of operation. The purpose of the book is not to survey the latest developments in this fast-growing industry. In the current information age, such information is best obtained on the Internet, since it requires updating at rates far exceeding the publication cycles of books and journal articles.

The focus of this book is analytical and forward-looking. I show that, despite the good intentions of its pioneers, Islamic finance has placed excessive emphasis on contract forms, thus becoming a primary target for rent-seeking legal arbitrageurs. In every aspect of finance – from personal loans to investment banking, and from market structure to corporate governance of financial institutions – Islamic finance aims to replicate in Islamic forms the substantive functions of contemporary financial instruments, markets, and institutions.

This supposed Islamization of contemporary financial practice is accomplished by means of modified premodern financial contracts (such as sales, leases, and simple partnerships). The contracts are designed by teams of (1) financial professionals who make and cater to the market for "Islamic" products, (2) lawyers who are skilled in the art of regulatory arbitrage, and (3) jurists or religious scholars who are familiar with medieval juristic texts (mostly in Arabic) and provide certification of the Islamicity of various financial products and services.

To make the classical juristic literature (on which the industry is built) accessible to English-reading audiences, I have provided a translation of one of the most comprehensive surveys of classical Islamic jurisprudence and its contemporary understanding; see Al-Zuhayli (2003). The book in your hands contains the argument that the classical jurisprudence in that survey aimed mainly to enhance fairness and economic efficiency, subject to the legal and regulatory constraints of premodern societies. In this regard, many of the intended economic and prudential regulatory functions of classical contract conditions are currently served by other means that were made possible through advances in communication, legal structures, and information technology.

By attempting to replicate the substance of contemporary financial practice using premodern contract forms, Islamic finance has arguably failed to serve the objectives of Islamic Law (*maqasid al-Shari'a*): Wherever the substance of contemporary financial practice is in accordance with Islamic Law, adherence to premodern contract forms (with or without modification) leads most often to avoidable efficiency losses, thus violating one of the main legal objectives that defined classical Islamic jurisprudence. Conversely, by focusing on Islamicity of contract forms rather than substance (in part to justify efficiency losses), Islamic finance has often failed to serve the economic purpose for which certain premodern contract structures were codified in classical jurisprudence. This book provides multiple examples of both types of departure from serving Islamic legal objectives. The case is also made that form-oriented Islamic finance is not sustainable in the long term, because of (1) inherent dangers of using sophisticated structured finance methods in Islamic countries with relatively unsophisticated regulators and (2) competitive pressures that dictate convergence to efficient conventional financial modes.

I propose refocusing Islamic finance on substance rather than form. This would entail abandoning the paradigm of "Islamization" of every financial practice. It would also entail reorienting the brand name of Islamic finance to emphasize issues of community banking, microfinance, socially responsible investment, and the like. In other words, I argue that the "Islamic" in "Islamic finance" should relate to the social and economic ends of financial transactions, rather than the contract mechanics through which financial ends are achieved. I provide specific examples of areas where such reorientation of the brand name may in fact provide value to individual customers of the industry, as well as society more generally.

A Note on Terms of Reverence

It is customary in Islamic writings to use terms of reverence when significant religious figures are mentioned. For instance, mention of the Prophet is traditionally followed by the phrase "*salla Allahu ʿalayhi wa sallam*" (may God bless him and give him peace), and the mention of his companions is traditionally followed by the phrase "*radiya Allahu ʿanhu*" (may God be pleased with him). However, Western academic writings conventionally eliminate the use of such terms of reverence. Following the latter convention, I shall not use terms of reverence in this book, as non-specialists and non-Muslims may find them distracting. In the meantime, I assure pious readers that I share their respect for all religious figures. I hope that they will not be offended by omission of printed terms of reverence, which readers may nonetheless vocalize at their discretion.

Mahmoud A. El-Gamal
Houston, December 2005

Glossary and Transliteration

Allāh – God.

amāna – trust, possession of.

ʿaqd – contract.

bāṭil – invalid (contract).

bayʿ – sale.

bayʿ al-amāna – variation on same-item sale-repurchase (*ʿīna*).

bayʿ al-ʿīna – same-item sale-repurchase.

bayʿ al-kāliʾ bi-l-kāliʾ – trading one deferred obligation for another, forbidden based on a tradition with questionable authenticity.

bayʿ al-ʿuhda – variation on same-item sale-repurchase (*ʿīna*).

bayʿ al-wafāʾ – variation on same-item sale-repurchase (*ʿīna*).

bayʿ bi-thaman ājil – credit sale.

companion – immediate follower of the Prophet.

ḍamān – guaranty, possession of.

ḍarar – harm or injury.

dayn – debt or liability for fungible property.

dīnār – Roman gold coins, adopted as currency in early Islam.

dirham – Persian silver coins, adopted as currency in early Islam.

fāʾida – (literally: benefit) interest, plural *fawāʾid*.

fāsid – defective (contract).

fatwā – religious edict or opinion, plural *fatāwā*, anglicized plural *fatwas*.

fiqh – juristic understanding or inference based on Sharīʿa.

fuḍūlī – uncommissioned agent.

gharar – risk or uncertainty, forbidden if excessive and avoidable.

ḥadīth – report of Prophetic or other early Islamic tradition.

Ḥanafī – belonging to the juristic school of Abū Ḥanīfa, see note 24, Chapter 2.

Ḥanbalī – belonging to the juristic school of Aḥmad ibn Ḥanbal, see note 24, Chapter 2.

ḥiba – gift.

ḥijra – the Prophet's migration from Makka to Yathrib (later called Madina).

ḥīla – ruse, legal stratagem to circumvent various prohibitions, plural *ḥiyal*.

ḥukm Sharʿī – Islamic legal status ruling.

īdāʿ – fiduciary deposit contract.

ijāra – lease or hire contract.

ijmāʿ – juristic consensus.

ijtihād – juristic inference.

ʿilla – juristic reason or grounds for analogy.

iqāla – contract revocation.

istiḥsān – juristic approbation, to overrule juristic analogy.

istiṣlāḥ – benefit analysis, to overrule juristic analogy.

istiṣnāʿ – commission to manufacture.

Jamāʿat-i-Islāmī – Islamist party founded by Pakistani writer Abu Al-Aʿlā Al-Mawdūdī.

jiʿāla – pledge to make payment.

jurist – *faqīh*, a specialist in Islamic jurisprudence.

kafāla – guaranty offered on behalf of some party.

Mālikī – belonging to the juristic school of Mālik ibn Anas, see note 24, Chapter 2.

manfaʿa – usufruct of a property.

maqāṣṣa – mutual debt clearance.

maṣlaḥa – public or private benefit, plural *maṣāliḥ*.

muḍāraba – silent partnership.

muftī – jurist who issues *fatwā*.

murābaḥa – cost-plus sale, often combined with *bayʿ bi-thaman ājil*.

Al-Ikhwān Al-Muslimūn – Muslim Brotherhood, Islamist group founded by Egyptian teacher Ḥassan Al-Banna.

qarḍ – loan of fungible property.

qirāḍ – silent partnership.

qiyās – juristic inference by analogy.

Qurʾān – ultimate Islamic canon, believed to be the revealed word of God.

rahn – collateral or pawned property in lieu of debt.

ribā – major prohibition of Islam, similar but not equivalent to either usury or interest, see Chapter 3.

ribawī – property subject to the rules of *ribā*.

ṣakk – bond or certificate, plural *ṣukūk*.

salam – forward sale with prepaid price.

sanad – bond or certificate, plural *sanadāt*.

ṣarf – currency exchange contract.

Shāfī ī – belonging to the juristic school of Muḥammad ibn Idrīs Al-Shāfiʿī, see note 24, Chapter 2.

Sharīʿa – revealed divine law in Qurʾān and *Sunna*.

sharika – partnership, see Chapter 7 for various types.

ṣukūk – bonds or certificates, plural of *ṣakk*.

Sunna – Prophetic or other early Islamic tradition.

tabarruʿ – voluntary contribution.

takāful – mutual guaranty or insurance, used differently in Islamic finance, see Chapter 8.

takhrīj fiqhī – juristic recharacterization of a contract or transaction (usually forbidden) in terms of another (usually permissible).

tawarruq – three-party variation on *bayʿ al-ʿīna*.

tawliya – sale at cost.

ʿurbūn – down payment on purchase, from which call options are routinely synthesized.

ʿurf – customary practice, appeals to which may overrule juristic analogy.

wadīʿa – fiduciary deposit.

waḍīʿa – sale below cost.

wakāla – agency.

waqf – trust or mortmain, plural *awqāf*.

zakāh – obligatory Islamic wealth tax.

I

Introduction

In his *Address to the Nobility of the German Nation* in 1520, Martin Luther wrote:

A cobbler, a smith, a peasant, every man, has the office and function of his calling, and yet all alike are consecrated priests and bishops, and every man should by his office or function be useful and beneficial to the rest, so that various kinds of work may all be united for the furtherance of body and soul, just as the members of the body all serve one another.[1]

A cobbler was said to have asked Luther how he could serve God within his trade of shoe making. Luther's answer was not that the cobbler should sell a "Christian shoe," but rather that he should make a good shoe and sell it at a fair price.[2] Most interesting in Luther's quote is the similarity of his message to Sunni Islamic traditions, wherein – at least in theory – there are no distinct categories of clergy and laity, and wherein all righteous acts – including fair dealings in the marketplace – are considered important parts of religious life.[3]

The term "Islamic finance" brings to mind an analogy to the concept of a "Christian shoe," rather than to good products that are fairly priced. Indeed, we shall see that the primary emphasis in Islamic finance is not on efficiency and fair pricing. Rather, the emphasis is on contract mechanics and certification of Islamicity by "Shari'a Supervisory Boards." To the extent that "Islamic" financial products also cost more than the conventional products that they seek to replace – partly because of relative inefficiency, and partly to cover otherwise unnecessary jurist and lawyer fees – one may make partial analogies between those certifications and the European pre-Reformation practice of selling indulgence certificates. Thus, quoting Luther at the outset seems doubly appropriate, since he was simultaneously driven to oppose religious peddling through the sale of indulgences as well as usurious practices camouflaged by the mechanics of legitimate business and finance.[4]

In fact, the expression "Islamic finance" suggests two competing forces at work. The noun "finance" suggests that Islamic financial markets and institutions deal

1

with the allocation of financial credit and risk. Thus, Islamic finance must be essentially similar to other forms of finance. On the other hand, the adjective "Islamic" suggests some fundamental differences between Islamic finance and its conventional counterpart. Observers of the theory and practice of Islamic finance sense this tension between attempts to be essentially similar to conventional finance (emphasizing competitiveness and efficiency) and attempts to preserve a distinctive Islamic character (emphasizing Arabic contract names and certification by religious scholars). We shall see in future chapters that this "Islamic" distinction often can be preserved only at a cost, and minimization of that cost – driven by competitive pressures – may render it a distinction of form without substance.

Finance without Interest?

Most readers encounter Islamic finance first through grossly simplistic statements such as "Islam (or the Qur'an) forbids interest." This has given rise to countless jokes about "how one can get an Islamic interest-free mortgage loan." Even relatively sophisticated journalists follow this process of false reductionism, followed by tongue-in-cheek qualifications. For instance, in a recent article in *Fortune* magazine, Useem (2002) reported on typical Islamic financing through credit sales, known by the Arabic name *murabaha*, the details of which we shall examine in some detail in Chapter 4. Reflecting on the transaction, he exclaimed:

> The result looked a lot like interest, and some argue that murabaha is simply a thinly veiled version of it; the markup [bank's name] charges is very close to the prevailing interest rate. But bank officials argue that God is in the details.

This tongue-in-cheek quotation of the statement that "God is in the details" may otherwise be viewed as offensive and condescending. However, it is surprisingly tolerated, and sometimes nurtured, within Islamic finance circles. It reflects the prevailing form-above-substance approach of that industry. Islamic financial forms are derived, albeit loosely, from classical sources of Islamic jurisprudence, which process of derivation gives the industry its "Islamic" label.

In fact, there are numerous instances wherein reporters begin by stating that the distinguishing feature of Islamic finance is the prohibition of interest and then proceed to report the interest rate that Islamic instruments pay. For instance, Reuters' August 13, 2002, coverage of Bahrain's $800 million *sukuk* (the Arabic term for "Islamic bonds") followed their characterization of Islamic financial products as "interest-free" with a report that those *sukuk* will pay "4 percent annual profit." Customary explanations that the transaction is asset-based, or that what appears similar to interest is in fact profit in a sale or rent in a lease, can often leave the uninitiated reader more perplexed about the "interest-free" characterization. To provide concrete understanding of the mechanics and justifications of Islamic finance, we now proceed to consider two examples of popular Islamic structures at the retail and investment banking levels.

Example 1: Home Mortgage Transaction

For the first example, we begin with a conventional mortgage transaction as conducted in many states in the United States. The main components of my mortgage loan transaction in the state of Texas are illustrated in Figure 1.1.

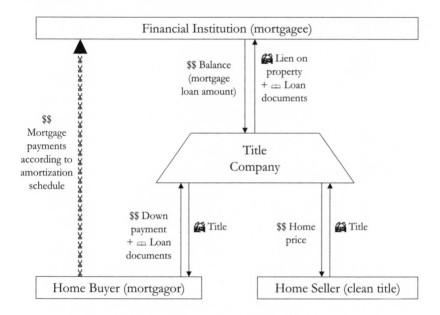

Fig. 1.1. Home Mortgage Transaction

The "closing" of this transaction took place at the title company offices. I brought a certified check for the amount of my down payment on the house (20 percent of the price plus closing costs), payable to the title company. The latter simultaneously collected the balance (80 percent) from my prospective mortgagee and subsequently issued a check to the seller for the sale price. I signed mortgage loan documents for the amount my mortgagee paid, promising to make mortgage payments according to the agreed-upon amortization schedule. I also had the option to prepay my balance, thus saving on financing charges, and obtaining clean title to the property at an earlier date, if I wished. In the meantime I received a title to the property, while my mortgagee obtained a lien thereon, thus restricting my ability to sell it without its permission.

The mechanics of this mortgage transaction are similar to numerous other forms of secured lending that evolved in modern times, made possible through searchable title databases that protect borrowers' and lenders' interests. Most Islamic jurists consider this transaction a form of forbidden *riba* (discussed in greater detail in Chapter 3), characterizing the various components of my mortgage as shown in Figure 1.2. According to this characterization, I borrowed a cer-

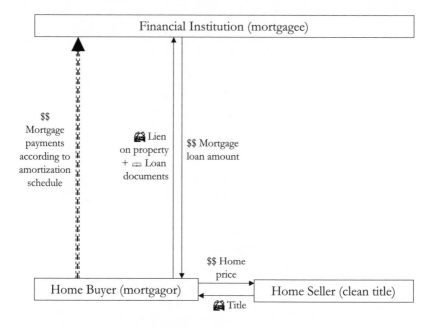

Fig. 1.2. Juristic Characterization of Mortgage Loan

tain amount of money from my mortgagee and promised to pay a larger amount of money in the future. This constitutes an interest-bearing loan of money, which the overwhelming majority of jurists (though not all) consider to be a form of the forbidden *riba*.[5] Thus, by separating the loan from the sale contract for which it was intended, jurists equally condemn secured loans (such as mortgages) and unsecured loans (such as credit card balances).

One "Islamic" alternative that has been very popular in Islamic finance is the use of multiple sales in a *murabaha* transaction, as shown in Figure 1.3. In this transaction the eventual mortgagee must first purchase the property from the seller, obtaining title either directly or through a special-purpose vehicle (SPV). Then, the bank may turn around and sell the property on credit to the mortgagor, using amortization tables that are often calculated based on the same interest rate

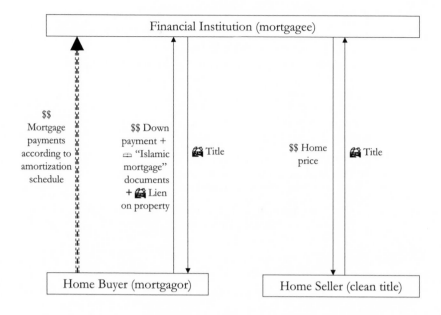

Fig. 1.3. *Murabaha* Alternative for Home Finance

used for conventional mortgages. One juristic difference, according to Islamic finance practitioners, is that the mortgagor in this case is involved in a credit sale contract, rather than a loan contract. In fact, because of requirements of some jurisdictions in the United States, and government-sponsored enterprises that assist with mortgage securitization, signed documents often contain terms such as "note," "loan," "borrower," and "interest." However, jurists have argued, the contract remains one of permissible trade rather than forbidden borrowing with interest. Depending on jurisdiction, the requirement of multiple sales, special-purpose vehicles, and documentations of title may add tax as well as legal costs. A second major difference to which jurists point is the peculiar structure that Islamic banks use for late payment penalties. We shall return to the basic secured lending transaction and its "Islamic alternative" in Chapter 4.

Example 2: Islamic Bond (Sukuk) Structure

For our second example, we consider a highly celebrated US$100 million corporate Islamic bond (*sukuk*) issue by Tabreed Financing Corporation in March 2004. The corporate entity "Tabreed Financing Corporation" is a limited company SPV incorporated in the Cayman Islands for the purpose of issuing the *sukuk* described here. The certificates issued by this SPV would act as an Islamic alternative to bond issues by the United Arab Emirates' National Central Cooling Company, nicknamed Tabreed (the Arabic word for "cooling"). The Shari'a advisors characterized the bond structure that they approved as follows:[6]

1. Structure and Mechanism

We have reviewed the proposed structure and the transactions entered into in respect of the Sukuks, the principal features of which are as follows:

1.1 On a future date to be agreed between the parties, ... , the Issuer will declare that it will hold the Trust Assets (defined below) upon trust absolutely for the holders of the Sukuks. The Trust Assets (the **"Trust Assets"**) comprise:

    1.1.1 Certain specified central cooling plants (the **"Initial Plant"**) which the Issuer will purchase from Tabreed on a future date to be agreed between the parties;

    1.1.2 ...

    1.1.3 ...

and will be purchased by the Issuer using the net proceeds received from the issuance and sale of the Sukuks.

1.2 The Issuer will lease the Plant back to Tabreed, for which Tabreed will be obliged to make rental payments to the Issuer. The Issuer will pass these rental payments on to the holders of Sukuks.

1.3 ...

1.6 ...

1.7 Upon maturity of the Sukuks, or if earlier, upon the acceleration of the Sukuk following the occurrence of a Dissolution Event under the documentation, Tabreed will purchase the Plant from the Issuer.

The bond structure is thus as illustrated in Figure 1.4. We shall study other lease-based as well as sale-based Islamic bond or *sukuk* structures that have become popular in recent years in Chapter 6. The example shown here is typical in many respects: Principal plus interest is passed to *sukuk* holders in the form of rent of a property that is sold to the SPV and purchased back at maturity. Any event that could interrupt the payment of "rent" (e.g., destruction of the leased property) is characterized as a "dissolution event," prompting the continuation of payments in the form of repurchase price. As we shall see in Chapter 6, this reduces the risk structure essentially to that of conventional bonds, allowing *sukuk* issuers to obtain the same credit ratings they would obtain for conventional bonds, and to pay the same interest they would pay based on that credit rating. Needless to say, however, transactions costs are increased because of the creation of SPVs, as well as payment of various jurist and legal fees for structuring the bond issuance. Moreover, there may be hidden legal risks in *sukuk* structures that get uncovered

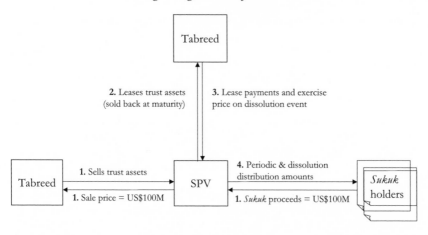

Fig. 1.4. Tabreed *Sukuk* Structure

only upon default. We shall discuss the potential advantages and disadvantages of various *sukuk* structures in Chapter 6.

1.1 Distinguishing Features of Islamic Finance

The most obvious distinguishing feature of Islamic finance (self-referentially) is the central importance of Islamicity certification (often called Shari'a compliance) for various contracts. Indeed, the recent Kuwaiti Islamic banking law, enacted in 2003 as an amendment to the Kuwaiti Central Bank and bank regulation law,[7] states explicitly that "Islamic banks are banks that perform banking operations – including all operations that the Trade Law lists, as well as those conventionally considered part of banking operations – according to the rules of Islamic Law (Shari'a)."[8] Most of the banking law amendment deals with licensing and capitalization issues (articles #87–92), relationship with the Central Bank (articles #94–5, 97–8), relationship to depositors and investment account holders (a unique feature of Islamic banks, article #96), and restrictions on ownership and trading in certain types of real assets (article #99).

Most of those legal provisions are similar for Islamic and conventional banks. In addition to the thorny issue of investment account holders (discussed in Chapter 8), the main distinguishing features of the Islamic banking section of the law are listed in articles #93 and #100:

93. An independent religious-law (Shar'iyyah) supervision board must be established for each [Islamic] bank, consisting of at least three members, to be appointed by the bank's general assembly. The incorporation documents and by-laws of the bank must dictate the existence of this board, its composition, portfolio, and means of performing its tasks.

If disputes should arise between members of the Shari'a supervision board regarding religious legal characterization [of some transaction], the bank's board of directors may forward the question to the *fatwa* board [issuer of religious edicts] of the Ministry of Awqaf and Islamic Affairs, which is deemed the ultimate authority on the matter.

The [Shari'a supervisory] board must submit an annual report to the bank's general assembly, containing its assessment of the degree of adherence of the bank's operations to Islamic Shari'a, and any comments or reservations that it may have in this regard. This document must be included in the bank's annual report.

100. On all matters not explicitly addressed in this special section [on Islamic banking], Islamic banks are subject to the [general] rules of this [banking] law, provided that they do not contradict Islamic Shari'a.

The tone of this Islamic banking law clearly illustrates the central role of jurists in Islamic finance, as well as the general nature of the industry.[9] In this regard, we may think of classical jurisprudence and modern finance as the two parents of contemporary Islamic finance. The Kuwaiti choice to add a section to the conventional banking law – highlighting deviations of Islamic banking practice wherever appropriate – makes it clear that the starting point in this formula is conventional financial practice, from which Islamic finance deviates only insofar as some conventional practices are deemed forbidden under Shari'a.

In other words, Islamic finance is not constructively built from classical jurisprudence. Rather, Islamic alternatives or modifications of conventional practice are sought whenever the latter is deemed forbidden. Thus, Islamic finance is a prohibition-driven industry. In this regard, the talented jurist Ibn Taymiyya (d. 728 A.H./1328 C.E.) famously stated that two prohibitions can explain all distinctions between contracts that are deemed valid or invalid: those of *riba* and *gharar*. We shall study those two prohibitions in great detail in Chapter 3. For now, we investigate the general economic advantages and disadvantages of a financial industry driven by religious prohibitions.

Prohibition-Driven Finance

Recent students of law and economics have maintained that the primary purpose of transaction law is often the enhancement of economic efficiency. For instance, Judge Richard Posner, perhaps the most significant figure in contemporary economic analysis of Anglo-American common law, wrote:

Often, the true grounds of legal decision are concealed rather than illuminated by the characteristic rhetoric of opinions. Indeed, legal education consists primarily of learning to dig beneath the rhetorical surface to find those grounds, many of which may turn out to have an economic character.[10]

In this regard, the majority of legal scholars engaged in this type of analysis have found prohibitions – injunctions against certain types of financial transactions conducted by mutual consent, such as interest-bearing loans – to be puzzling. For instance, Posner denounced Adam Smith's support for laws against interest-based borrowing and lending as paternalistic and efficiency reducing.[11] Students of this field also find usury laws (against charging excessive interest) imposed in most states to be puzzling. Jolls, Sunstein, and Thaler (2000) expressed this puzzlement as follows:

> *Puzzle.* A pervasive feature of law is that mutually desired trades are blocked. Perhaps most puzzling amid this landscape ... are bans on conventional "economic" transactions, such as usurious lending, price gouging, and ticket scalping. Usury, or charging an interest rate above a certain level, is prohibited by many states in consumer lending transactions. ... Not surprisingly, economists and economically oriented lawyers often view these laws as inefficient and anomalous.

Mutual consent also plays a crucial role in Islam. The Qur'an reads: "let there be among you trade by mutual consent."[12] The same emphasis is echoed in the Prophetic tradition: "I shall meet God before I give anyone the property of another without the latter's consent, for trade requires mutual consent."[13] However, mutual consent in this context is considered a necessary but not-sufficient condition for validity of economic transactions. For instance, the majority of jurists strongly denounced the December 2002 *fatwa* issued by al-Azhar's Institute of Islamic Jurisprudence, which the public viewed as legitimizing the collection of interest on bank deposits. The *fatwa* (discussed in some detail in Chapter 8) characterized the depositor-bank relationship as that of an investor and his investment agent and legitimized collection of a fixed profit percentage (interest) as follows:

> Those who deal with the International Arab Banking Corporation – or any other bank – thus forwarding their funds and savings to the bank to be their investment agent in the bank's permissible dealings, in exchange for a predetermined profit that they receive at pre-specified time-periods. ...

> This transaction, taking this form, is permissible and beyond any suspicion, since there is no text in the Book of Allah and the Prophetic tradition that forbids such a transaction wherein the profit or return is prespecified, provided that both parties mutually consent to the transaction. ...[14]

Despite this appeal to mutual consent, most jurists, including all those involved in the area of Islamic finance, vehemently opposed the *fatwa*.

Recall that Posner rejected Adam Smith's attitude toward interest-bearing loans as paternalistic and efficiency-reducing. Within the quasi-religious context of Islamic jurisprudence and finance, there is no doubt that religious injunctions are by definition paternalistic. Indeed, the charge of "paternalism" sounds compassionate when attributed to the Divine and therefore will not be contested. With regard to efficiency reduction, consider the following simple and well-known example, which suggests that paternalistic injunctions against dealings to which parties mutually consent can in fact be efficiency-enhancing.

Player 2

		Cooperate	Defect
	Cooperate	4,4	0,5
Player 1	Defect	5,0	1,1

Fig. 1.5. Prisoners' Dilemma

In the standard two-prisoners' dilemma shown in Figure 1.5, each player has a choice to cooperate or defect, with the shown payoffs (the first payoff in each cell is for the row player, and the second is for the column player). For each of the two players, the dominant strategy, regardless of the opponent's choice, is to defect (and get 5 instead of 4, or 1 instead of 0, depending on opponent's action). Thus, the unique Nash equilibrium (wherein each player plays the best response to the other's selected action) is defection for both players, whereby each player would receive 1.

In this well-known game, it is very clear that the equilibrium outcome of the prisoner's dilemma, to which players will gravitate if left to their own devices, is inefficient. Mutual cooperation would yield 4 for each, instead of 1. In this case, a paternalistic divine command "thou shalt not defect" can in fact be efficiency-enhancing. In a dynamic setting, Glaeser and Sheinkman (1998) explained ancient usury laws, which forbade all interest on loans, as a form of a priori social insurance. In societies with pervasive poverty, the cooperative charitable lending rule provides transfers from fortunate individuals born with wealth to those less fortunate. Thus, the prohibition of mutually consensual interest-based lending can enhance ex ante efficiency by encouraging the cooperative outcome.

In Chapter 3 we shall see that classical jurists envisioned the two major prohibitions in Islamic jurisprudence of financial transactions – those against *riba* and *gharar* – to be efficiency-enhancing. That is not to say that the manner in which injunctions against *riba* and *gharar* have been obeyed in Islamic financial practice necessarily achieved such increases in efficiency. On the contrary, form-driven Shariʿa arbitrage routinely reduces efficiency relative to conventional financial practices.[15] In many instances, secular legal and regulatory constraints would have eliminated the dangers and inequities targeted by the two prohibitions. Thus, efficiency losses due to Shariʿa arbitrage in such cases can be considered dead-weight losses. In other cases, where Islamic alternatives are required to avoid *riba* or *gharar*, the form-above-substance orientation of Shariʿa arbitrage often adds to transactions costs without avoiding the harmful substantive effects of the forbidden factors.

Jurists, Shariʿa Boards, and Innovation

We have already noted the prominent role of Shariʿa boards in the development and marketing of Islamic financial products and services. The most public role played by those jurists is certification of Islamicity of various products, both in theory as well as in practice. Regulators have mandated formal inclusion of Shariʿa board reports in annual financial statements and the like. Along with this official capacity, Shariʿa boards also play an informal marketing function: by participating at various conferences and workshops and by publishing various writings that explain to the public why certain products are deemed Islamic, whereas others are not.

Eventually Islamicity criteria for well-established Islamic financial products become standardized, in part through efforts of industry-sponsored institutions such as the Accounting and Auditing Organization for Islamic Financial Institutions (AAOIFI) or regulatory bodies such as the State Bank of Pakistan.[16] Products that reach this level of maturity become the focus of various workshops for bankers and regulators, who generally understand the mechanics of those standardized products quite well.[17] Once products reach this level of maturity, and become sufficiently widely accepted, the role of Shariʿa boards is reduced substantially. Moreover, widespread understanding of those modes of finance reduces barriers to entry in Islamic finance, thus increasing competitive pressure and reducing profit margins. In turn, reduced profitability, coupled with a reduced need to educate the public about those well-established products, drives the industry toward constant innovation in search of new profit margins in new market segments.

This brings us to the other main functions that jurists on Shariʿa boards play in various product development stages. Interactive discussions between bankers, lawyers, and jurists commonly start with an existing conventional product for which no Islamic alternative is available. The three groups then engage in a process of financial reengineering of the product, replacing its various conventional components that are deemed un-Islamic with others that can be presented to the public and defended as Islamic. In the later stages of product development and marketing, the vehicle of choice has been modification and adoption of premodern nominate financial contract names. Coverage of the premodern contracts in classical jurisprudence texts thus makes the new products identifiable as Islamic. To maintain credibility, industry practitioners insist on using Arabic names of contracts, for instance, "*ijara*" instead of the equivalent "lease," or "*murabaha*" instead of the equivalent "cost-plus sale." In many cases, the contemporary practice marketed under some premodern Arabic name bears only very superficial similarity to the premodern financial practice discussed in classical jurisprudence.

The pursuit of profit margins through innovation is best exemplified in the development of "Shari'a-compliant" mutual funds and, eventually, hedge funds, discussed in Chapters 7 and 10. The first stage of development in this area was pioneered by Al-Baraka's Investment and Development Company and then copied and popularized by Dow Jones Islamic Indexes (DJII) and Financial Times' FTSE Islamic Indexes (developed in cooperation with Kuwait-based The International Investor). The simple initial idea was to use standard fund management techniques, applied to a restricted universe of equities. Various screening rules were adopted to exclude stocks of companies in "sin industries" (e.g., breweries), as well as those of companies with significant forbidden practices (including the payment and collection of interest on loans).

In the early stages of introduction of "Islamic mutual funds," various providers experimented with different screening rules, and many expressed skepticism regarding some of those screens (especially debt ratios). However, standardization eventually took hold. The standardized process was particularly hastened by the fact that screens selected in the late 1990s heavily favored booming technology stocks (especially after DJII changed its cutoff debt ratio from 33 percent of assets to 33 percent of market capitalization). The technology stock bubble of that period created a strong incentive to hasten the widest possible acceptability of this "Shari'a-compliant" debt screen.[18]

In the early twenty-first century, the need for further innovation in this area became pressing. This need was caused not only by reduction in industry-wide rents as others learned to replicate standardized screens, but also by the bubble in technology stocks bursting. In fact, the debt screen that had become standard – exclude companies with debt-to-market capitalization above 33 percent – forced fund managers who bought stocks when the denominator of that ratio was at its peak to sell them as their prices fell, whether or not that was the best investment strategy.

Rather than recognize that any fixed debt-to-market-capitalization rule leads to such "buy-high, sell-low" tragedies, jurists turned to investigation of means to provide innovative Islamic investment alternatives that would perform well in "bear markets." Some attention was paid to Real Estate Investment Trusts (REITs), returns of which tend to be uncorrelated with market indices such as the Standard and Poor's 500. However, the biggest race quickly began for development of the first "Islamic hedge fund." In this regard, being first is very significant, since it allows fund managers who can successfully market some hedge fund strategy – say, basic long-short trading – to attract significant funds under management, in part through free indirect advertisement that would be otherwise illegal. In turn, once "Islamicity" of a shorting methodology is established, it can (and will) be soon replicated, thus increasing competition and reducing management fees.

I have chosen this example to illustrate a simple point: the mode of operation of our three parties in Islamic finance (financial providers, jurists, and lawyers) necessarily dictates chasing past returns and past trends in conventional finance. In the process, short-term profit margins are created for first-movers in the Islamic space, based on access to captive markets and free indirect publicity. However, as one should expect, medium- to long-term returns are severely limited for any industry that chases past returns.

Lawyers and Regulatory Arbitrage

While jurists assist in reengineering and marketing Islamic alternatives to conventional financial products, lawyers help Islamic financial providers take this product to market in two ways. First, they ensure that the reengineered product is compatible with legal and regulatory systems. This can be accomplished both by ensuring that the reengineered structure is as similar as possible to the conventional product with which regulators are familiar, and by helping to explain the new structure (and its minimal deviation from conventional practice) to those regulators. Second, lawyers strive to make reengineered products as efficient as possible, especially due to tax considerations and the need to incorporate special-purpose entities for various Islamic structures.

Discussions between lawyers and jurists thus center on a tradeoff between efficiency (proximity to conventional product being mimicked) and ease of marketing the product as Islamic (which requires noticeable, if superficial, differences). We shall turn to this tradeoff between efficiency and perceived legitimacy of the Islamic financial label in Section 1.2.

First, we conclude this section with a simple illustration of the functions that lawyers play in Islamic finance. Consider the case of an Islamic alternative to home-mortgage loans, as in Example 1. The two most common Islamic modes of home financing are *murabaha* (cost-plus credit sale) and *ijara* (lease) financing. We shall discuss how the premodern contracts carrying those names were transformed into modes of financing in Chapters 4 and 6. For the purposes of this section, suffice it to say that in both financing modes, as envisioned by contemporary jurists, the financier needs to own the property for some period of time (either directly or through an SPV). In the case of *murabaha* financing, the financier buys the property and then sells it to the customer on a credit basis (usually with a markup benchmarked to a conventional interest rate, such as the London Interbank Offer Rate [LIBOR]). Indeed, it is this financier ownership of the property, for any period of time, however short, that jurists use to differentiate between an interest-bearing mortgage loan, deemed forbidden, and a *murabaha* financing contract, deemed valid.

The mechanics of a *murabaha* financing transaction sometimes blur the boundaries between interest-bearing loans and credit-sale financing. In many *murabaha* transactions, the customer is appointed as the financier's agent. Thus, the customer may proceed as the financier's buying agent to purchase some property on its behalf, and then as the financier's selling agent to sell that property to himself. Technically, jurists argue, the financier in fact owns the property during that period of time between the two agency sales and bears the risk, for instance, of its destruction by lightning.[19] In the case of lease financing, jurists insist that permissible *ijaras* are operating leases, rather than financial leases, thus forcing the financier to maintain substantial ownership of the property throughout the lease period. Thus, both *murabaha* and *ijara* financing models require financiers to engage in purchase and sale of properties. Indeed, Islamic finance jurists highlight this "asset-based" nature of Islamic finance as one of its distinguishing features that allow avoidance of the forbidden *riba*.

In sharp contrast, most regulatory frameworks for banks define them as financial intermediaries and forbid them from owning or trading real properties (including real estate, dubbed in the United States as OREO – an acronym for "Other Real Estate Owned"). Moreover, in the case of lease-to-purchase real estate financing, the customer pays a monthly contribution toward eventually owning the property. Later in the mortgage, the customer may in fact have paid off 90 percent or more of the property's price and yet be exposed to the risk of losing the property if the financier is sued, loses, and declares bankruptcy. Both considerations call for the construction of bankruptcy-remote SPVs that hold title to the property and serve as parties to various agreements regarding obligations for repairs and insurance as required by jurists.

Islamic finance lawyers utilize skills that they honed in the area of structured finance during the boom of the 1980–90s to ensure that Islamic finance structures are as efficient as possible in terms of legal fees, costs of incorporation, and taxation. Lawyers also play a pivotal role in comparing and contrasting the risk allocations to the financier and customer under conventional and Islamic arrangements. In the context of *murabaha* and *ijara* financing in the United States, their arguments have successfully convinced the Office of the Comptroller of the

Currency (OCC, which regulates nationally licensed banks) that both modes as practiced constitute examples of the normal business of secured lending as conducted by commercial banks. The primary mover at the time was United Bank of Kuwait's Al-Manzil program for home financing in New York. The two OCC letters of understanding dealing with *murabaha* and *ijara* are available on the Web site www.occ.treas.gov. Two excerpts follow:

OCC #867, 1999: Lending takes many forms. . . . Murabaha financing proposals are functionally equivalent to, or a logical outgrowth of secured real estate lending and inventory and equipment financing, activities that are part of the business of banking.

OCC #806, 1997: Today, banks structure leases so that they are equivalent to lending secured by private property . . . a lease that has the economic attributes of a loan is within the business of banking. . . . Here it is clear that United Bank of Kuwait's net lease is functionally equivalent to a financing transaction in which the Branch occupies the position of a secured lender.

Those conclusions beg the question: If the economic substance of Islamic home finance is deemed to be functionally equivalent to conventional banking forms of secured lending, why should we not say that secured lending is more akin to trade or leasing than to forbidden interest-based cash loans? In fact, as we shall see in Chapter 4, the argument for equating interest-based secured borrowing as practiced today to interest-bearing monetary loans of premodern times appears very weak according to the standards of premodern jurisprudence. Thus, applying the classical rules of *riba* in that jurisprudence to contemporary financial practices may be unwarranted, especially in the presence of anti-usury laws, truth-in-lending regulations, and elaborate bankruptcy law protections.

1.2 Islamic Transactions Law as Common Law

English and American lawyers have found financial engineering within the context of Islamic jurisprudence to be a natural exercise. Indeed, many Islamic finance lawyers have found Islamic and English common law sufficiently similar that they decided to make most Islamic financial structures subject to the latter. A student of Islamic law expressed his realization of similarities between the two legal systems as follows:

In the course of studying Islamic law in its everyday practice I have been increasingly struck with its similarities to the common law form in which I have also been trained in the United States.[20]

This inherent familiarity with the modes of analysis in Islamic jurisprudence stems from its close relationship with Anglo-American common law. Although most historical studies trace the origins of common law during the reign of Henry II to

Roman and canon laws,[21] some recent historical scholarship has traced the roots of some parts of the common law of financial transactions to Islamic origins. One of the earliest studies in this area traced the British system of trusts to the Islamic institution of *waqf*.[22] More recently, John Makdisi traced the origins of many innovations in British contract law to Islamic origins.[23] Indeed, similarities extend to the very methodology of legal inference based on case studies of legal precedents and reasoning by analogy.

This explains the relative success of Islamic finance in the Anglo-American world and in Islamic countries that have had a history of British rule (e.g., Gulf Cooperation Council (GCC) countries or Malaysia). In the meantime, divergence between the common-law nature of Islamic jurisprudence, on the one hand, and the rhetoric of interpreting the Islamic canon, on the other, has led to fundamental failures of Islamic finance in countries that attempted to "Islamize" their entire financial systems (Iran, Pakistan, and Sudan). Rosen (2000, p. 64) correctly explained those failures of contemporary attempts at de jure implementation of Islamic Law as follows:

in Pakistan and Sudan the simple use of Islamic law as an arm of the state has slipped through the fingers of those at the center. The reason, I believe, is that these regimes have been trying to apply a common law variant as if it were a civil law system.

This confusion is even more acute in countries that have not been officially Islamized. Many of those countries' official legal systems were derived from European civil codes: Swiss in the case of the Turkish republic (1926), French in the cases of Egypt (1949), Syria (1949), and Iraq (1953).[24] The architect of those codes, 'Abdal-Razzaq Al-Sanhuri, argued successfully before the Egyptian parliament in 1948 that they contain all the aspects of Islamic jurisprudence that agreed with widely accepted principles of modern legal theory.[25] Yet, we continue to hear calls for "application of the Islamic Shari'a" in Egypt, post-Baathist Iraq, and other countries.

The legal environment for Islamic finance is made more complicated by statements about the supremacy of Islamic law, even in countries that are relatively secular. For instance, Egyptian Constitution Article 2, amended in May 1980, stated that all subsequent laws and legislations must be derived from Islamic Law. This constitutional requirement was further strengthened through a later Egyptian Constitutional Court's ruling:

It is therefore not permitted that a legislative text contradict those rules of Shari'a whose origin and interpretation are definitive, since these rules are the only ones regarding which new interpretive effort (*ijtihad*) is impossible, as they represent, in Islamic Shari'a, the supreme principles and fixed foundations that admit neither allegorical interpretation, nor modification. In addition, we should not contemplate that their meaning would change with changes in time and place, from which it follows that they are impermeable to any amendment, and that it is not permitted to go beyond them or change their meaning. The authority of the High Constitutional Court in this regard is limited to safeguarding their implementation and overruling any other legal rule that contradicts them.[26]

Islamic finance thrives mainly in Islamic countries with officially adopted civil laws, but it is driven primarily by a canon-law-like interpretation of Islamic scriptures. However, one can readily see that the canon-like nature of Islamic jurisprudence is mostly rhetorical. The true nature of Islamic jurisprudence of financial transactions is very similar to Western-style common law. In particular, contemporary developments in Islamic finance owe more to juristic understandings of the canonical texts and previous juristic analyses than they owe to the canon itself. According to one of the most prominent jurists working in this field:

> It must be understood that when we claim that Islam has a satisfactory solution for every problem emerging in any situation in all times to come, we do not mean that the Holy Quran and Sunna of the Holy Prophet or the rulings of Islamic scholars provide a specific answer to each and every minute detail of our socioeconomic life. What we mean is that the Holy Quran and the Holy Sunna of the Prophet have laid down the broad principles in the light of which the scholars of every time have deduced specific answers to the new situations arising in their age. Therefore, in order to reach a definite answer about a new situation the scholars of Shariah have to play a very important role. They have to analyze every question in light of the principles laid down by the Holy Quran and Sunna as well as in the light of the standards set by earlier jurists enumerated in the books of Islamic jurisprudence. This exercise is called *Istinbat* or *Ijtihad*. ... [T]he ongoing process of *Istinbat* keeps injecting new ideas, concepts and rulings into the heritage of Islamic jurisprudence.[27]

In other words, by "injecting new ideas, concepts and rulings," Islamic jurists make law in a manner very similar to common-law judges presiding over cases for which there are no common-law precedents.

Precedents, Analogies, and Nominate Contracts

It is worthwhile noting that the process of juristic inference (*ijtihad*) discussed above is restricted in Sunni schools to reasoning by analogy (juristic rather than logical). Early jurists used a variety of tools, including benefit analysis (*istislah*) and juristic approbation (*istihsan*). However, most surviving Sunni schools have chosen to follow the rules of Islamic legal theory as established by Al-Shafi'i, who declared that "*ijtihad* is *qiyas*" (i.e., the only permissible form of juristic inference is through analogical reasoning).[28] It is also worth noting at this point that the operation of a hybrid common-civil-law system, which nonetheless focuses on reasoning by analogy from precedent, is not unique to Islamic finance.[29]

As a consequence of this reliance on analogies to legal precedents in Islamic law, jurists looking for alternatives to conventional financial products frequently search through classical books of jurisprudence for precedents that can be used – directly or in modified form – to accomplish their goal. For instance, the earliest writers on Islamic finance envisioned a two-tiered silent partnership system, modeled after the *mudaraba* contract of classical Islamic jurisprudence.[30] As we shall see in Chapter 8, this model continues to be utilized on the liabilities sides of Islamic banks, giving rise to many regulatory and corporate governance problems. It is also used appropriately in a variety of securitization schemes, such as mutual funds and mortgage-backed securities.

For Islamic bank assets, the most popular mode of financing has been a variation on the classical *murabaha* (cost-plus sale) contract, modified by the late Sami Humud as a means of extending credit without violating the Islamic prohibition of interest-based loans. Humud (1976) seems to be the first prominent instance of proposing the use of cost-plus *murabaha* in a credit sale setting (*bay' bithaman 'ajil*), with an added binding promise on the customer to purchase the property, thus replicating secured lending in a "Shari'a-compliant" manner. Islamic banking began its steady growth shortly after this idea was popularized and adopted by jurists in the late 1970s. While the liabilities of Islamic banks continue to be structured in terms of "investment accounts" on a profit-and-loss-sharing basis, *murabaha* and other debt-financing forms have dominated the assets side of Islamic banks' balance sheets.

Numerous books on Islamic finance define the subject in terms of "permissible" classical nominate contracts (*murabaha, mudaraba*, etc.) that are commonly used in modified forms today. This contrasts sharply with a general rule in Islamic jurisprudence stating that the default ruling in financial transactions is permissibility, exceptions being based on prohibitions of *riba* and *gharar*. Jurists active in the area of Islamic finance readily admit this reality. However, they have found constructive analogies to classical nominate contracts – known to be devoid of *riba* or excessive *gharar*, or allowed as exceptions to the general prohibitions – to be more fruitful. The alternative would have been to allow the default ruling to stand, abstaining from issuing opinions on any new financial contracts, unless and until a valid analogy is constructed to determine that any given transaction contains forbidden *riba* or substantial *gharar*.

There are many reasons for Islamic finance adopting the Arabic names of premodern contracts, not least of which is the desire to create an independent identity and brand name for Islamic finance. In this regard, the use of classical nominate contracts helps to connect the current financial practice to the revered classical Islamic age. On the other hand, this adherence to variations on ancient and medieval nominate contracts and the associated need to preserve as many of the conditions stipulated by classical jurists to keep those contracts devoid of *riba* and excessive *gharar* are the primary reasons that Islamic finance has heretofore fallen significantly short of its potential.

Convergence of Sunni and Shi'i Approaches

The modes of Shari'a arbitrage discussed in this book are predominantly practiced in Sunni-majority regions, such as GCC countries, Malaysia, Pakistan, and Sudan. However, extrapolation from the experiences of Islamic finance in those countries to Shi'a-dominated regions appears justified, despite some basic differences in jurisprudence.

In principle, Shi'i jurisprudence can reach very different conclusions from its Sunni counterpart. That is not only because of minor differences in recognized canonical traditions, which differences also exist between the various Sunni schools. The primary distinction is that most Shi'i schools do not restrict juristic inference on matters that were not addressed in canonical texts to the use of analogy. In Chapter 2 we shall see that some progressive Sunni jurists – such as the Azhari jurist 'Abdul-Wahhab Khallaf – also argued for allowing all forms of juristic inference in the domain of financial transactions. However, the majority of contemporary Sunni and Shi'i jurists alike have gravitated toward the comforts of analogical reasoning and use of classical nominate contracts, as discussed in this chapter.

Some flexibility is given to Muslims living in non-Muslim lands. The *fatawa* (religious edicts) issued by Ayatullah Sistani (Iraq's most prominent Shi'i cleric) seem to accommodate many forms of conventional finance for those Muslims. For instance, he allowed depositing funds with banks, and collecting interest thereof, on the basis of permissibility of charging interest to non-Muslims in those lands. Moreover, he allowed Muslims to take mortgage loans from non-Islamic banks – even with knowledge that they will pay principal plus interest – provided that they do so with an intention other than "borrowing" in the classical sense of "*iqtirad.*"[31] Likewise, the prominent Sunni jurist Yusuf Al-Qaradawi issued a similar *fatwa* allowing Muslims in North America to finance their home purchases with conventional mortgages. He based this ruling on three considerations: (1) the opinion of Abu Hanifa that permitted dealing with *riba* in non-Muslim lands, (2) determination that the mortgagor is the primary beneficiary from mortgage home financing, and (3) invoking the rule of necessity.[32]

The rules are much stricter for Muslims living in Islamic lands, within both the Sunni and Shi'i schools. Within that context, Sistani appears to revert to Shari'a-arbitrage alternatives that have been popular in Sunni-majority Islamic countries. For instance, in answers (543–6) on his Web site, he forbade borrowing from private or public banks with stipulated conditions of paying interest, which he thus characterized as forbidden *riba*. His proposed alternatives are trade- and lease-based contracts, for which he uses the Arabic names *bay* and *ijara*. Recognizing that those contracts are used to synthesize interest-based loans, he ruled merely that conditions that render the underlying loan transparent must be deemed invalid, much like Sunni jurists have permitted operating leases but forbade financial leases (as we shall see in Chapter 6). Based on the same analysis, he disallowed depositing funds with conventional banks.[33]

Thus, whether – and if – Iraq imposes Islamic transactions law according to the juristic views of the Shi'i majority, or according to the juristic views of the Sunni minority, the resulting system of Islamic finance would likely follow the same Shari'a arbitrage path currently charted in places like GCC, Malaysia, and Pakistan. Evidence of convergence between the Shi'i and Sunni Islamic financial modes of operation is clear in Iran's recent efforts to issue *sukuk* that imitate the lease-based structures utilized in the Sunni-majority regions. Collaborative efforts to create liquid Islamic money and capital markets have led to convergence within Sunni Islamic financial jurisprudence, for example, to allow Malaysia to tap funds from more conservative GCC investors. Likewise, Islamic countries with Shi'i majorities are likely to continue their own process of juristic convergence to gain access to those growing Islamic financial markets.[34]

Tradeoff between Efficiency and Legitimacy

Throughout this book we study the current practice of Islamic finance, which has adopted a peculiar form of regulatory arbitrage that is best characterized as Shari'a arbitrage. The practice of Shari'a arbitrage proceeds in three steps:

1. Identification of a financial product that is generally deemed contrary to the percepts of Islamic Law (Shari'a).

2. Construction of an "Islamic analog" to that financial product. Examples include Islamic home (mortgage) or auto financing – commonly using the Arabic-nominate contracts *murabaha* or *ijara*, as well as Islamic bonds or certificates commonly marketed under Arabic names like *sukuk al-ijara* or *sukuk al-salam*. In fact, an important step in executing Shari'a arbitrage is finding an appropriate Arabic name for the Islamic analog product, preferably one that was extensively used in classical Islamic legal texts.[35] Differences in contract forms and language thus justify and lend credibility to the "Islamic" brand name.

3. In the meantime, an Islamic financial structure marketed under an Arabic name must be sufficiently similar to the conventional structure that it aims to replace. Sufficient similarity would ensure that the Islamic structure

is consistent with secular legal and regulatory frameworks in target and origin countries.[36]

Legitimacy of declarations that an Islamic analog product is Islamic, whereas the conventional financial product it aims to replace was not, increases with deviations of the analog's financial structure from its conventional counterpart (in both form and substance). This may require the creation of otherwise unnecessary SPVs or the addition of superfluous financial transactions. Those additional economic entities and activities necessarily increase transaction costs and reduce efficiency of the resulting Islamic financial products and services.

Consequently, professionals structuring an Islamic financial product have to examine the tradeoff between their product's efficiency, on the one hand, and its credibility in target Islamic financial markets, on the other. Depending on target markets for the various products (e.g., Malaysia vs. Sudan, as two historical extreme points), one may choose different structures (e.g., favoring efficiency in Malaysia and credibility in Sudan). For instance, Malaysian bankers had developed repurchase markets for Government Investment Certificates (GICs) since the mid-1980s, allowing Islamic banks to use interbank markets for liquidity management and Bank Negara to engage them in open market operations. More generally, Malaysian jurists continue to allow various forms of debt trading, which enhance liquidity and efficient pricing of various instruments. In contrast, the Sudanese have until very recently maintained that *musharaka* (partnership) certificates built on profit-and-loss sharing are the only ideal forms of Islamic bond alternatives. Sudanese Islamic banks have generally purchased those certificates and held them to maturity. Lack of liquidity in those Sudanese instruments has resulted in inefficient pricing and absence of effective monetary policy through open market operations, ultimately leading to demonetization and the general weakness of the Sudanese financial system.

1.3 Limits and Dangers of Shari'a Arbitrage

Consider the previously discussed Tabreed *sukuk* structure in Example 2, as a quintessential exercise in Shari'a arbitrage. Tabreed wished to issue bonds and pay bondholders an interest rate commensurate with market rates. This would be interest-bearing debt, which is deemed by most jurists as forbidden *riba*. The Shari'a-arbitrage approach in this case required structuring the transaction as a lease of one or more assets (cooling plants). The assets were sold to an SPV created for the purpose of this transaction. The SPV proceeded to lease the asset back to Tabreed, collecting interest in the form of rent, and distributing it to certificate holders. At lease end, the SPV sells its assets back to Tabreed.

We shall return to this and similar transactions involving sale and resale of the same property in Chapter 4. Premodern jurists discussed at length same-item sale-repurchase (most commonly called *bay' al-'ina*), which was a known ancient legal arbitrage method to circumvent the prohibition of interest-based lending. In this regard, the *sukuk* structure involves sale of property (including its usufruct), followed by temporary repurchase of usufruct (lease), and then full-fledged repurchase of the property and its remaining usufruct. In Chapters 4–6 we shall discuss at some length the juristic grounds for questioning various bond-alternative or *sukuk* structures, which differ from conventional bonds only in superficial form. For now, we focus on other legal problems that *sukuk* structures may cause.

Risk of Mispricing

To the extent that differences in form may also lead to substantive differences between *sukuk* and bonds, such potential differences may lead to legal problems:

1. If the company issuing lease-based *sukuk* had previously issued regular (conventional) bonds, how would its issuance of *sukuk al-ijara* affect earlier bond-holding creditors? In particular, would the debt owed to those earlier creditors be de facto subordinated to the new debt by virtue of implicit collateralization? If the company defaults on earlier debts, how are the respective rights of bond and *sukuk* holders to be determined, and under which legal system? How would a third party's entitlement (*istihqaq*) to the leased property affect the lease structure, under Islamic jurisprudence and under relevant secular law?

2. Can this procedure be abused as a means of shielding company assets from existing creditors?

3. To avoid credit downgrades if the sold and leased-back property ceases to produce usufruct (and thus to yield rent to *sukuk* holders), *sukuk* are made essentially callable by designating such circumstances as "dissolution events." How can one price this embedded option? Unlike standard pricing based on credit-risk models, the callability in this case relates also to operational risk factors. In general, pricing Islamic finance instruments becomes increasingly difficult because of its characteristic bundling of multiple risk factors.

In fact, to avoid most of those problems, *sukuk* are structured legally to replicate the seniority and risk structures of conventional debt instruments. To the extent that lawyers have been successful in replicating conventional bond structures, *sukuk* as an asset class should eventually be recognized merely as expensive bonds. Moreover, credibility of those instruments may come into question. For instance, the highly respected and learned Saudi scholar 'Abdullah ibn Mani' retracted his approval of Bahraini government-issued *ijara-sukuk* after he was convinced that ownership of the underlying properties was not fully transferred to the lessor, as required in *ijara* (leasing) contracts discussed in great detail in classical jurisprudence books.

In the meantime, errors may be made in replicating the risk structure of conventional bonds in *sukuk*, thus mispricing of embedded options may eventually cause divergence between the two asset classes, leading to collapse of *sukuk* markets. This possibility should not be dismissed. The GNMA CDR experience due to mispricing embedded options in interest-rate derivatives was not foreseen prior to that market's collapse, even by the most astute financial professionals; see Johnston and McConnell (1989). Interestingly, this mispricing in modern financial innovation occurred despite the focus of conventional finance on disentangling various risks to price them more efficiently. In this regard, the use of premodern contract forms in Islamic finance essentially reentangles the various risks, for example, by allowing an increase in price due to embedded options, while disallowing sale of those options separately. In certain instances, as argued in Chapter 3, this bundling of risks may enhance efficiency and reduce harmful speculation. However, the more likely result of approximating modern transactions with premodern ones is increased risk of mispricing and inefficiency.

Legal and Regulatory Risks

Another set of risks discussed in Chapter 10 relate to issues of money laundering and criminal finance. The structured finance technologies utilized in Islamic finance aim primarily to separate would-be borrowers or lenders from interest-bearing loans – the process we have labeled Shari'a arbitrage. The degrees of separation introduced for that purpose – in the forms of multiple trades, or special purpose vehicles, and the like – dangerously resemble the "layering" tools of money launderers and criminal financiers. In addition, the use of those tools of structured finance often require utilization of offshore financial centers to reduce tax burdens and minimize incorporation costs for various SPVs.

Of course, both of these sets of concerns are not unique to Islamic finance. Indeed, the means and venues of structured finance characteristic of Shari'a arbitrage were originally devised in the Anglo-American world as tools of regulatory arbitrage – mainly aiming to minimize tax burdens for corporations, trusts, and high-net-worth individuals.

However, there is considerable cause for concern regarding the use of those sophisticated tools of regulatory arbitrage in Islamic finance. Recent corporate scandals in the United States have shown that Western regulators lack the requisite sophistication to understand and track complicated financial structures. In this regard, one must recognize that financial regulators and law enforcement officials in the Islamic world lag significantly behind their Western counterparts in sophistication and understanding of structured finance.

This makes the chance for abuse by money launderers and criminal financiers higher in Islamic finance than elsewhere. To the extent that such criminal financiers always seek the weakest link in regulation and law enforcement, this makes Shari'a-arbitrage-oriented Islamic finance potentially vulnerable to such abuse. Moreover, the industry's "Islamic" brand name has been tarnished and abused in the past, for example, as part of the BCCI affair or Egyptian "fund mobilization companies" rumored to have run pyramid schemes in the 1980s.[37]

Beyond Shari'a Arbitrage

Returning to the economic concerns of inefficiency and mispricing, we should recognize that nominate contracts in classical Islamic jurisprudence – valuable vehicles that they were for the time those texts were authored – can serve only a very limited number of financial functions. At the time those classical texts were authored, the number of financial markets was extremely limited. Hence, financial instruments that eventually became classical nominate contracts (credit sales, leases, etc.) had to serve multiple functions in terms of allocation of credit and risk. In contrast, modern financial markets and institutions (money markets, capital markets, options markets, etc.) were designed to disentangle various risks, in a manner that allows us to price them more efficiently.

In this regard, adherence to classical nominate contracts necessarily amplifies the aforementioned tension between efficiency and credibility objectives. This, in turn, must force the industry to choose one of two directions:

1. Classical conditions of nominate contracts may be systematically relaxed to enhance efficiency, in which case they would have served no purpose. We shall see examples of this in practice, especially in the area of *murabaha* financing. The risks of this approach are twofold:

    (a) Practically, the target audience of Islamic finance may grow progressively more disenchanted by the lip service it pays to classical texts, without adhering to the conditions therein.

    (b) Theoretically, any hope for recovering the substantive content of various Islamic legal and religious provisions may be lost forever. Indeed, some have argued that it was precisely this fear of losing religious substance that prompted some scholars in the thirteenth century C.E. to declare that the doors of *ijtihad* (juristic inference) must be closed.

2. Islamic finance may continue to be an inefficient replication of conventional finance, always one step behind developments in the imitated sector. Eventually, sophisticated clients of the industry may lose hope that it can ever provide a bona fide alternative to conventional finance – the primary reason they tolerate its form-above-substance approach. At that stage, Islamic finance would lose large portions of its constituency and become a mere footnote in financial history.

The alternative, to which this book is dedicated, is to try to understand and apply the substantive spirit of Islamic Law. This can be accomplished by understanding the economic functions served by classical legal provisions and the general principles that prompted classical jurists to pursue those functions within their economic and legal environment. This, in turn, can pave the road for developing financial products that may be marketed more effectively to Muslims and non-Muslims alike, without need for Arabic names of classical nominate contracts, and without hiding behind the "Islamic" brand name.

2

Jurisprudence and Arbitrage

The previous chapter highlighted the irony in reports that "Islam forbids interest" or "the Qur'an forbids interest," followed by a statement of the interest rate paid by Islamic instruments (e.g., *sukuk*). Some practitioners may be more cognizant of this problem and choose to report that the "profit rate" or "return" paid on their interest-free bond is a fixed 4 percent, or floating LIBOR plus 50 basis points. Indeed, many Islamic finance practitioners would be genuinely offended if someone asked them about the interest rate they charge, say, on Islamic mortgages. They may be slightly less offended if asked about "the implied interest rate," computed from the deferred price they charge in a credit sale, or the rent they charge in a lease-to-purchase or declining-partnership agreement.

Such discrepancies between rhetoric and practice are not only problematic from an intellectual standpoint. They also lead to disillusionment with the industry for many educated Muslims, who may otherwise be its primary customers. Similarly, this rhetoric drives away many conventional financial providers, who could otherwise be the primary providers of Islamic financial services. To those practitioners, it is clear that there is no such thing as finance without interest. They find endless "research" on whether or not discounting is allowed in Islam to be silly and decide to ignore the industry altogether. Last but not least, this rhetoric encourages a pietist antirational approach to the field, as shown by the previous chapter's quotation from the *Fortune* magazine article that "God is in the details."

The long-term solution to this problem requires substance-oriented revival of Islamic jurisprudence. This would in turn require an economic analysis of classical Islamic jurisprudence to uncover the substantive considerations that gave rise to premodern Islamic contract forms. A comprehensive economic analysis of Islamic theories of property, contract, tort, and the like is beyond the scope of this book. However, to understand the short-term inadequacy of Islamic finance as currently practiced, the reader needs to acquire a basic understanding of the nature of Islamic law and jurisprudence in the premodern and contemporary periods. A brief summary of Islamic jurisprudence is provided in this chapter, and an in-depth analysis of the two prohibitions that define the character of contemporary Islamic finance is provided in Chapter 3. The goal of both chapters is to illustrate that the form-oriented nature of Islamic finance as practiced today is unjustified. As we shall see, the objective of classical Islamic jurisprudence has been to enhance economic efficiency, according to the best benefit analyses of premodern jurists. Thus, contemporary adherence to inefficient premodern forms is insufficient for earning the "Islamic" brand name.

2.1 Islamic Law and Jurisprudence

We have asserted in Chapter 1 that Islamic jurisprudence is in fact a common-law system, built primarily on analogy to precedents. In fact, religious rhetoric and formal Sunni Islamic legal theory dictate that permissible juristic inference is restricted to analogies in relation to the Islamic canon. However, we shall see that, in reality, good classical jurisprudence of financial transactions was driven by benefit analyses, which were sometimes disguised by the characteristic formalism of juristic analogy and reference to the canon.

The Canon: Qur'an, Tradition, and Consensus

The primary canonical text of Islam is the Qur'an (lit. The Recitation), which is self-referentially called "The Book."[1] Indeed, accounting for average verse length and repetitions of nonlegal verses, Goitien (1960) has shown that the relative legal content of the Qur'an is not less than its counterpart in the Torah, which is often called "The Law."[2] Thus, Islamist rhetoric suggests that the Qur'an is at least in large part a legal document that should be applied.

However, careful reading shows that most Qur'anic legal verses (especially outside the domain of criminal penalties) tend to be general in nature, with few detailed exceptions on issues of marriage and inheritance. For instance, in the economic realm, the Qur'an orders believers to fulfill their contractual obligations [5:1] and declares generally that "God has permitted trade and forbidden *riba*" [2:275].[3] However, the Qur'an does not state clearly which contracts are valid, and thus must be kept, and which are invalidated and voided (e.g., based on the prohibition of *riba*).[4]

In this regard, it is useful to recall the following statement of 'Ali ibn Abi Talib, the fourth Caliph. When asked to let the Qur'an arbitrate his political dispute with Mu'awiyah ibn Abi Sufyan, he said famously: "The Qur'an does not speak; men [claim to] speak on its behalf." Legal content of the Qur'an thus required explanation through Prophetic *Sunna*, as well as juristic analyses in later centuries.[5]

The Prophetic *Sunna* consists of reported sayings and actions of the Prophet, as well as the practices that he witnessed and approved implicitly.[6] Al-Shafi'i (1939) established Prophetic *Sunna* as a legal source of equal authoritativeness to the Qur'an.[7] Although the Qur'an was reportedly recorded in writing very early in Islamic history, reports of the Prophetic *Sunna* survived for centuries in the form of oral tradition. This allowed for contradictory traditions to exist and left room for jurists to disagree over means of reconciling them to reach appropriate legal rulings.

Al-Shafi'i (1939) further argued that consensus over a ruling elevates it to the canonical level.[8] However, most jurists ruled that local consensus of scholars in a particular country or region is not deemed authoritative.[9] Together with the possibility of dissent by unknown parties, this effectively limits viable invocation of the principle to consensus reached during the early Islamic period. Moreover, Islamic legal theorists have argued that consensus based on juristic inference is not permanently part of the canon, since it may be abrogated by later juristic inference constructed for different circumstances or based on different analysis.[10]

Juristic Inference (Ijtihad) and Benefit Analysis

In the absence of legislative canonical texts or canonized consensus, jurists had to resort to some process of juristic inference. Most Sunni jurists have agreed formally to limit juristic inference to reasoning by analogy, following Al-Shafi'i (1939, p. 477). The general term for juristic analysis is *ijtihad*, which literally means "doing one's utmost" (to reach the most appropriate ruling). Earlier juristic methods of approbation (*istihsan*, mainly in the Hanafi school), benefit analysis (*istislah*, mainly in the Maliki school), and reliance on local customs ('*urf*) were thus denounced by Al-Shafi'i as illegitimate forms of human legislation.[11] Strict adherence to reasoning by analogy has played an important role in the development of an inefficient Islamic finance industry focused on premodern nominate contracts. However, careful examination of classical jurisprudence shows that many of the best classical jurists based their rulings mainly on benefit analyses that were guided by their economic understanding.

In this regard, Zahiris (those who only adhere to apparent meanings of canonical texts) and Shi'i schools officially continued to allow their jurists to utilize any means of inference on matters not directly addressed by the Islamic canon. However, the freedom accorded Shi'i jurists – which theoretically permitted them to use reason ('*aql*) without restriction to formal analogies – was tempered by the principle of caution (*ihtiyat*) to ensure adherence to the paths of their Imams.[12]

Moreover, the notion of following or imitating (*taqlid*) the opinions of a learned jurist (*marji' fiqhi*) is also very similar to the concept of following a particular jurist or a particular school of jurisprudence in Sunni Islam. Finally, while Shi'i jurisprudence has traditionally had a formal hierarchy of jurists, Sunni Islam in various countries has developed similar hierarchies through, for example, posts of grand muftis and memberships of various prestigious jurisprudence academies. Consequently, the structural dynamics of mainstream Shi'i and Sunni jurisprudence have shown many more similarities than differences.

Indeed, although Sunni jurists are formally required to restrict their inference to reasoning by analogy, effective jurists of the main Sunni schools have managed to base their rulings on benefit analysis and other rational devices. For instance, Hanafi jurists continued to use juristic approbation by rephrasing it in terms of "abandoning the most apparent analogy in favor of more subtle hidden analogy," or appealing to the rule of necessity. Maliki jurists did not even search for hidden analogies, simply rejecting apparent analogies if their resulting rulings contradicted customary practice, prevented apparent benefits, or led to significant harm.[13] In this regard, the Maliki jurist-philosopher Ibn Rushd (d. 594 A.H./1198 C.E.) equated Hanafi juristic approbation and Maliki benefit analysis thus: "in most cases, juristic approbation means consideration of benefits and justice."[14]

In general, jurists enumerated four criteria for invoking benefit analysis: (1) allowing apparent benefit, (2) preventing apparent loss/harm, (3) preventing means of circumventing the Law, and (4) consideration of specific circumstances in time and place.[15] Jurists also had to decide on priorities when benefit analysis contradicted the apparent meanings of canonical texts (Qur'anic verse or Prophetic tradition). Islamic legal theorists addressed this problem by classifying canonical texts into (1) specific (dealing with a particular case) versus general ones and (2) well-established (in terms of meaning and authenticity) versus vague or inauthentic ones. Although all schools of Sunni jurisprudence disallowed overruling an explicit and specific canonical ruling, they differed in opinion regarding areas wherein some jurist discretion was allowed (e.g., to restrict general rulings based on benefit analysis). In this regard, the Hanafi and Maliki schools were the most liberal in using benefit analysis, and the Shafi'i and Hanbali schools were the most conservative.[16] However, one must be careful not to jump to the conclusion that the Hanbali school (which is dominant in the GCC region) is the strictest in practice. Indeed, it is only within the Hanbali school that some jurists approved the practice of *tawarruq* (a three-party multiple sale to synthesize interest-based lending, as discussed in Chapter 4), whereas luminaries of the Hanafi school – including Abu Hanifa's associate Al-Shaybani – condemned the practice unequivocally.[17]

Thus, we have seen that benefit analysis should guide the development of Islamic finance, rather than formalist analogy to premodern practices. In this regard, the great twentieth-century Azhari jurist and legal theorist ʿAbdul-Wahhab Khallaf clearly stated that benefit analysis should be the final arbiter in the area of financial transactions: "Benefit analysis and other legal proofs may lead to similar or different rulings. ... In this regard, maximizing net benefit is the objective of the law for which rulings were established. Other legal proofs are means to attaining that legal end [of maximizing net benefits], and objectives should always have priority over means."[18]

The undiscriminating quest in Islamic finance to replace "conventional," that is, contemporary, financial practice is particularly perplexing, given that classical jurists considered adherence to convention (ʿurf) to be an important legal consideration. In fact, there are five general rules in *Majallat Al-Ahkam Al-ʿAdliyya* (Ottoman codification of Hanafi jurisprudence circa 1293 A.H./1876 C.E.) that directly contradicted canonical texts and were defended by jurists on the basis of hardships in altering customary practice.[19] Similarly, the great Hanafi jurist Al-Sarakhsi wrote in *Al-Mabsut* the general principle that "establishment [of rights, etc.] by customary practice is akin to establishment by canonical texts."[20] In addition, recognizing that conventions change from one historical period to another, the 39th article of *Majallat Al-Ahkam Al-ʿAdliyya* stated that juristic rulings must keep up with the times.[21]

Consequently, the bias in contemporary Islamic finance should be for maintaining conventional practice, rather than seeking alternatives thereof, especially if those alternatives are inefficient. In this regard, many of the contemporary practices in conventional finance already have built into them protections that were intended by classical juristic rulings. Thus, instead of seeking to replace the mechanics of conventional financial practices with inefficient analogs synthesized from premodern contract forms, Islamic finance should focus on the substance of Islamic Law with regard to how financial instruments are used, rather than how they are constructed.

2.2 From Classical to Contemporary Jurisprudence

The history of Islamic jurisprudence is customarily divided into eight periods.[22] The first period ended in 11 A.H./632 C.E., when revelation stopped with the Prophet's death. The second period, characterized by personal interpretations of the canon by the Prophet's companions, lasted until 50 A.H./670 C.E.[23] From the year 50 to the early second century A.H., tension emerged between a traditionist approach to jurisprudence in western Arabia and a rationalist approach in Iraq. This gave rise to the golden age of classical Islamic jurisprudence, which extended from the early second to the mid-fourth century A.H. The eight most significant schools of Sunni and Shi'i jurisprudence emerged during that period.[24]

From the mid-fourth to mid-seventh century A.H., Islamic jurisprudence was limited to elaborations within the main juristic schools. Then began the dark age of Islamic jurisprudence, following the fall of Baghdad to the Tatars in the mid-seventh century A.H. (thirteenth C.E.). Rebirth of jurisprudence occurred in 1293 A.H./1876 C.E., when the Ottomans codified Hanafi jurisprudence in the *Majalla*. From the late nineteenth to the mid-twentieth century C.E., a number of juristic revival movements began, following exposure to Western legal and technological progress. This period produced progressive jurists such as Muhammad 'Abduh and legal pioneers such as 'Abdal-Razzaq Al-Sanhuri, who aimed to reinterpret classical jurisprudence in modern form. In the latest episode of Islamic revival, which began in the mid-twentieth century C.E., Islamist trends have been predicated on rejection of Western social and legal advances and a quest for building Islamic states, Islamic social science, Islamic economics, and Islamic finance. As a result, classical (premodern) jurisprudence is mostly read uncritically today, and attempts to adhere to its conditions have given rise to inefficiencies and rent-seeking Shari'a arbitrage activities.

Jurisprudence, Revival, and Codification

For Islamic societies to go beyond formalistic adherence to premodern jurisprudence, they needed to revive the substance of classical Islamic jurisprudence in an enlightened modern manner. Some contemporary jurists have made efforts in that direction, such as Al-Qaradawi (1996). His and similar proposals for renewed juristic inference have centered mainly on the notion of "collective *ijtihad*," in order to overcome classical taxonomies of jurists and their authorities. In the classical hierarchy of jurists, the two top categories of unconstrained-independent and unconstrained-dependent jurists (the difference being that the former type develop their own legal methodology) are generally restricted to the great Imams of the golden age of jurisprudence.[25] Thus, the only recognized categories of jurists today require varying degrees of dependence on classical jurisprudence. However, proponents of reviving *ijtihad* argued, groups of jurists may attain sufficient modern authoritativeness through collaboration.

Calls for such collective *ijtihad* began shortly after the fall of the Ottoman empire, which had codified Hanafi jurisprudence in the year 1293 A.H./1876 C.E. and imposed the code as *Majallat Al-Ahkam Al-'Adliyya*. When the Ottoman empire fell after World War I, that code had become outdated, and many regions sought to apply juristic principles in transactions law that were more liberal than those of the strict Hanafi school.[26] To provide appropriate forums for collective *ijtihad*, various Islamic countries began to establish national as well as multinational juristic councils.[27] Most prominent among those councils were the Institute of Islamic Research (Majma' Al-Buhuth Al-Islamiyya) at Al-Azhar University (established in Cairo, 1961), the Islamic Jurisprudence Council (Al-Majma' Al-Fiqhi Al-Islami) of the Muslim World League (established in Makka, 1979), and the Fiqh Academy (Majma' Al-Fiqh Al-Islami) of the Organization of Islamic Conference (established in Jeddah, 1984). It was within this framework that "Islamic finance" was born in the mid-1970s, backed by a series of juristic rulings from the various international juristic councils, as well as national councils and independent Shari'a supervisory boards. Those boards in part rely on general rulings issued by the international jurisprudence councils, and some members of those boards simultaneously serve on or advise those councils.

In recent years, bank-sponsored institutions such as the Accounting and Auditing Organization for Islamic Financial Institutions (AAOIFI) have put in place their own Shari'a boards to set general standards for contracts used in Islamic finance. The jurists serving on AAOIFI's board constitute a major subset of the jurists serving on Shari'a boards of various financial institutions. Moreover, some of those jurists serve on the major multinational juristic councils mentioned above, and others serve as expert witnesses who help to shape the opinions of those councils. Thus, there is today a small number of jurists retained by and directly advising and supervising Islamic financial providers, setting standards at institutions such as AAOIFI, and engaged in global collective *ijtihad* to define the nature of contemporary Islamic financial jurisprudence. One of the most important aspects in this contemporary *ijtihad* is its reliance on the classical institution of *fatwa* (elicitation of juristic response to a question, modeled after the Roman system of *responsa*). In this regard, the bulk of finance-related questions considered by the various juristic bodies are posed to them by practitioners of Islamic finance.[28]

Institution of Fatwa and Islamic Finance

The institution of *fatwa* has been central to the development of jurisprudence, dating back to the time of the Prophet, whose answers to various legal questions are codified as part of the Islamic canon. In later decades the Prophet's companions fielded questions on all aspects of Islamic law, often leading to codification of their opinions as "consensus of the early community in Madina." During those early periods, the two institutions of *fatwa* (providing nonbinding answers to legal questions) and *qada'* (court legal rulings) were confounded to some extent. In later periods the two institutions became clearly distinct, with *qadis* (state-appointed court judges) legislating through *qada'*, and *muftis* of official or unofficial status legislating to those who accepted their opinions through the institution of *fatwa*. In the Muslim world, a vacuum ensued in the areas of *qada'* and official jurisprudential codification following the Ottoman empire's fall after World War I. Consequently, the institution of *fatwa* effectively became the only vehicle for legislation in Islamic jurisprudence of financial transactions.

In this regard, *fatwa* played a central role in the birth of Islamic finance. The proposals of Humud (1976) inspired a *fatwa* at the First Conference of Islamic Banks (Dubai, 1979), which ushered the birth of contemporary Islamic banking. This *fatwa* (based on an otherwise obscure opinion of the Maliki jurist Ibn Shubruma) stated that an Islamic financial institution may require its customer to sign a binding promise that he will purchase the financed property on credit (with an agreed-upon mark-up) once the bank buys it based on his order. The resulting contract came to be known as *murabaha l-il-'amir b-il-shira'* (mark-up sale to the one who ordered the purchase).[29] Further modifications in this contract allowed banks to assign the eventual buyer as buying agent (to purchase the property on behalf of the bank), as well as selling agent (to sell the property to himself, again on behalf of the bank).

This *fatwa* is similar to other Islamic-finance-related *fatawa* in many respects: Bankers, lawyers, and other practitioners in the field of Islamic finance pose questions to members of juristic councils, or their own retained Shari'a supervisory boards. Jurists then rule whether or not the transaction as described to them is permissible, and if not, what permissible alternatives may be available. Some of those *fatawa* are advertised publicly,[30] whereas others issued by Shari'a boards of Islamic financial institutions may be kept confidential.[31]

We have noted in Chapter 1 that Islamic jurisprudence of financial transactions in fact proceeds as a common-law system, relying on precedent and analogy. In the above-mentioned central *fatwa*, which allowed Islamic finance to grow in the late 1970s, the precedent of Ibn Shubruma's opinion was required to justify a practice that contemporary jurists would have found difficult to base directly on canonical texts. Note, moreover, that within the institution of *fatwa*, jurists contemplate only questions posed to them. In this regard, the questioner has a decisive primary-mover advantage in choosing the question and its wording.

Consider, for instance, the manner in which an Islamic bank can offer a liquidity facility to a customer who did not wish to buy a capital good that can serve as collateral. In fact, a number of Islamic financial institutions, including some of the most conservative, structured unsecured corporate lending practices often in terms of *murabaha*. Thus, if a customer needed to borrow $1,000,000, and the "Islamic bank" was willing to lend him $1,000,000 at 5 percent interest, a simple intermediary trade solved the problem of Islamicity: The bank bought $1,000,000 worth of a commodity with relatively stable prices over the short term (e.g., some metal traded on a commodity exchange) and then sold the commodity to the customer on credit, with a deferred price of $1,050,000. This transaction falls within the framework of *murabaha* financing and thus would be approved by the bank's Shari'a board with little hesitation, given the centrality of *murabaha* to Islamic banking practice since its inception.

Of course, the customer may have no interest in the commodity except to turn around and sell it for $1,000,000 (perhaps less a brokerage fee), thus obtaining the desired liquidity. Interestingly, in two celebrated *murabaha* cases (Islamic Investment Company of the Gulf v. Symphony Gems NV in 2002, and Beximco Pharmaceuticals v. Shamil Bank of Bahain EC in 2004), plaintiffs attempted to use the argument that the credit facilities were in fact interest-bearing loans and thus did not adhere to the Shari'a, as stipulated in the contracts. In both cases, English courts ruled exclusively according to English law, deeming Shari'a issues nugatory, since contract provisions did not stipulate applying the law of any recognized sovereign state. Thus, the Islamic banks in both cases received their principals plus interest on the synthetic loans.

The transaction costs associated with multiple metal trades were sufficiently small for corporate customers borrowing large sums of money. Thus, *murabaha* structures were sufficient for this purpose and utilized for decades. However, to cater to small borrowers at the retail level, Islamic banks in GCC countries needed to reduce those transaction costs. Thus, they resorted to the transaction known as *tawarruq* (literally: monetization), which was approved by a number of Shari'a boards of Islamic financial institutions, based on its acceptability to some Hanbali jurists. In Chapter 4 we shall discuss the mechanics of *tawarruq*, which allow for lower transaction costs and raise a number of reservations, even for Hanbali jurists who had approved the contract's limited and unsystematic utilization. The practical difference between *murabaha* and *tawarruq* is quite minimal: The latter makes the final sale for cash a formal part of the transaction, often conducted by the bank on its customer's behalf. Of course, for the retail customer, this "innovation" allows better approximation of conventional bank products, as multiple trades are performed in the bank's back office, and the customer merely gets the interest-bearing loan amount in cash (rather than aluminum).

Thus, at the initiative of bankers, progressively smaller groups of jurists have issued *fatawa* that allowed progressively closer approximations of conventional banking practice: (1) In the 1970s and 1980s, large numbers of jurists approved *murabaha* financing as a de facto form of secured lending, (2) in the 1980s and 1990s, smaller numbers of jurists allowed commodity-purchase *murabaha* financing to provide de facto unsecured loans to corporate customers, and (3) in the early 2000s, a small group of GCC jurists have allowed unsecured lending to retail and corporate customers through *tawarruq*. Similarly, as we shall see in Chapter 6, multiple-sale-based bond structures were approved and used by the

Bahrain Monetary Agency to issue treasury-bill-type debt instruments. The gradual progression in approximation of conventional financial products (loans and bonds) illustrates the fundamental role bankers and lawyers play in the development of Islamic jurisprudence itself (rather than merely the Islamic finance built thereupon).

Thus, the combination of form-oriented jurisprudence and first-mover advantage given to financial industry practitioners has enabled those practitioners to shape Islamic jurisprudence of financial transactions for future generations. Indeed, the current generation of observing Muslims have already grown accustomed to reading religious books that list *murabaha* and the like as Islamic modes of finance. This makes it difficult for future jurists to develop a sensible jurisprudence that is both efficient and Islamic. A frequent argument made by industry jurists and practitioners states that one had to start somewhere. Even if the current modes of Islamic finance are imperfect, the argument goes, they are a good starting point toward developing a bona fide juristic understanding and accompanying Islamic financial industry. However, the history of Islamic finance belies that optimistic vision. As we cover most aspects of Islamic finance in this book, it will become painfully obvious that the modus operandi of this industry – rent-seeking Shari‘a arbitrage – is incapable of developing new products and services, and impervious to calls for adherence to the substance of Islamic law. Thus we end up with inefficient finance (that chases past returns) without the substantive personal protections of religious law and de facto codification of bad jurisprudence for generations of Muslims to come.[32]

2.3 Arbitraging Classical Jurisprudence

We briefly review the classical juristic treatment of property and contracts in this section and that of the forbidden *riba* and *gharar* in Chapter 3.[33] We shall see based on those reviews that the essence of classical Islamic jurisprudence of financial transactions was simply to maximize efficiency and equity in exchange. However, understanding the mode of operation in Islamic finance (reviewed in Chapters 4–9) requires some familiarity with the classical juristic views and contract forms upon which the industry was built.

For instance, the most common vehicle for Islamic bond alternatives relies on securitization of the usufruct of an eligible property, such as land or machinery. Since the most common *sukuk* structure involves selling property and leasing it back, the property must satisfy all the classical conditions of eligibility for sale as well as lease. A special-purpose corporate entity is created to buy and lease back the property. That entity must therefore be eligible to take part in such contracts. Moreover, the special-purpose entity issues certificates (*sukuk*), the holders of which receive rental income in place of bond coupons. This imposes certain conditions on certificate holders' degree of ownership – through the SPV – of the leased assets, which ownership justifies the collection of rent. Thus, the process of Shariʿa arbitrage curiously combines such classical conditions on property (and its transfer through nominate contract) with modern corporate forms that were adopted only recently in the Islamic world.[34]

Shariʿa-Arbitraging Classical Property Law

For an object to qualify as property (*mal*) in classical Islamic law, it must satisfy two conditions: (1) possibility of physical possession and (2) having potential beneficial uses. The first condition makes it impossible to define intangibles such as knowledge and health as property. Thus, if one pays a doctor or teacher, one would pay them for their time (as proxy for effort and service) rather than for the goods they provide.[35] The second condition ensures the existence of considered value for objects deemed to constitute property. The two conditions were jointly crucial for determining legal status of various economic institutions and financial transactions.

Those conditions were invoked by the majority of contemporary jurists who deemed commercial insurance impermissible, based on their characterization of its "object of sale." In this regard, if the object of an insurance contract were defined as "security," with its premium viewed as price, the contract may have to be deemed valid. However, many jurists argued, "security" does not qualify as an object of sale, since it does not constitute a tangible good or service. Similarly, jurists adhering to classical taxonomies of property could not classify any disembodied contingent claims as eligible objects of sale. Instead, those jurists argued, the object of sale in a commercial insurance contract is the amount of money that the insured party receives in compensation for loss, which is uncertain. The contract thus characterized is deemed invalid based on excessive *gharar*, since the price (premium) is known, but the object of sale (paid claim) is uncertain, as discussed in Chapter 3.

Valued vs. Unvalued Property: Shariʿa-Arbitrage Opportunity

Classical jurists further classified property (*mal*) according to a system of binary taxonomies, of which we list the most important three. First, they classified property as either (a) valued property (*mal mutaqawwam*), if it is privately owned and has permissible uses for its legitimate possessor, or (b) unvalued property (*mal ghayr mutaqawwam*). The second category includes two subcategories: (1) properties that are not currently possessed, for example, public property, and (2) properties with no permissible uses under normal circumstances, for example, wine and pork. Most contracts for total or partial ownership transfer (e.g., sale or lease, respectively) are permissible for valued, but not for unvalued, properties. This distinction allows lawyers in structured Islamic finance some leverage. For instance, if a company's assets included both valued and unvalued assets, they can either bundle the two sets of assets or disentangle them to maximize Shari'a-arbitrage profits. For instance, classical jurists would allow a Muslim investor to buy a farm with pigs living on it, or a house with a wine cellar, but would disallow sale of those impermissible properties that are unvalued for Muslims. However, the use of SPVs – to which ownership rights of various assets are assigned – can allow non-Muslims to own the impermissible properties or sell them, compensating Muslim investors indirectly through inflated prices of the valued components of the bundled property being acquired.

Another source of Shari'a-arbitrage profits stems from contemporary jurists' prohibition of owning companies with debt ratios exceeding a certain threshold. Islamic investment banks can transform a company from impermissibility to permissibility merely by structuring the leveraged acquisition through leases of eligible company property. In this regard, classical jurists differed over the eligibility of usufruct (*manfa'a*) as unbundled property eligible for sale, thus accepting or refusing characterization of leases as sale of usufruct. Shafi'i and Maliki jurists accepted usufruct as valued property, but early Hanafi jurists argued that the legal right to extract usufruct does not exist separately from other ownership rights, except by virtue of the lease contract. Differences in characterization of the same contract as sale of usufruct versus lease (*ijara*) can result in numerous differences in lease conditions, including rights and responsibilities for maintenance. Given a desired structure, those differences in characterization may require the creation of additional SPVs (in addition to the one that holds title for the master lease) to transfer those rights and obligations under classical *ijara* conditions back to their optimal parties under contemporary regulation and legislation. Another consequence of characterizing usufruct as a sale object – which has received surprisingly little attention in the literature – is the resulting sale repurchase characterization of sale-lease-back structures extensively used in structuring *sukuk* and corporate acquisitions in Islamic investment banking. We shall discuss various juristic and legal problems raised by this and similar sale-repurchase structures below.

Portability and Sukuk Structures

Second, properties are also classified into (a) immovable (*'aqar*) properties such as real estate and (b) movable or easily transportable (*manqul*) properties. Legal status of a number of transactions is affected by the portability of property. For instance, reselling purchased items prior to taking possession is deemed by some Hanafi jurists to be valid for immovable objects but not for movable ones. This makes many Islamic financial transactions (e.g., *murabaha*-based mortgage financing) particularly cost-effective for banks whose offices may not be in physical proximity to the financed real estate. Another important distinction based on transportability of property pertains to preemption rights (*haqq al-shuf'a*, the right of first refusal to buy a neighbor's or partner's property at whatever price offered by third parties), which are deemed valid only for immovable properties. This also has potentially significant legal consequences for sale-lease-back-repurchase *sukuk* structures, wherein owners of adjacent properties may have preemption rights that are negated by the bond structure.

A third important consequence of the distinction between movable and immovable properties for structures of *sukuk* and other debt instruments is that movables (and hence more liquid) properties of a delinquent or bankrupt debtor are liquidated first, thus inducing implicit debt-subordination rules in asset-based structures. There are many other legal consequences of portability of property, including ineligibility of movable properties for easement rights, and their ineligibility for establishment as mortmain or trusts (*waqf*), which play an important role in contemporary structured finance and investment banking.[36]

Fungibility and Entitlement

Third, properties are divided into fungibles (*mithli*), measured by weight, volume, length, or numbers, and nonfungibles (*qimi*), each item of which is unique and differs in value significantly from other items of the same genus and kind. A main legal effect of this distinction is eligibility of fungible properties for establishment as liabilities, for example, as deferred prices, or objects of prepaid forward sales (*salam*). Many rulings also follow from divisibility and uniformity of fungibles, including the possibility of partial in-kind compensations. This distinction is important for various Islamic finance products, including trade- and lease-based *sukuk* commodity trade financing. In case of nondeliverability of goods in trade-based finance, liability for delivery of the goods (rather than their value) remains intact.

This may clearly induce significant transaction costs, for example, for contracts based on *salam*, wherein holders of the short position are required to deliver the commodities for which they contracted. On the other hand, in leases of nonfungible properties, destruction of the property would require compensation for its market value. In fact, Islamic finance structures utilizing *salam* and *ijara* stipulate sufficient conditions to ensure equivalence to the debt structures of conventional bonds (see Chapter 6 for details). However, unless and until specific lawsuits are brought to bear on this point, it is not clear how those conditions interact with stipulations that contracts are made in accordance with Shari'a. At worst, such lawsuits may expose gaps in the legal structures that render the Islamic products substantially different from mimicked conventional counterparts (in which case those instruments would have been mispriced). More likely, highly publicized lawsuits may question the legitimacy of calling the products "Islamic," where the brand name rests on the assertion that classical Islamic contract conditions are observed.

Most significant for Shari'a-arbitrage purposes is that rules of *riba* (increase in one of two exchanged items of the same genus and kind without compensation) do not apply to nonfungibles. Thus, while a usurer is not allowed to trade one ounce of gold for two, he is allowed to trade one nonfungible item (e.g., a diamond) for two diamonds, each of equal market value to the first. Moreover, a usurer may legally sell a diamond worth $10,000 today for a deferred price of $20,000 tomorrow. The buyer may have no interest in the diamond and sell it for $10,000 in cash. Thus, the usurer would legally collect overnight interest of 100 percent in a valid contract that avoids *riba* in form (though obviously usurious in substance). This clearly illustrates that the prohibition of *riba* cannot possibly be limited to questions of interest or exorbitant interest, since interest can be hidden in sales (as in *murabaha* and *tawarruq*), and it can easily be made exorbitant while avoiding the formalistic rules of *riba*.

Ownership

Article #125 of *Majallat Al-Ahkam Al-'Adliyya* defined owned property as "anything owned by a human being, be it a specified property, or usufruct of a property." Thus, Hanafi jurists, who did not recognize usufruct and disembodied legal rights as property, did recognize ownership thereof. Conversely, some properties (e.g., rivers, public infrastructure, parks) are not eligible for private ownership. Thus, attributes of properties and owned objects must be studied separately in terms of eligibility as objects of various contracts. Although the *Majalla*'s basic definition restricted ownership rights to humans, jurists have lately adopted legal entities such as corporations (genuine or special-purpose entities) and allowed them to own properties, usufruct, and legal rights.

Whereas modern legal scholarship recognizes ownership as a bundle of rights, which may be distributed across a number of human and corporate entities, classical jurisprudence recognized total and partial ownership only in terms of separating property (*raqaba*) from its usufruct (*manfa'a*).[37] Thus, classical jurists defined ownership of the property and its usufruct as total, and ownership of one without the other as partial ownership. Participants at Al-Baraka's sixth jurisprudence symposium in 1990 utilized this separation of a property from its usufruct to devise an innovative structure in lease-to-purchase models for Al-Baraka lease-based home financing in London. Under the proposed structure, the property itself would be sold at the outset, thus allowing the eventual buyer of the property to receive title immediately. However, the bank would retain ownership of the usufruct, for which they can put a lien on the property and collect rent according to the contract. In recent years this structure has not been used. Instead, title is typically assigned to an SPV constructed for each lease-to-purchase transaction.[38]

Advances and Restrictions on Partial Ownership

Sale of usufruct, and its possible resale through subleasing, has given rise to time-sharing arrangements, primarily for housing units near the two holy mosques in Makka and Madina. Through this structure individuals own a multiyear right, for example, to usage of a housing unit next to the holy mosque in Makka for one week each year. The Saudi government did not contemplate the problematic prospect of selling land adjacent to the mosque (which may be needed later for expanding it). Instead, the government leased the land long term to a legal entity that in turn issued usufruct certificates (*sukuk al-manfaʿa*) that entitle their owners to extract usufruct during certain periods. This structure, with tradable usufruct extraction rights, was possible since all certificate holders would use the property in the same manner.[39] This is a positive example of using partial ownership provisions to develop a useful financial vehicle.

However, other useful implications of partial ownership were not developed in the industry. For example, within the conventional mortgage example of Chapter 1, contemporary jurists had the option to recognize partial ownership in more advanced terms than had their classical predecessors. Thus, instead of allowing mortgage financing only through credit sales (*murabaha*), lease (*ijara*), or full-fledged partnership (*musharaka*), they could have determined that liens (which could not have existed in premodern times, without searchable title databases) are a form of ownership right different from the classic *rahn* (pawning) contract. Indeed, modern legal dictionaries define a lien primarily as "a conveyance of title to property that is given to secure an obligation (as a debt) and that is defeated upon payment or performance according to stipulated terms."[40] Based on this legal definition and reality, jurists could have viewed the mortgagee's lien on property as a form of partial co-ownership for the mortgage period (until the debt is fully paid). Thus, conventional mortgages could have been characterized in terms of diminishing partnership between mortgagor and mortgagee.

Full development of this juristic argument is beyond the scope of this book and the author's area of expertise. However, we should note that such characterization of conventional mortgages would have led to more efficient outcomes that are deemed "Islamic." Of course, this efficiency would be attainable in part through elimination of Shariʿa-arbitrage opportunities, which have sadly become the main incentive mechanisms for Islamic finance. We shall discuss an alternative approach to Islamic finance in Chapters 3 and 4, based on understanding the prohibition of *riba* in terms of equity in exchange through marking to market within the framework of conventional financial tools such as mortgage financing. Within that framework the role of Islamic financial institutions would be acting as de facto financial advisers for their customers.

Trust, Guaranty, and Interest

Classical jurists recognized two types of property possession based on liability risk: possessions of trust and possessions of guaranty. Possessions of trust (which result, e.g., from deposits, leases, and partnerships) make the possessor responsible to compensate the owner only for damage to property caused by the trustee's own negligence or transgression. In contrast, possession of guaranty implies that the possessor guarantees the property for its owner against all types of damage, including damage not caused by the guarantor's own negligence or transgression. Classical jurists further stipulated that both types of possession cannot coexist. Thus, if a property is held in trust according to one consideration and in guaranty according to another, the possession of guaranty is deemed stronger and dominant, and rules of guaranty are thus applied.

Hence, most contemporary jurists have analyzed bank deposits thus: A classical depositary would hold the depositor's funds in trust. However, if the deposited amount is guaranteed, then the contract is no longer a valid deposit (*ida*ʿ), and many jurists have argued that the closest contract resulting in possession of guaranty is the loan (*qard*) contract (without specifying the metric used for determining contract proximity). Hence, if the principal is guaranteed by the bank, the depositor-bank relationship is viewed by those jurists as lender-borrower, and bank interest on deposits is thus viewed as forbidden *riba*. This line of reasoning was utilized in the conclusions of the fourteenth session of Majlis Majmaʿ Al-Fiqh Al-Islami held in Duha, Qatar, January 11–16, 2003. This logic was thus used to reject the earlier *fatwa* by Majlis Majmaʿ Al-Buhuth Al-Islamiyya of Al-Azhar, issued in Cairo on November 28, 2002, which had characterized bank deposits as legitimate investments paying fixed profit rates. El-Gamal (2003) proposed a synthesis of the two positions, which seems to have anticipated more recent developments of Islamic bank savings accounts that guarantee deposit principals in the United States and United Kingdom, as discussed in Chapter 8. Similar considerations of trust and guaranty are used by contemporary jurists to justify the Islamicity of *murabaha* financing, wherein the Islamic bank charges the same fixed interest rate it would charge on conventional mortgages, for instance. We shall discuss this issue in greater detail in Chapter 4.

Arbitraging Classical Contract Conditions

The most important condition for contract validity is mutual consent.[41] Toward that end, jurists enumerated some contract cornerstones without which this meeting of minds cannot be ensured. Those pertain to (1) parties of the contract, who must be eligible to conduct the contract, (2) contract language, and (3) object of the contract. A contract was not considered concluded if any of its cornerstones were violated. Conditions of contract conclusion may be grouped into conditions pertaining to (1) contracting parties (must be discerning, of legal age, etc.), (2) contract language (correspondence of offer and acceptance, elimination of unnecessary uncertainty), (3) unity of contract session, and (4) permissibility of object for specific contract.

A concluded financial contract was deemed valid if it avoided six main factors: (1) ignorance about object, price, time period, and the like, (2) coercion, (3) conditions contrary to a contract's nature (e.g., sale for a fixed period, or wherein the buyer 's use of his property is restricted), (4) unnecessary ambiguity in contract language, (5) encroachment on others' property rights, and (6) unconventional conditions that benefit one party at the other's expense. Returning to our mortgage example of Chapter 1, notice that jurists based their conclusion of impermissibility of conventional mortgage loans on the view that the mortgagor borrowed a certain sum of money (cash loan) and pays a larger amount in the future. However, in a classical loan contract (*qard*), ownership of the lent amount would be transferred to the borrower.[42] Thus, the jurists' analysis appears to be incoherent.

Conditions that reinforce the lender's ability to ensure debt repayment (including *rahn* or premodern mortgage of some property) were allowed. However, restrictive covenants that determine how the borrower must use the lent money (in modern mortgages, to buy a particular property that is then mortgaged) negate ownership of the money being transferred from lender to borrower. Hence, according to the classical rules of loan contracts, condition (3) is violated, and the mortgage loan's characterization in terms of premodern *qard* would be invalid. Development of a modern Islamic theory of secured lending is beyond the scope of this book. However, it is clear that Shariʿa-arbitrage opportunities in the mortgage market have been based on inaccurate matching of a contemporary term "loan" (especially within the context of secured lending) with the premodern *qard* contract. In this regard, we have seen in Chapter 1 that the OCC was convinced that Islamic mortgage alternatives through credit sale (*murabaha*) and lease (*ijara*) financing were in fact substantively equivalent to secured lending as practiced by banks. Instead of using this arbitrage opportunity to market costlier mortgages to Muslim customers, Islamic finance jurists and practitioners should have developed a new Islamic theory of secured lending, which is a modern transaction with no direct analogs in classical jurisprudence.

Another interesting subversion of conditions of classical contracts is evident in the structure of *murabaha* (cost-plus) financing. Classical jurists had stipulated that in *murabaha* and other "trust sales" (where buyer relies on seller revealing his cost), knowledge of the initial price is a condition of validity. When jurists adapted *murabaha* contracts for financial intermediation, they maintained this condition in terms of revealing the initial cash price paid for the property later sold on credit. However, it is clear that financial intermediaries, Islamic or otherwise, serve a primary function of transforming financial liabilities into financial assets, rather than trading in homes or automobiles. Thus, in *murabaha* financing, for example, and certainly in its *tawarruq* incarnation, the Islamic bank's business is in fact extension of credit, rather than sale of property. The requirement to reveal the initial price should translate in this financing framework into revelation of the bank's cost of funds and spread paid by the customer (e.g., we pay LIBOR + 100 basis points for those funds, and we charge you LIBOR + 200 basis points). This would in fact add economic value for Islamic bank customers, who are currently – at best – informed of their own cost of funds under truth-in-lending provisions such as regulation Z in the United States. In contrast, the current Islamic bank procedure is to reveal only the cash price, thus claiming that the difference between that cost and the credit price – which can be 200 percent or more of the original price, that is, the customer's cost of financing – is the bank's profit. This obviously does not satisfy the original intent in classical *murabaha*, since the relevant cost and profit margin for the financier are not in fact disclosed to the customer.

Other examples of arbitraging classical contract conditions to synthesize contemporary financial practices are provided throughout the book. In many cases, we shall argue that contemporary jurists' characterization of contemporary practices in terms of classical contracts may render those contracts invalid or defective according to the classical conditions. In this regard, it is worthwhile noting that Hanafi scholars distinguished between those two types of nonvalid contracts: defective (*fasid*) and invalid (*batil*). They ruled that a contract is invalid if it fails to satisfy any of its cornerstones, uses inadmissible contract language, or has an impermissible object (e.g., wine or pork). They further ruled that invalid contracts were not in fact concluded and thus may not result in any transfer of property, legal rights, and the like. In contrast, they deemed a contract defective if it satisfies all normal legal requirements but contains some illegal characteristics (e.g., a sale that contains excessive uncertainty, or *gharar*). Hanafis uniquely allowed certain types of defective contracts to revert to validity, for instance, if an appended corrupting condition that is not integral to the contract is removed. Moreover, they ruled that a valid contract to which defective conditions are appended remains valid, and the defective conditions are disregarded as nugatory provisions.

Thus, Hanafi and other jurists relied on nominate contract conditions to ensure validity of various contracts. Contemporary selective adherence to some of those conditions can be used for Shari'a-arbitrage purposes, as shown in the previous examples and throughout this book. In contrast, contemporary juristic and economic analysis may be used to justify many contemporary financial practices. Within the latter context, study of classical nominate contracts would focus on their substantive economic content within their specific historical context, rather than outdated formal mechanics. To the extent that modern regulatory and legal systems share the main objectives of Islamic law (*maqasid al-Shari'a*, of which the highest are preservation of life, wealth, mind, etc.), conventional modern regulatory restrictions can often be considered sufficient substitutes for classical contract conditions. To the extent that religious law aims to provide personal protections beyond the minimal ones afforded by secular regulatory frameworks, the substance of classical jurisprudence should be used to devise new individual protections within the modern conventional practice.

Arbitrage, Ruses, and Islamic Finance

Blind or cynical adherence to classical contract conditions may violate a fundamental principle in Islamic legal theory as expressed by Al-Shatibi:

> Legal ruses (*al-hiyal*) in religion are generally illegal. ... In this regard, legal provisions (*al-a'mal al-Shar'iya*) are not ends in themselves, but means to legal ends, which are the benefits intended by the law. Thus, one who keeps legal form while squandering its substance does not follow the law.[43]

However, there have been historical differences in opinion among jurists regarding some of the most obvious ruses, including some for which canonical prohibition is claimed. The most obvious example, discussed in detail in Chapter 4, is same-item sale-repurchase (*bay' al-'ina*). Some jurists – including the prominent Hanafi scholar and judge Abu Yusuf – deemed this practice valid, and others including the Hanafi scholar Al-Shaybani and most Shafi'i and Zahiri jurists deemed it valid but reprehensible, provided that the second sale is not stipulated as part of the initial contract.[44] In contrast, Maliki and Hanbali jurists ruled that the contract is invalid, since it is clearly a device for circumventing the prohibition of *riba* and based on two Prophetic traditions, the authenticity of which was accepted within those two schools but rejected by other jurists. However, some Hanbali jurists allowed a slightly more elaborate version of the same-item sale-repurchase procedure by including a third party. Contemporary *tawarruq* emerged based on this introduction of a third party.

We have thus seen that contemporary Shari'a arbitrage is made possible mainly through the utilization of nominate contracts and selective application of their classical conditions. In this regard, the influential jurist Ibn Taymiyya noted in his lengthy discussion of nominate contracts that early Maliki and Hanbali jurists (including Imam Ahmad himself) had deemed contracts invalid if they could not find appropriate precedents permitting similar ones.[45] Traces of this original bias are readily seen in the use of classical nominate contract names in Islamic finance. Contemporary jurists assert that the default ruling in economic transactions is permissibility, but it is clear that many Muslims hold the view that contemporary Islamic financial contracts need to adhere to classical forms. Whether this bias is based on belief of impermissibility of transactions without classical precedents or merely aims to derive comfort from such precedents, it is likely that legal forms will continue to play a prominent role in Islamic finance for the foreseeable future. The best we can hope to accomplish in the short term is to ensure that this focus on form does not exclude consideration of economic substance entirely. Optimistically, one may hope that modest inclusions of substantive considerations in Islamic finance in the short to medium term may later serve as catalysts in long-term development of a viable modern Islamic jurisprudence.

3

Two Major Prohibitions: *Riba* and *Gharar*

We have shown in Chapter 2 that Islamic finance is a prohibition-driven industry. In this regard, the instigating factor for prohibition-based contract invalidation can almost always be attributed to the two factors labeled *riba* and *gharar*. We have also shown in Chapter 1 that mainstream contemporary scholars of economic analysis of the law consider such prohibitions of mutually agreeable financial transactions paternalistic and conducive to efficiency losses. The form-oriented nature of Islamic finance has done little to counter this claim for Islamic prohibitions.

Participants in the industry, especially ones who are not themselves devout Muslims, operationally respect Muslims' religious observance and devise financial solutions that avoid various prohibitions according to juristic opinion. This attitude has contributed further to the form-above-substance approach in Islamic finance: Lawyers and bankers are loath to challenge jurists' solutions as merely inefficient replications of what they had deemed forbidden transactions. To provide proper understanding of Islamic finance as practiced today, this chapter covers the economic substance that we believe was intended by the prohibitions. In later chapters we shall compare the economic substance of prohibitions and premodern nominate contract conditions in greater detail, comparing the form-oriented approach of contemporary Islamic finance to the substance-oriented classical jurisprudence.

Paternalism of Prohibitions

In the process of highlighting economic substance of prohibitions of *riba* and *gharar* in this chapter, we need to address two charges against prohibitions: paternalism and efficiency reduction. The paternalism charge is freely admitted, since devout Muslims – and indeed most religious people – do not shy away from a paternalistic image of God. In this regard, Islamic jurists and legal theorists have maintained that God never forbids anything that is good. When God forbids

46

something that contains some good, legal theorists argued, it must be because of the potential for greater hidden harm.[1] For instance, the second of three Qur'anic stages of gradual prohibition of wine and gambling state explicitly: "They ask you about wine and gambling, say: 'Therein is great sin and some benefit, and their sin is greater than their benefit' " [2:219].

Human irrationality in the face of addictive activities such as drinking and gambling appears to be at the heart of this prohibition. This is suggested by the conjunction of wine and gambling in the cited verse as well as the final stage of categorical Qur'anic prohibition of addictive drinking and gambling activities: "O people of faith: Wine, gambling, dedication of stones, and divination with arrows are abominable works of the devil. Thus, avoid such activities so that you may prosper" [5:90].

More generally, one may consider four types of activities based on *net* benefit or harm: (1) beneficial ones that are apparently beneficial, (2) beneficial ones that are not clearly beneficial, (3) harmful ones that are apparently harmful, and (4) harmful ones that are not apparently harmful. No injunctions or prohibitions are needed for the first and third types of activities, whereas injunctions to perform the first type of acts, and prohibitions against the fourth, are necessary. In this regard, the verse [2:219] clearly explained that drinking and gambling belong to the fourth category: Humans may be lured by the apparent benefits and thus lose sight of the greater harm.

This is easily explained in the context of drinking, which may not be harmful in small measure, but can be extremely dangerous because of human irrationality in the face of addictive and intoxicating substances. The intoxication effect was highlighted in the first stage of prohibition of wine: "O people of faith, do not approach prayers while you are intoxicated" [4:43], wherein gambling was not mentioned. The addictiveness effect and resulting tendency to create acrimonious and irresponsible behavior were highlighted by conjoining wine and gambling in the two subsequent stages of prohibition in [2:219] and [5:90].

Bounded Rationality and Paternalism

In the case of wine and gambling, the Qur'anic solution was complete avoidance thereof, since those activities are not essential. In contrast, transfers of credit and risk are at the heart of finance, without which an economic system cannot function. The Islamic legal solution in this case was to impose restrictions on the means of transferring credit and risk, through prohibitions of *riba* and *gharar*. In this chapter I shall argue that – in finance – the forbidden *riba* is essentially "trading in credit," and the forbidden *gharar* is "trading in risk," as unbundled commodities.

In other words, Islamic jurisprudence uses those two prohibitions to allow only for the appropriate measure of permissibility of transferring credit and risk to achieve economic ends. As many observers and practitioners in financial markets will testify, trading in credit and risk (perfected through derivative securities) is as dangerous as twirling a two-edged sword. Although those vehicles can be used judiciously to reduce risk and enhance welfare, they can easily entice otherwise cautious individuals to engage in ruinous gambling behavior. While financial regulators seek to limit the scope of credit and risk trading to prevent systemic failures, Islamic jurisprudence introduces injunctions that aim also to protect individuals from their own greed and myopia.

What to Forbid? Balancing Benefits and Risks

The objective of balancing economic freedom (allowing more contracts to enable more economic activities) with risk of abuse (if too much freedom is allowed) is made clear by the fact that some contracts that contain *riba* and/or *gharar* are permitted in the canonical and juristic texts. This is the case with prepaid forward sales (*salam*), which contain significant *gharar* (unnecessary risk and uncertainty), since the object of sale typically does not exist at contract time. However, this *gharar* is deemed minor relative to the potential gains from financing agricultural and other activities through *salam*. Thus, this benefit consideration overruled the contract's invalidity based on *gharar*, as would be dictated by analogical reasoning alone. Similarly, credit sales can easily be used as vehicles for *riba*, as shown in the previous chapter (e.g., through same-item sale-repurchase, either as *'ina* or *tawarruq*). In both of those examples, the benefits from allowing production of nonexistent goods through *salam*, and consumption of goods against claims to future income through credit sales, respectively, outweigh the potential dangers of abuse. Hence the contracts were permitted despite the corrupting factors.

The discussion in Chapter 2 of various juristic opinions on *'ina* (same-item sale-repurchase) is illustrative of juristic cost-benefit analysis. Obviously, one cannot forbid all spot sales or credit sales, since that would lead to economic ruin. On the one hand, jurists unanimously forbid same-item sale-repurchase if the second sale is stipulated in the first.[2] On the other hand, if the two transactions are executed under separate contracts, some jurists forbade the practice to prevent abuse (the Maliki juristic rule of preventing means of circumventing the law, known as *sadd al-dhara'i'*), whereas others (e.g., Al-Shafi'i, who restricted juristic reasoning to analogy) felt compelled to deem the practice valid. Of course, in Islamic finance, jurists may be asked to validate each contract separately, without explaining the entire financial structure for which they will be used.

This example is indeed central for understanding our subsequent discussion of contemporary Islamic jurisprudence and finance. By definition, almost all novel financial transactions, and variations thereof that were considered by jurists on Islamic banks' Shari'a boards, are sufficiently complex to generate multiple juristic opinions based on analogy, prevention of abuse, benefit analysis, and the like. Variations in opinions allow Islamic financial providers to exercise price discrimination by segmenting the market according to degree of conservatism, thereby extracting greater Shari'a arbitrage rents from more conservative customers.

3.1 The Prohibition of *Riba*

The three-letter past-tense root of the term *riba* is the Arabic verb *raba*, meaning to increase.[3] Therefore, jurists defined the forbidden *riba* generally as "trading two goods of the same kind in different quantities, where the increase is not a proper compensation."[4] Naturally, the lexical meaning of the term (which covers increase of all types) is not the object of prohibition. Thus, numerous jurists have analyzed the juristic meaning of the forbidden *riba* over the centuries. While most contemporary jurists have denied any uncertainty about the juristic definition of forbidden *riba*, studies such as the two in Rida (1986) clearly show that premodern and contemporary jurists have expanded the definition of the forbidden *riba* considerably beyond its original domain.[5]

In this regard, the distinction between legitimate compensations and forbidden *riba* is the most fundamental distinguishing feature of Islamic finance, as a prohibition-driven industry. However, the distinction – as defined by contemporary jurists – is exploited mostly by adopting premodern forms rather than mechanisms that ensure fairness of contract pricing. In this regard, understanding the canonical prohibition of *riba*, and contemporary interpretations thereof, is central to understanding the industry as it exists today, as well as any likely alternative "Islamic" structure. We thus turn now to the task of providing an economic analysis of the canonical texts on *riba* and the classical juristic analyses thereof. We begin by considering the canon.

Canonical Texts on Riba

There are two main types of *riba* recognized by all scholars, with Shafi'i scholars providing a further refinement of the second type. The first type is called *riba al-nasi'a*.[6] The worst form of this *riba*, known as *riba al-jahiliyya* (practiced in pre-Islamic Arabia), was strictly forbidden in the Qur'an, to the point that Imam Malik is reported to have described its prohibition as the severest one in Islam.[7]

The first mention of *riba* in the Qur'an was in Makka, and it discouraged collection thereof, without explicitly prohibiting it: "That which you lend to increase in the property of others will not increase with God; but that which you give out in charity, seeking God's pleasure, it will surely multiply" [30:39]. The first verses regarding *riba* that were revealed in Madina only forbade pre-Islamic *riba* of Arabia, whereby interest was charged at the maturity of debts from interest-free loans or credit sales, and compounded at later maturity dates. Thus, the principal due on the debtor was described in the Qur'an as "*riba* doubled and multiplied" [3:130].[8] Among the very last Qur'anic verses to be revealed, the verses [2:275–9] ordered Muslims to abandon all remaining *riba* (presumably of the same form defined in [3:130]), otherwise to expect a war from God and His Messenger.

Main Juristic Taxonomies of Riba

Most jurists have expanded the strict Qur'anic prohibition of pre-Islamic *riba* to cover all forms of interest-bearing loans, subsumed under the term *riba al-nasi'a*. They provided three explanations of the rationale for this prohibition: (1) one might potentially exploit poor debtors who need to borrow money or commodities, (2) trading money may lead to fluctuations in currency values and monetary uncertainty, (3) trading foodstuffs for larger amounts of future foodstuffs would lead to shortages in spot markets for those foodstuffs (presumably because many traders would withhold the goods in the hope of getting more in the future!).[9]

None of those explanations seems particularly convincing. After all, a usurer can equally easily exploit a needy debtor by selling him a property of market value $100, say, for a deferred price of $1,000, without violating the rules of *riba* as envisioned by jurists. The second explanation seems equally weak on economic grounds. Relative prices of commodities may fluctuate based on supply and demand changes, regardless of the possibility of extending interest-based credit.

Finally, the logic of the argument on foodstuffs is clearly defective: Traders prefer deferment only as long as the terms of trade exceed their time preference and vice versa – indeed, that is how implicit interest rates would be determined in equilibrium, based on market participants' rates of time preference. Moreover, if credit trading in foodstuffs could cause the problems of which classical jurists spoke, those same problems would result from selling deferred claims on foodstuffs for an immediate monetary price, or selling foodstuffs for deferred monetary prices, both of which are allowed by jurists with implicit compensation for time value. In fact, jurists of all major schools, declaring that "time has a share in the price," recognized the legitimacy of seeking compensation for time value in credit and *salam* sales, including where the objects of sale are foodstuffs.[10]

The second category of *riba* recognized by jurists is called *riba al-fadl* (the *riba* of increase, also called *riba al-Sunna*). It prohibits trading goods of the same genus and kind in different quantities, based on a valid Prophetic tradition: "Gold for gold, silver for silver, wheat for wheat, barley for barley, dates for dates, and salt for salt, like for like, hand to hand, and any increase is *riba*."[11] Non-Zahiri jurists agreed that those six commodities were given only as examples. Hanafi jurists extended the prohibition to all fungible goods measured by weight or volume, whereas Shafi'i and Maliki jurists restricted it to monetary commodities (gold and silver) and storable foodstuffs.

In our discussion of currency exchanges (*sarf*), we shall discuss Prophetic traditions that dealt exclusively with spot- and deferred-price trading of gold for gold, silver for silver, and gold for silver. Those traditions explicitly forbade a standard trick used by Medici bankers to circumvent the early Catholic Church's prohibition of interest, by subsuming interest rates in exchange rates.[12]

Riba Is Not the Same as Interest

There are reports that some prominent early companions of the Prophet, including the brilliant jurist 'Abdullah ibn 'Abbas, did not recognize the strict prohibition of *riba* that does not involve a time factor. He, Usama ibn Zayd ibn Arqam, Ibn Jubair, and others ruled that the only type of definitively forbidden *riba* is that which contains a time factor (*riba al-nasi'a*), even citing a Prophetic tradition to that effect: "There is no *riba* except with deferment."[13] Later reports by Jabir suggest that this tradition referred to trading different goods, such as gold for silver or wheat for barley, and that Ibn 'Abbas reversed his opinion and joined the majority opinion of prohibition of *riba al-fadl*.[14]

Jurists listed two reasons for the prohibition of *riba al-fadl*, which does not include a time factor: (1) spot trading of the same commodity for different quantities can be easily combined with credit sales to bring about the same effect as deferment *riba* (hence *riba al-fadl* is forbidden to prevent circumvention of the law – *saddan lil-dhara'i*), and (2) such trading includes excessive *gharar* (avoidable risk and uncertainty), since neither party knows whether the trade is beneficial or harmful to them.[15] Ibn Rushd based his central analysis of *riba*, on which we shall elaborate below, on the latter explanation of the prohibition (uncertainty regarding equity in exchange).

The inclusion of *riba al-fadl* under the general heading of forbidden *riba* is very important for understanding the economic substance of the prohibitions. However, most contemporary jurists and scholars of Islamic finance wish to exclude discussions of this topic, precisely to continue the mistaken one-to-one rhetorical association of "*riba*" with "interest." In fact, equivalence of the two terms is far from appropriate.

First, even the most conservative contemporary jurists do not consider all forms of what economists and regulators call interest to be forbidden *riba*. A simple examination of *riba*-free Islamic financial methods such as mark-up credit sales (*murabaha*) and lease (*ijara*) financing shows that those modes of financing are not "interest-free." Indeed, truth-in-lending regulations in the United States force Islamic and conventional financiers to report the implicit interest rates they charge their customers in such financing arrangements. Thus, the practice of Islamic finance itself illustrates the fact that some forms of interest (e.g., in credit sales and leases) should not be considered forbidden *riba*.

Conversely, the prohibition of *riba al-fadl* illustrates definitively that there are forms of forbidden *riba* (illegitimate increase in exchange) that do not include interest. Indeed, as some Hanafi jurists have noted, the six-commodities Prophetic tradition cited in the previous section stipulated two conditions: "hand to hand" and "in equal amounts." Thus, if one traded an ounce of gold today for a deferred price of one ounce of gold next year, the transaction would still be deemed *riba*, despite the zero interest rate, because of violation of the "hand-to-hand" restriction. Those Hanafi jurists reasoned as follows: An ounce of gold today is clearly worth more than an ounce of gold in one year (recognizing the time value of money). Thus, one would never trade an ounce of gold today for an ounce of gold next year, unless one is getting something else in return (which is not disclosed in the sales contract). Whatever that extra benefit may be, they argued, it constitutes *riba*. Our subsequent analysis of the prohibition of *riba* – in terms of ensuring economic efficiency and equity in exchange – would simply explain the prohibition at zero interest based on the same general principle, applied to any other interest rate: How do we know that zero percent is the fair rate in exchanging gold today for gold in one year?

Economic Substance of the Prohibition of Riba

In his seminal work on comparative jurisprudence, the Maliki jurist, judge, and philosopher Ibn Rushd (also known as Averroës, d. 595 A.H./1198 C.E.) adopted the Hanafi generalization of rules of *riba* (based on the six-commodities tradition) to all fungible commodities, based on the following economic analysis:

It is thus apparent from the law that what is targeted by the prohibition of *riba* is the excessive inequity it entails. In this regard, equity in certain transactions is achieved through equality. Since the attainment of equality in exchange of items of different kinds is difficult, we use their values in monetary terms. Thus, equity may be ensured through proportionality of value for goods that are not measured by weight and volume. Thus, the ratio of exchanged quantities will be determined by the ratio of the values of the different types of goods traded. For example, if a person sells a horse in exchange for clothes ... if the value of the horse is fifty, the value of the clothes should be fifty. [If the value of each piece of clothing is five], then the horse should be exchanged for 10 pieces of clothing.

As for [fungible] goods measured by volume or weight, equity requires equality, since they are relatively homogenous, and thus have similar benefits. Since it is not necessary for a person owning one of those goods to exchange it for goods of the same type, justice in this case is achieved by equating volume or weight, since the benefits are very similar.[16]

Thus, Ibn Rushd articulated the conditions for efficiency in exchange: that the ratio of traded quantities should be determined by the ratio of prices, and the latter should be equal to the ratio of [marginal] utilities.[17] This restriction was never made part of the rules of *riba*, since monitoring market prices of all goods would be a very tedious task. Thus, the prohibition is imposed only for equality in exchanging fungible goods, with the understanding – as suggested by Ibn Rushd – that if significant quality differences existed, one would avoid directly exchanging low-quality goods for high-quality ones of the same kind in barter.

A number of Prophetic traditions clearly support the notion of equity through equality when trading fungibles and illustrate the alternative of avoiding direct barter in cases of different good qualities. In this regard, Bilal and Abu Hurayrah narrated that a man employed in Khaybar brought the Prophet some high-quality dates. The Prophet inquired if all Khaybar dates were similar to that kind, and the man told him that they traded two or three volumes of lower-quality dates for one volume of higher-quality ones. The Prophet told him – angrily – never to do that again, but to sell lower-quality dates and use their proceeds to buy the higher-quality ones.[18]

Equity and Efficiency through Marking to Market

Selling the first type of dates (at the highest available market price), and buying the other type (for the lowest available market price), ensures that exchange takes place at the ratio dictated by market prices. Naturally, traders would trade only at that ratio if they valued the marginal units differently. Allowing for diminishing marginal utilities, whereby the buyer of each type of dates will value successive marginal units less, trading eventually halts by equating the ratio of marginal utilities to the ratio of market prices. Hence (Pareto) efficiency in exchange is attained, as dictated by contemporary neoclassical economic theory. Thus, the injunction against this type of *riba al-fadl* can be readily seen as a mechanism that precommits those who observe the prohibition to collection of information about market conditions, and marking terms of trade to market prices. This protects individuals against engaging in disadvantageous trades and enhances overall exchange efficiency. In this regard, notice that trading at any ratio that deviates from that of market prices will – by necessity – be disadvantageous to one party. Hence, justice and efficiency both dictate following this mark-to-market approach to establishing trading ratios.

Extending this logic to exchange over time (through credit sales, leases, or other transactions) is not difficult. In the context of credit sales and lease-to-purchase financing, the substantive prohibition of *riba* – aiming to ensure equity in exchange – dictates that credit in such transactions must be extended at the appropriate interest rate. In this regard, conventional finance has played a very important role for contemporary Islamic finance, by determining the market interest rates for various borrowers, based on creditworthiness and security of the posted collateral.

Here, benchmarking the implicit interest rate in Islamic credit sales and lease-to-purchase transactions to conventional interest rates is quite appropriate. Indeed, if, for instance, the market interest rate for a particular borrower and particular collateral was 6 percent, but customer and financier agreed on a credit sale at 10 percent implied interest, one would object that this clearly violates the spirit of Islamic prohibition of *riba*, even if it uses a sale-based ruse to stay clear of the ancient forbidden form. In this regard, Al-Misri (2004) has argued that Islamic banks are well advised to abandon characterizing their mark-up in credit sales as "profit," and list it instead as "interest," since the former is potentially unlimited whereas the latter is capped by various contemporary anti-usury laws that protect those in need of credit against predatory lenders.

Islamic Finance: Form and Substance Revisited

Why, then, would we need an Islamic finance? Why would we go through the trouble of forcing an Islamic bank to buy a property first and then sell it to the customer on credit if the actual objective can be achieved more directly, through a secured lending transaction? Those questions must be answered in two steps: The first step is recognition that individuals engage in myopically excessive borrowing behavior if left to their own devices. Adherence to religious law can serve as an effective precommitment mechanism to ensure that individuals do not abuse the availability of credit to their own detriment.

The second step is recognition that adherence to religion has been historically ensured through adherence to forms, equally in the areas of ritual and transactions. In this regard, classical jurists developed contract forms and conditions thereof in a manner that encapsulated the spirit of the law to the best of their ability. When contemporary jurists attempt to help Muslims adhere to the spirit of the law, they feel safest working within the formal and informal methodologies of Islamic jurisprudence. We have seen in earlier chapters that Islamic jurisprudence is in fact a common-law system (if dressed in the garb of canon law), with emphasis on precedent and analogy. The resulting contemporary process of adapting classical contract forms to modern needs necessarily produces interim inefficiency.

This inefficiency would be tolerable only if we ensure that the spirit of the Law that gave rise to adopted forms is protected. Otherwise, it would be shameful merely to copy or adapt inefficient historical forms and squander the substance of Islamic law. Ideally, contemporary jurists would develop a modern jurisprudence that embodies the substance of premodern laws within the context of contemporary legal and regulatory frameworks. This ideal may be approachable in the long term but seems impossible in the short term. In this regard, earlier jurists had the luxury of seeking efficiency by adopting Roman or other legal forms. However, later jurists have to work under the heavy burden of sacred history, including unreasonable admiration of the presumed timeless wisdom of their predecessors. Thus, practical Islamic solutions for the short to medium term may abandon premodern forms only gradually.

Multiple Paternalistic Parties

Earlier in this chapter, we discussed the paternalistic nature of prohibitions in general. We now turn to the prohibition of *riba* in particular, which aims substantively to protect individuals from getting excessively indebted, as well as paying or receiving unfair compensations for receipt or extension of credit. Naturally, one might argue that secular regulators also strive (paternalistically, one might add) to prevent individuals from borrowing excessive amounts, or falling prey to unfair predatory lending. However, regulators care primarily about the general health of the financial system – their concern about financial health of specific individuals being secondary at best. Thus, regulators may allow certain types of transactions that are hazardous to a few individuals, based on the tradeoff between that particular group's well-being (which is not their primary mandate) and overall systemic well-being (e.g., economic growth).

A second group of economic agents who aim to prevent excessive indebtedness are bankers, who use debt payments relative to income and other criteria for credit extension. However, bankers and loan officers work primarily for financial corporations that care little about systemic or individual financial health and care mostly about their own profitability. Thus, they would generally allow large numbers of customers to borrow excessively if the expected rate of repayment remains sufficiently high to ensure profitability.

Human Time Inconsistency and Precommitment Solutions

Thus, restrictions imposed by regulators and financial professionals require supplementary protections for individuals against their own irrational behavior – a function that can be fulfilled by religious law. In this regard, it is well documented in psychological and behavioral economic research that humans exhibit fundamental forms of irrationality in time preference, against which precommitment mechanisms (including those based on religion) can protect them. For instance, most individuals would prefer $100 today over $105 in one year, but prefer $105 in twenty years over $100 in nineteen. Those and other "time preference anomalies" suggest that individuals will be "dynamically inconsistent" in their saving, spending, and borrowing behavior.[19]

The conclusion of this research is that individuals tend to discount the immediate future (e.g., one year from now) much more severely than they discount over a similar period later in the future (e.g., between nineteenth and twentieth years). Thus, in the previous example, an interest rate of 5 percent looks low for the current year, but sufficiently high for an arbitrary year further in the future. An individual exhibiting this type of time preference will choose to borrow $100 today, planning (genuinely) to save in the future and pay off his loan. However, once the future arrives, present consumption is again valued substantially more than future consumption, and the individual borrows even more, under the illusion that he will later save enough to pay off both loans. The debt cycle never ends. Some of those individuals may experience sufficiently fast growth in their incomes, so that they can eventually pay off their debts without increasing their saving rates. However, many other debtors may get buried under a debt cycle and eventually have to declare personal bankruptcy, which has become a mini-epidemic in some Western societies.

Good Loans and Bad

Why, one may wonder, would banks extend those bad loans that lead to bankruptcies? The answer is that loans are very rarely bad at their inception. When economic conditions are favorable, many borrowers experience income growth, and banks have an incentive to continue lending to them, since the number of defaults and bankruptcies will be too small to affect their profits. Sometimes, for example, in Asia during the 1990s, borrowed funds are invested in real estate and other fast-appreciating assets, making loans that are secured by those overpriced assets seem less risky than they are in reality. As economic conditions worsen, and asset market bubbles burst, too many of those loans may turn bad simultaneously, threatening the financial system. Hence, regulators impose restrictions to ensure that banks' operations do not threaten the system, albeit in a reactive manner that often fails to protect against later banking crises. In contrast, religious law aims to protect each and every individual by ensuring that they do not borrow excessively.

For instance, consider a Muslim customer who wishes to finance a home purchase through lease financing. If the housing market in question happens to be experiencing a speculative bubble, that fact should become clear to the customer by comparing the "rent" he would have to pay his Islamic bank (which is benchmarked to mortgage market interest rates) to the actual market rent of the property. If mortgage payments are excessively high relative to rent, that is generally an indication that the customer is about to borrow an excessive amount of money relative to the long-term value of the property serving as collateral. Thus, marking the interest rate to market lease rates should prevent the individual from engaging in excessive borrowing to purchase that property. In the process, the customer is also assured that the implicit interest rate he pays is marked to the market-determined time value of the property serving as security for the debt.

If such considerations are ignored, the Islamic bank in this example would merely allow the customer to become "house-poor" or bankrupt, but do it "Islamically" through partial adherence to classical contract forms. That would be shameful abuse of religion and finance. Consequently, although we have accepted the necessary inefficient Islamic financial adherence to classical contract forms, it is equally if not more important to ensure adherence to the substance of Islamic law, which premodern jurists attempted to enshrine in those classical forms.

Digression on Loans in Islamic Jurisprudence

We have thus seen that the classical prohibition of *riba* in finance refers to the unbundled sale of credit, wherein it is difficult to mark the interest rate to market. In this regard, the simplest form of an unbundled credit sale is an interest-bearing loan. Indeed, if loans were viewed as commutative financial contracts (i.e., if repayment of the loan were viewed as compensation for the lent amount), then even interest-free lending would have been deemed forbidden *riba*. Al-Qarafi argued in *Al-Furuq* (a legal-theory book dedicated to explaining juristic distinctions) that lending is exempted from the rules of *riba* because of its charitable nature. Religiously, one who extends a loan does not seek repayment as the compensation, but rather seeks to give the time value of lent money, or usufruct of lent property, in charity.[20]

Thus, the Prophet's companions and early jurists said that they preferred to lend a coin, have it repaid, and lend it again, rather than to give it away in charity. Goodly loans have direct charity built in, as a needy debtor would be absolved if he cannot pay. On the other hand, a needy borrower retains dignity relative to recipients of explicit charity, through the possibility of repaying the principal. Even in case of repayment, the lender gains religious credit through sacrificing the time value of his property, and proving his willingness to sacrifice the property itself if necessary. Hence, Islamic jurisprudence excluded lending from the arena of finance, to retain its goodly charitable nature. This is possible since all the financial ends that can be served through commercial lending can be equally if not better served through other forms of commutative contracts (such as sales, leases, and the like).

3.2 The Prohibition of *Gharar*

We have explained prohibitions in terms of boundedly rational human behavior, in particular with regard to highly addictive behavior such as drinking and gambling. In particular, we have argued that the prohibition of *riba* may very well be based on the potentially addictive nature of borrowing and living beyond one's means. In this section we deal with the prohibition of *gharar*, which was characterized by prominent jurists in light of its similarity to gambling. In this regard, the late Professor Mustafa Al-Zarqa defined the forbidden *bayʿ al-gharar* as "the sale of probable items whose existence or characteristics are not certain, the risky nature of which makes the transaction akin to gambling."[21]

Numerous historical examples of forbidden *gharar* sales are enumerated in classical jurisprudence books.[22] Generally speaking, *gharar* encompasses some forms of incomplete information and/or deception, as well as risk and uncertainty intrinsic to the objects of contract. Since complete contract language is impossible, some measure of risk and uncertainty is always present in contracts. Thus, jurists distinguished between major or excessive *gharar*, which invalidates contracts, and minor *gharar*, which is tolerated as a necessary evil. In his seminal paper summarizing classical opinions on *gharar* and applying them to contemporary transactions, Professor Al-Darir listed four conditions for *gharar* to invalidate a contract.[23]

First, *gharar* must be excessive to invalidate a contract. Thus, minor uncertainty about an object of sale (e.g., if its weight is known only up to the nearest ounce) does not affect the contract. Second, the potentially affected contract must be a commutative financial contract (e.g., sales). Thus, giving a gift that is randomly determined (e.g., the catch of a diver) is valid, whereas selling the same item would be deemed invalid based on *gharar*.[24] This condition is extensively used in designing *takaful* (cooperative insurance) as an alternative to commercial insurance solutions. *Takaful* companies, stockholder and mutually owned, use noncommutativity structures of voluntary contribution (*tabarruʿ*) and agency (*wakala*), respectively, to resolve the *gharar* problem on the basis of which most contemporary jurists forbade commercial insurance. We shall discuss those structures in greater detail in Chapter 8.

Third, for *gharar* to invalidate a contract, it must affect the principal components thereof (e.g., the price or object of sale). Thus, the sale of a pregnant cow was deemed valid, even though the status of the calf may not be known. Indeed, the price of a pregnant cow would be higher than the price of the same cow if it were not pregnant. However, the sale of its unborn calf by itself is not valid based on *gharar*. In the first case, the primary object of sale is the cow itself, whereas in the latter case the object of sale is the unborn calf, which may be still-born.

Finally, if the commutative contract containing excessive *gharar* meets a need that cannot be met otherwise, the contract would not be deemed invalid based on that *gharar*. A canonical example is *salam* (prepaid forward sale), wherein the object of sale does not exist at contract inception, giving rise to excessive *gharar*. However, since that contract allows financing of agricultural and industrial activities that cannot be financed otherwise, it is allowed despite that *gharar*. Similarly, while contemporary jurists forbade commercial insurance based on excessive *gharar* and availability of noncommutative (*takaful*) alternatives, they currently allow *takaful* companies to deal with conventional reinsurance companies, since re-*takaful* alternatives are not yet available.

Definition of Gharar

The distinction between major and minor *gharar*, as well as considerations in the fourth criterion for *gharar* to invalidate contracts, suggests a strong cost-benefit analysis as the foundation for prohibition. Indeed, a number of classical jurists explicitly highlighted this central cost-benefit analysis:

[The Prophet's] prohibition of *gharar* sales (*bay' al-gharar*) render such sales defective. The meaning of "*gharar* sale," and God knows best, is any sale in which *gharar* is the major component. This is the type of sale justifiably characterized as a *gharar* sale, and it is unanimously forbidden. However, minor *gharar* would not render a sales contract defective, since no contract can be entirely free of *gharar*. Consequently, scholars differ in opinion regarding which contracts are thus rendered defective, based on their assessment of the extent of *gharar* in the contract. Thus, each scholar would invalidate a contract if he deems its *gharar* component substantial, and would otherwise declare the contract valid if the *gharar* is deemed minor.[25]

Scholars said that the criterion for invalidity of a contract based on *gharar*, or validity despite the existence of *gharar*, is this: If necessity dictates allowing *gharar*, which thus cannot be avoided without incurring an excessive cost, or if *gharar* is trivial, the sale is deemed valid, otherwise it is deemed invalid. ...Thus, differences in opinion among scholars are based on this general principle, where some of them render a particular form of *gharar* minor and inconsequential, while others render the same form substantial and consequential, and God knows best.[26]

In this regard, the corrupting factor in *gharar* is the fact that it leads to dispute, hatred, and devouring others' wealth wrongfully. However, it is known that this corrupting factor would be overruled if it is opposed by a greater benefit.[27]

Perhaps the best literal and juristic translation for "*bay' al-gharar*" is "trading in risk."[28] In this regard, the *Encyclopedia of Islamic Jurisprudence* also lists cheating (*tadlis*) and fraud (*ghubn*) as special cases of *gharar*.[29] Thus, *gharar* incorporates uncertainty regarding future events and qualities of goods, and it may be the result of one-sided or two-sided and intentional or unintentional incompleteness of information.

The factor that is common in all those categories is significant (possibly unquantifiable) risk and uncertainty. The possibility of unanticipated loss to at least one party may be a form of gambling or may lead to ex post disputation between contracting parties. The prohibition of *bay' al-gharar* (the sale of *gharar*) may thus be seen as a prohibition of the unbundled and unnecessary sale of risk. Of course, the most extreme form of unbundled sale of risk is gambling: paying a predetermined price for some unproductive game of chance (e.g., spinning a roulette wheel and winning a larger sum of money if the ball falls on black). Various forms of *gharar* are assessed based on proximity to this extreme form.

Economic Substance of Prohibition

The most significant developments in finance over the past three decades have been in the area of separating various financial credit and risk components for accurate pricing. This was accomplished through advances in securitization and development of financial derivatives. We admitted earlier that finance (Islamic or otherwise) is about allocation of credit or risk. Moreover, we have argued that the two main prohibitions in Islamic jurisprudence, those of *riba* and *gharar*, are best characterized as trading in unbundled credit and trading in unbundled risk, respectively. For the case of *riba*, we argued that disallowing unbundled trading of credit can protect individuals who are vulnerable to excessive borrowing from falling into debt cycles and ensured marking interest rates to market. Similarly, it can be seen that the prohibition of trading unbundled risk aims to protect individuals from exposure to excessive financial risk or payment of mispriced premia to eliminate existing risks.[30]

Bounded Rationality in the Face of Risk

Starting with the early experiments by Allais in 1953, behavioral economists and psychologists have documented a number of basic patterns in human behavior under risk and uncertainty. Kahneman and Tversky (1979) summarized the most important patterns under four headings, the most important being (1) the excessive weight humans place on events considered certain, relative to ones that are highly probable, (2) the overweighting of losses compared to gains, and (3) risk-loving behavior over losses. A recent literature has emerged in finance, using those documented idiosyncrasies of human behavior under risk to provide explanations for a host of otherwise puzzling human and market behaviors.[31]

The above-mentioned idiosyncrasies drive individuals to take too much risk, and then to pay too much for insurance. For instance, when one buys a computer at a retail store in the United States, the computer commonly comes with only a one-year manufacturer's limited warranty. At the check-out, just before one pays for the computer, the sales clerk offers the buyer an extended warranty. This insurance sales tactic is used to capitalize on individuals' loss aversion. If the insurance was offered bundled with the computer (e.g., if it sold for $1,000 without warranty, and for $1,200 with extended warranty), buyers will tend to view safety as an attribute of a computer they do not yet own, and would thus be unwilling to pay a high price for the embedded insurance. In contrast, once the buyer is ready to pay for the computer, thus considering it his property, loss aversion will drive him to pay more for insurance than he would have otherwise.

Some experimental evidence suggests that financial professionals are no less susceptible to those documented human idiosyncrasies in decision making under risk and uncertainty.[32] Most humans seem to exhibit loss aversion or asymmetric assessment of small gains versus small losses. This loss aversion produces willingness to pay too much for insurance, once the new "reference point" – with respect to which "prospects" are evaluated – makes one think of more events in terms of loss. In addition, since humans also tend to exhibit risk-loving behavior over losses and risk-averse behavior over gains, they treat the same prospect differently, depending on how it is presented to them. Those human idiosyncrasies in decision making under risk and uncertainty lead to dynamically inconsistent behavior. Precommitment, through prohibition of selling the unbundled insurance, helps to protect consumers against that dynamic inconsistency.

Insurance and Derivatives

If we accept the definition of forbidden *bay' al-gharar* as trading in risk, we can readily understand contemporary jurists' prohibition of conventional insurance and derivatives trading. Those topics will be discussed in much greater detail in Chapter 8. Thus, our coverage in this chapter only briefly links juristic analysis of the prohibition of *gharar* to our economic understanding of its legal substance. In this regard, we have noted in Chapter 2 that jurists argued that "safety" or "insurance" itself does not qualify as the object of sale. Hence, the object of sale in that contract would have to be defined as a contingent claim, akin to an option: The insured party has a legal right to receive compensation for damages in the event of loss stipulated in the insurance contract.

Based on this interpretation, jurists have forbidden commercial insurance dating back to the late nineteenth century C.E., when the prominent Hanafi jurist Ibn 'Abidin, whose work and opinions were central to the Ottoman *Majalla*, forbade maritime insurance on similar grounds. Likewise, jurists forbade naked options (calls and puts), which give their holders a legal right (respectively, to buy or sell the underlying assets). In this regard, the legal right to exercise the option was also viewed to be ineligible as object of sale. Thus, in both insurance and options, the price (insurance premium or option price) is certain, but its compensation (insurance payment or profit from exercising option) is uncertain, and hence the trade is forbidden based on *gharar*.

Notice that, in both instances, it is the sale of an unbundled contingency claim or legal right that jurists have forbidden. Jurists have not forbidden the inclusion of warranty in sale, whether the warranty is provided by the manufacturer or the retail seller. This bundled sale of insurance was allowed, just as the bundled sale of credit was (e.g., by allowing a manufacturer or dealer to sell cars with deferred payments, whereas financially equivalent loans are considered forbidden unbundled sales of credit). Likewise, jurists have not forbidden the sale of bundled options. Indeed, juristic analyses of sales contracts include lengthy discussions of permissible options in sales, an area in which the highly respected Hanbali jurists Ibn Taymiyya and his student Ibn Qayyim were particularly liberal.

3.3 Bundled vs. Unbundled Credit and Risk

We have thus argued that the two major prohibitions in Islamic jurisprudence of financial transactions, those against *riba* and *gharar*, are in fact prohibition of trading in unbundled credit and unbundled risk, respectively. We have further argued that the paternalistic nature of those prohibitions is understandable, in light of human idiosyncrasies that would lead to dynamically inconsistent behavior, much like wine drinking can lead to dynamically inconsistent behavior for most humans. Unlike the consumption of intoxicating beverages, which is not necessary for life, transfer of credit and risk is fundamental to the functioning of financial systems and economies. Hence, classical jurisprudence evolved methods of bundled trading in credit and risk while maintaining the prohibition of unbundled trading thereof.

That being said, one must recognize that classical contract forms – specific means of bundling credit and/or risk with other economic activities – can be used as apparently legitimate means toward illegitimate ends. This is obviously the case in *tawarruq*, for instance, where the stated purpose is to extend credit and provide liquidity to some customer. Economic activities camouflaging the underlying sale of credit (two spot sales and one credit sale of some commodity) do little to protect individuals from borrowing or lending excessively, for the wrong reasons, or at the wrong interest rate.

In the case of legitimate credit sales or lease-to-purchase financing secured by real estate, vehicles, equipment, and the like, marking-to-market rental value of the financed instrument can help individuals and lenders determine whether or not the implicit loan is justifiable. In contrast, the "rental" value on commodities used in *tawarruq* is precisely the rental value on money: that is, market interest rates that are not linked to the object of sale in any meaningful way. In other words, the "bundling of credit" in this transaction serves no economic purpose. It is a mere legal stratagem or ruse (*hila*) to legalize otherwise forbidden interest-based lending. That is why jurists of most schools have forbidden this transaction, which takes the form of multiple valid sales but does not serve the desired substance of Islamic law.

In later chapters we shall see that some classical nominate contract-based solutions to the prohibitions of *riba* and *gharar* seem to serve the form and substance of classical jurisprudence, while others clearly do not. In cases where current practice in Islamic finance serves legal form alone, and ignores substance, we have seen the credibility of the industry erode (e.g., in scholarly and public attacks on the contemporary practice of *murabaha* financing as merely inefficient lending).[33] This in turn led to the development of better alternatives (e.g., increased use of lease-based financing, including in *sukuk* issuances, in which marking-to-market rent is more straightforward). By attempting to analyze forms and economic substance of classical jurisprudence simultaneously, we hope to make it easier for industry participants to develop instruments that serve the latter. In the longer term, that emphasis on the economic substance of transactions may eventually rid Islamic finance of outdated and inefficient modes of operation. Thus, the Islamic brand name of the industry may be redefined in terms of consumer protection and social development, rather than contract mechanics.

4

Sale-Based Islamic Finance

As noted in earlier chapters, nominate contracts in classical Islamic jurisprudence play a very prominent role in contemporary Islamic finance. This prominence is in large part a function of the common-law nature of Islamic jurisprudence. Contemporary jurists are generally reluctant to declare that a contemporary financial practice is permissible under Islamic law, even though the default rule in transactions is permissibility. Thus, jurists seek precedents in classical jurisprudence to justify proposed contemporary practices.

To illustrate, consider the Chapter 1 example of conventional mortgage loan transaction and the Islamic version based on *murabaha* financing. Background credit checks, and other financial considerations to determine whether or not credit should be extended to a particular customer, are identical in both settings. Indeed, the mark-up charged to a customer under the Islamic model can be determined based on the customer's credit rating and benchmarked to interest rates on potential conventional loans to the customer. The main difference between conventional and Islamic financing procedures is thus inherent in the contracts used.

In the case of conventional mortgage lending, the bank collects principal plus interest on debt documented as a loan. In contrast, the *murabaha* model of Islamic finance is predicated on the permissibility of charging a credit price that is higher than the spot price of a property. Thus, the Islamic bank collects principal plus interest on debt documented as a credit price. As noted previously, the price mark-up can mimic conventional interest rates, and indeed the amortization table for a *murabaha* financing facility may be identical to the corresponding table for a mortgage loan. However, the *murabaha* financing return on capital is characterized rhetorically as profit or price mark-up in a sales transaction rather than interest on a loan.

One problem in applying the credit sale *murabaha* model directly to mortgage financing is that the bank does not own the property it finances. In fact, most banks in the West are prevented from owning real estate or trading it. Thus, the Islamic model requires that the bank must first purchase the property (possibly through a special-purpose vehicle) and then sell it (or lease it then sell it, in *ijara* financing) to the customer. This imposes a number of additional transaction costs, including legal fees and sales taxes.

Some of those costs may be reduced by lobbying regulators. For instance, the Financial Services Authority (FSA) recently made *murabaha* financing, for example, as practiced in the United Kingdom by HSBC, more affordable by eliminating double-duty taxation when the two sales are executed to facilitate financing.[1] Other costs can be reduced by allowing the customer to act as the bank's agent, thus buying the property on the bank's behalf and then selling it to himself. Those and other steps allow the Islamic model progressively to approximate the conventional model's procedures and costs.

Islamic finance as practiced today serves a primary goal of replicating conventional financial products and services, as efficiently as possible, utilizing classical contract forms (such as sales and leases). Toward the end of enhancing efficiency in Islamic finance, bankers and lawyers venturing in the field need to understand some of the basic features of classical nominate contracts, which are used to mimic conventional financial products and services. However, one can hope that as the industry matures, its practitioners will look beyond mimicking contemporary financial practices utilizing those classical contract forms. As we review the main classical contract forms, we should reflect on our Chapter 3 analysis of the main prohibitions in Islamic financial jurisprudence, their economic merit, and the way classical nominate contracts implemented the principles enshrined in the jurisprudence. This can help in our quest for a thoroughly contemporary Islamic financial model that retains the substance of classical jurisprudence, rather than falling into superficial adherence to classical contract forms while possibly violating the substance of Islamic law.

4.1 Basic Rules for Sales

Sale is the ultimate permissible contract, as indicated by the Qur'anic verse asserting that God has permitted trade and forbidden *riba* [2:275]. Sales generally are characterized by classical jurists as exchanges of owned properties, including services and some property rights for non-Hanafi jurists. A sales contract requires offer and acceptance, with a meeting of minds for buyer and seller. For Hanafis and Malikis, a sale is concluded and binding on both parties on the expression of offer and acceptance. On the other hand, Shafi'is and Hanbalis ruled that buyer and seller retain the option to rescind the sales contract as long as they have not parted from the contract session. This is called the "contract session option" (*khiyar al-majlis*), which is based on an authentic Prophetic tradition: "The two parties to a sale have the option [to rescind it] as long as they have not parted, and one of them may give the other the option for a longer period."[2]

A number of restrictions on objects of sale were put in place, in part to ensure that sales contracts are not used as ruses for *riba*, and in part to protect the interests of contracting parties. With the exception of prepaid forward sales (*salam*) and commissions to manufacture (*istisna'*), to be discussed separately in later chapters, objects of sale must exist at the time of the contract. Moreover, for a sale to be executed, objects of sale must be owned by the seller, in his possession, and deliverable to the buyer. This set of conditions is central to the practice of Islamic financial institutions, wherein the financial institution must own a property in order later to sell or lease it to its customer. As noted above, this requirement results in additional legal costs for the extra sale and establishment of SPVs, as well as potential additional sales taxes, licensing fees, and the like. Interestingly, although the Shafi'is and Hanbalis listed the seller's ownership of an object of sale as a condition of conclusion of the sale contract, Hanafis and Malikis deemed it only a condition of execution of the sale. Thus, the latter two groups of scholars deemed sales by an "uncommissioned agent" (known in Arabic as *bay' al-fuduli*) concluded but suspended pending the [ultimate] seller's approval.[3]

The Underused Uncommissioned Agent (Bay' al-Fuduli) Structure

In this regard, while most areas of Islamic finance tend to be dominated by the Hanafi and Hanbali schools of jurisprudence,[4] there is ample evidence that opinions from other schools of jurisprudence have been accepted in the industry. For instance, in the classical *murabaha* practice, wherein the bank buys a property and then sells it on credit to customer, jurists and banks have accepted a Maliki opinion of the jurist Ibn Shubruma – to allow the bank first to obtain a binding promise by its customer that he will buy the property after the bank buys it. It appears that developments along the "uncommissioned agent" opinions of the Hanafis and Malikis can greatly reduce the transaction costs in *murabaha* financing, by approximating conventional procedures more accurately.

Thus, the bank may act as an uncommissioned agent for the seller, selling his property to the customer on credit. At this stage the customer will owe the seller that property's price plus mark-up as determined by market interest rates, if the seller were to accept it. The seller may accept to provide financing to the customer directly, in which case the bank would be entitled only to its agency commission. On the other hand, if the seller demands receiving the price in cash, the bank – as agent – may conclude the sale by paying him the cash price he demanded, while collecting from the customer the credit price he agreed to pay. Thus, the bank would act as a traditional financial intermediary, with the associated lower costs, rather than trading in property.

Although this alternative structure based on uncommissioned agent trading (*bay' al-fuduli*) may not necessarily be acceptable to all jurists, it appears to have been used in Islamic finance in the GCC. For instance, *fatwa* #62 for Dalla Al-Baraka and *fatawa* #17 and #24 for Kuwait Finance House all permitted the uncommissioned agent structure, arguing that ex post acceptance of the Islamic bank (that the customer bought on its behalf) is equivalent to ex ante agency authorization.[5]

Trust Sales: Murabaha, Tawliya, Wadi'a

The most common type of sale in Islamic jurisprudence is negotiated-price sale *bay' al-musawama*), wherein the two parties agree on a price at which they are both willing to conclude the transaction. However, there are three other types of sale, wherein the two parties agree on a profit or loss margin, and the buyer relies on the seller's truthful revelation of his cost. In *murabaha* the two parties agree to trade at a price equal to the cost plus mark-up or profit, in *tawliya* they trade at cost, and in *wadi'a* they agree to trade at a marked-down price.[6]

In *murabaha* and *tawliya*, jurists ruled that the seller must be the owner, otherwise it is impossible for the seller to disclose the cost at which he obtained the property. The most common method of financing by Islamic financial institutions is "*murabaha* to order." It is based on a concatenation of two opinions, one by Al-Shafi'i that permitted a potential buyer to tell a seller "buy this property, and I will buy it from you at x percent mark-up," and an opinion of the Maliki jurist Ibn Shubruma that allows the potential buyer's promise to be made binding. In the first conference of Islamic banks in Dubai (1979), participants concluded that "this type of promise is legally binding on both parties based on the Maliki ruling, and religiously binding on both parties for all other schools." This ruling was reiterated in 1983, at the second conference of Islamic banks in Kuwait, reasoning that "this [*murabaha*] sale is valid as long as the bank is exposed to the risk of destruction of the good prior to delivering it to the buyer, as well as the obligation to accept return of the good if a concealed defect is found therein."

Led by the Pakistani jurist and retired Justice M. Taqi Usmani, jurists who are involved in Islamic finance have allowed the rate of return in *murabaha* to be benchmarked to conventional interest rates. In this regard, the rate of return earned by the bank was justified by two risks: (1) the risk of ownership between the two sales, and (2) the risk that the property may be returned to the bank (as seller) if a defect is found therein. We must note, however, that the risk of ownership can be made minimal by restricting the time period between the two sales to minutes, if not seconds. Moreover, although jurists insist that any cost of insurance of the property during that period must be borne by the Islamic financial institution, the bank may negotiate a mark-up that compensates it for that cost. Similarly, the cost of insuring against the risk of having to accept the return of defective merchandise can be transferred easily back to the original seller or forward to the buyer. Thus, the only material risks to which the bank is exposed are credit risk and interest rate risk, which conventional banks specialize in managing. Indeed, many of the transaction costs associated with Islamic finance arise precisely for the purpose of eliminating all other (e.g., commercial) risks, which banks are not particularly well equipped to manage.

Currency Exchange (Sarf)

The well-known Prophetic tradition on *riba*, discussed in Chapter 3, listed six commodities that should be traded hand-to-hand and in equal quantities. In a variation on this Prophetic tradition that applied exclusively to monetary commodities, ʿUmar ibn Al-Khattab said, "Do not sell gold for gold or silver for silver except in equal quantities. Moreover, do not trade gold for silver with one of them deferred. Even if your trading partner asks you to wait until he can fetch the money from his house, do not accept the deferment. I fear that you will fall in *riba*."[7] Thus, *murabaha* financing cannot be applied to trading gold for silver with deferment for equal or different quantities.

Of course, gold and silver represented the bimetallic monies of the time, and thus trading gold for gold, silver for silver, or gold for silver were all grouped together under the title "currency exchange," or *sarf*. In those trades the aforementioned Prophetic tradition requires the exchange to be hand-to-hand (i.e., without deferment), and if the two compensations are of the same genus, then they must be equal in weight. No conditions or options are allowed in this contract, which is deemed binding at its conclusion.

The earliest jurists reasoned by analogy that currency exchange contracts may not be used to settle existing debts (e.g., settling a debt for gold with payment in silver). However, later jurists reasoned by juristic approbation that clearing a debt in one currency with payment in another currency is permissible if both parties consent to it, regardless of when and how the debt was initiated, and in some cases, the exchange would be enforced without need for mutual consent.[8]

Contemporary jurists have allowed regular currency-trading transactions, in which a payment in one currency is made in one country, and receipt of another currency is made in a different country, possibly at a later time. This practice was characterized as an instantaneous currency exchange contract in the first country, followed by an interest-free loan to be repaid at the later date in the other country.[9] Of course, the underlying assumption is that exchange will be carried out at the spot exchange rate of the initiation date, to avoid suspicion of *riba*. On the other hand, those familiar with the evolution of modern banking in Europe will recognize bills of exchange along those lines (known by the Arabic name *suftaja*) as the classical forms through which Medici bankers managed to embed interest rates in exchange rates, to circumvent the classical Catholic prohibition of "usury."[10]

Metals and Tawarruq

Another interesting development in Islamic finance is that some precious metals (e.g., platinum) were exempted from rules of currency exchange. For instance, the Rajhi Investment Company's Shari'a board reasoned as follows in its *fatwa* #101:

> Platinum is a precious metal that does not inherit the legal status rulings of gold and silver, even though some people call it "the white gold." Thus, mutual receipt during contract session is not required for platinum, and it may be sold with deferment in exchange for currency.

> In general, platinum is subject to legal status rulings for metals other than gold and silver. Thus, if the company [Al-Rajhi] wishes to deal in this metal when it is not present [in the seller's possession], it may only buy it through *salam* [prepaid forward contract], subject to all the conditions of that contract. Moreover, the company must receive the metal prior to reselling it.[11]

Thus, although the classical rules of currency exchange very strictly ensured that an interest-bearing loan cannot be manufactured out of trade, recent developments in jurisprudence have allowed trade-based financing to replicate loans. This is especially prevalent today through the *tawarruq* contract that is increasingly practiced in GCC countries. Thus, if a customer wishes to borrow $10,000 and pay 5 percent interest, and the bank wishes to lend him the money at that rate, the bank needs only to buy $10,000 worth of platinum from a dealer, sell to the customer on a credit basis for $10,500 to be paid later, and then sell the platinum on behalf of the customer back to the dealer, thus generating the desired result. Needless to say, all interest-based financial transactions (including loans and bonds) can be (and are in fact) generated through such trade cycles, which involve a credit component through either credit sales or prepaid forward sales.

In the context of *tawarruq* as practiced by Islamic banks, it is noteworthy that most classical jurists deemed it impermissible for one entity to execute a sale as agent for both trading parties, with the exceptions of judges, plenipotentiaries, and parents.[12] This restriction was intended to ensure that sales contracts are legitimate, and that they are perceived by all parties to be beneficial to them. One particularly troublesome practice that would be voided by this restriction applies to banks engaging in "trade" for the purpose of *tawarruq* financing, whereby the bank acts as an agent for its customer and the merchant – buying commodities from the merchant, selling to the customer on credit, and then selling back to the merchant for the amount of cash desired by the customer.

4.2 Same-Item Sale-Repurchase (*'Ina*)

Most recent developments in Islamic finance involve the utilization of a commodity or property as one degree of separation to recharacterize an interest-bearing loan in the form of trade. Thus, we have just described the most common form of *tawarruq* financing that has become increasingly popular in Saudi Arabia, UAE, and other GCC countries in recent years. This practice was common in earlier decades for larger corporate customers of Islamic banks and financial institutions. For those larger customers, the bank did not need to provide agency services for all sales. Indeed, larger customers were capable of borrowing through a simple *murabaha* transaction for platinum, and they had the necessary recourses to sell the platinum on the spot market to obtain desired liquidity. This was particularly advantageous to bankers who operated in countries wherein *tawarruq* was unacceptable, whereas *murabaha* was.

As noted briefly in previous chapters, most Islamic bond (*sukuk*) structures developed in recent years also involve the sale and repurchase of some property or commodity. Thus, short-term bill-like instruments are manufactured through prepayment (*salam*) sale of commodities, and long-term bondlike instruments are manufactured through sale of a property, followed by leasing back the same property, and possibly buying it back at lease end. In this section we shall review classical and contemporary juristic rulings on same-property sale-repurchase and their implications for Islamic finance.

Same-Item Trading in *'Ina* and *Tawarruq*

The classical *bay' al-'ina* (same-item sale-repurchase to circumvent the prohibition of interest-based lending) was discussed extensively in the classical juristic literature.[13] Discussion centered mostly around Prophetic traditions, the authenticity of which were accepted by some jurists but not others. In the simplest form of *'ina* sale to produce interest-based debt, the "borrower" sells some property to the "lender" and receives its cash price. Then, the "lender" turns back and sells the same property to the "borrower" on credit, at a higher price equal to the "principal," or cash price, plus interest. Classical jurists also recognized that a third party may be introduced as an intermediary, whereby A (dealer) sells to B (bank) in cash, B sells to C (customer/borrower) on credit, and C sells to A in cash. Of course, if jurists were to forbid same-item repurchase through one intermediary, more degrees of separation – for example, trading parties D and E – may be added.

Abu Hanifa had generally ruled that the validity of sales is determined by contract language. However, he ruled that same-item sale-repurchase without an intermediary third party is defective, based on a tradition of Zayd ibn Arqam.[14] He also reasoned that if someone sells a property on credit, and then the buyer sells it back to him for cash, the second sale would not be valid. He based that ruling on the view that the deferred price in the first sale would not have been received, and thus the second sale (which is contingent on the first) could not be definitively concluded. Of course, the latter objection can be circumvented formally in Islamic banking by asking the customer first to sell any property to the bank for cash, and then turn around and buy it back on credit.

The two closest associates of Abu Hanifa differed in opinion regarding this contract. Thus, the judge Abu Yusuf ruled that the contract is valid and not reprehensible, whereas Muhammad Al-Shaybani found it extremely reprehensible, as an obvious stratagem invented to circumvent the prohibition of *riba*. Similarly, Shafi'i and Zahiri jurists ruled that the contract is valid, since it satisfies the cornerstones and language of valid sales, and since Al-Shafi'i himself did not accept the tradition of Zayd as authentic. However, they reasoned, it is reprehensible since the intent to legitimize *riba* through sales is clear, although their legal theory did not allow them to invalidate a contract based on such analysis of intent.[15]

Interestingly, Maliki and Hanbali jurists ruled that same-item sale-repurchase without a third-party intermediary is forbidden, by invoking the rule of preventing means of legitimizing illegitimate ends (*sadd al-dhara'i*). However, if a third-party intermediary is present (as in the case of *tawarruq*), most Malikis and some Hanbalis reasoned that the contract is merely reprehensible. Since the use of *tawarruq* has been spreading quite rapidly in the GCC region (especially Saudi Arabia and UAE) based on its permissibility among some Hanbali jurists, it seems appropriate to review some of the more recent classical and contemporary juristic opinions regarding this contract.

Hanbali Denunciation of Organized Tawarruq

Ibn Qayyim Al-Jawziyya, a prominent Hanbali jurist and star student of Ibn Taymiyya, said the following regarding Ibn Taymiyya's attitude toward *tawarruq*:

and our teacher (God bless his soul) forbade *tawarruq*. He was challenged on that opinion repeatedly in my presence, but never licensed it [even under special circumstances]. He said: "The precise economic substance for which *riba* was forbidden is present in this contract, and transaction costs are increased through purchase and sale at a loss of some commodity. Shari'a would not forbid a smaller harm and permit a greater one!"[16]

Similarly, Al-Ba'li reported in his selection of juristic rulings of Ibn Taymiyya that the latter had forbidden *tawarruq*.[17] More recently, two very prominent juristic councils, both housed in Saudi Arabia, tackled the issue of *tawarruq*. The more prominent Fiqh Academy of the Organization of Islamic Conference, in Jeddah, Saudi Arabia, forbade *tawarruq*. The second and generally less prestigious Fiqh Academy of the Muslim World League, in Makka, Saudi Arabia, issued two rulings on the transaction. The first opinion was issued in the fifteenth session of the academy in October 1998. It permitted the contract subject to the condition that the customer does not sell the commodity to its original seller, to avoid direct evidence of *'ina* as a legal stratagem to circumvent the prohibition of *riba*. In the seventeenth session of the academy, held in December 2003, they tackled the issue of "*tawarruq* as practiced by Islamic banks today" and forbade it. They based their decision on the following characterization and reasoning:

After listening to presented papers on the subject, and discussions thereof, the Academy recognizes that some banks practice *tawarruq* in the following manner:

The bank routinely sells a commodity (other than gold or silver) in global markets or otherwise to the customer on credit, wherein the bank is bound – by virtue of a contract condition or convention – to sell the commodity to another buyer for cash, which the bank delivers to the customer.

After study and deliberation, the Academy ruled as follows:

First, *tawarruq* as described above is not permissible for the following reasons:

1. The seller's obligation to act as the buyer's agent to sell the commodity to another buyer, or making similar arrangements, makes the dealing akin to the forbidden *'ina*, whether that obligation is spelled out as an explicit contract condition, or determined by custom.
2. In many cases, this type of transaction would result in nonsatisfaction of receipt conditions that are required for validity of the dealing.
3. The reality of this transaction is extension of monetary financing to the party characterized as a *tawarruq* customer, and the buying and selling operations of the bank are most often just meant for appearances, but in reality aim to provide the bank an increase in compensation for the financing it provided.

Some banks have attempted to address those concerns of the Muslim World League Fiqh Academy by ensuring that all trasanctions are bona fide sales and purchases, with corresponding transfer of commodity risks. Towards that end, many banks in Saudi Arabia have begun to emphasize that all commodities used for *tawarruq* are bought and sold in domestic markets, with real merchants delivering the goods or reassigning their ownership as dictated by trade. However, it would appear that this increased emphasis on forms misses the argument made by Ibn Taymiyya as reported by Ibn Qayyim: that the difference between what is permitted and what is forbidden cannot possibly be determined by the amount of transaction costs involved (with higher transaction costs favored!).

Returning to our analysis of *riba* in Chapter 3, it appears that the true demarcation should be determined by "marking to market." We explained the canonical prohibition of trading dates for dates in different quantities by arguing that when dates are sold for money, one seeks the highest bid, and when one uses the money to buy dates, one seeks the lowest offer. This enhances efficiency in markets (especially if added transaction costs are negligible) and ensures equity in exchange. Similarly, if financing is replaced by bona fide trade, as both Fiqh Academies have agreed, then the financing charge in *murabaha* financing (whether or not the customer plans to sell the commodity for cash) will be determined by the difference between actual cash and credit prices in the marketplace.

In contrast, a *tawarruq* transaction is usually structured by banks to equate financing charges to market interest rates on loans to similar borrowers, regardless of the actual underlying commodity. It is thus possible to understand the Fiqh Academies' opinions in terms of rejection of robbing the trading components of Islamic finance of all economic significance, thus squandering the potential efficiency-enhancing provisions built into Islamic jurisprudence. The distinction based on marking to market is more significant in Islamic transactions structured through leases, where a market lease rate may be computable and useful for comparison to the interest rate being charged on similar financial products.

Custody Sale (Bay' Al-'uhda) and Sukuk Al-ijara

We have described the recent lease-backed Islamic bonds briefly in the introduction, and we shall discuss them in much greater detail in Chapter 6. The structure quite simply proceeds as follows. The entity that desires to issue bonds (be it a sovereign government, a corporation, etc.) creates an SPV that sells certificates (*sukuk*) for the amount of the bond issuance. The SPV uses the proceeds to buy some property (typically, land, buildings, machines, etc.) from the issuer and proceeds to lease the property back to the seller. The issuer pays rent, which is passed through the SPV to certificate holders. At lease end, the issuer typically buys the property back from the SPV (although in at least one structure that we shall discuss in detail, the property will be given back as a gift from the SPV to original seller).

We have noted in Chapter 1 that there are two elements of same-item sale-repurchase in this structure: (1) the property and its usufruct are sold to the SPV, and then the usufruct is purchased back through the lease, and (2) the property itself (and all of its remaining usufruct) is purchased back at lease end. This raises the issue of *'ina*, which would deem the contract forbidden. However, same-item sale-repurchase has been approved in lieu of debt by some schools of jurisprudence. That sale form is called fulfillment sale (*bay' al-wafā'*), wherein a property is sold on condition that once the seller returns the price, the buyer must return the property. Shafi'i jurists call this trade *bay' al-'uhda* (custody sale), and the Hanbalis call it *bay' al-amana* (trust or faithfulness sale).

Maliki and Hanbali jurists, as well as early Hanafi and Shafi'i jurists, ruled that such sales are defective, since they were viewed as legal stratagems to reach illegitimate ends (forbidden *riba*) through legitimate sale means. In this regard, they forbade the practice by characterizing the apparent sale as a loan of the price, with usufruct of the property being the profit or interest collected on the loan. Interestingly, this ruling is reinforced in *sukuk* structures, wherein the usufruct is further monetized through leasing the property back to the seller. However, some later jurists have allowed the contract based on convention, thus paving the road for its contemporary utilization.[18]

In general, Islamic jurisprudence does not forbid the same property being sold back to its original seller, provided that the two sales are not stipulated in the original contract. Otherwise, a sales contract that requires the buyer to sell the property back is not a sale at all, since the buyer never in fact obtains ownership rights, which include the right not to sell the property, and certainly the right not to sell it to any given individual or entity (e.g., the original seller). However, the precedent of fulfillment sale mentioned in this section opened the door for the possibility of constructing the *sukuk* structures that have become popular in recent years, which we discuss in Chapter 6.

Now, we may return once more to the issue of "marking to market," which we argued to be at the heart of the prohibition of *riba*. Many Islamic finance practitioners have hailed the ability of countries and corporations to engage in secured lending through sale-lease-back-repurchase certificates, which may – in theory, if not in practice – allow them to borrow at lower rates. Indeed, because of the recent preponderance of those issuances, Standard and Poor's has developed a rating methodology for such lease-backed bonds (discussed in Chapter 6), and the country of Bahrain has progressively used that tool to refinance substantial amounts of its conventional debt at lower interest rates. Invariably, however, the interest rates on those secured bonds are benchmarked to interest rates for conventional bonds with similar credit ratings. We must thus turn to this issue of benchmarking Islamic financing rates to conventional interest rates.

4.3 Cost of Funds: Interest-Rate Benchmarks

Contemporary jurists have simultaneously lamented benchmarking implicit interest rates in Islamic sale- and lease-based financing to conventional interest rates (such as the London Interbank Offer Rate [LIBOR]) and argued that such bench-marking by itself would not deem the financing un-Islamic. A favorite argument of contemporary jurists' has been drawing an analogy to two lines of business, one legitimate and the other illegitimate. Just the fact that the legitimate business (say, a carpenter's shop) may demand the same profit rate as the illegitimate one (say, a brewery, which earns a 6 percent profit rate), they argued, does not render the legitimate business illegitimate. Other analogies that one hears at Islamic conferences compare the price of *halal* chicken (chicken slaughtered according to Islamic standards) to the prices of chicken processed otherwise, again arguing that numerical equality of prices does not imply similar legal status of the priced properties.

Needless to say, those analogies are patently fallacious: The object of sale in Islamic finance does not differ from the object of sale in conventional finance the way carpentry differs from brewing, or even the way *halal* or kosher chicken differ from regularly slaughtered chicken. When an Islamic financial provider structures an "alternative" to conventional finance (say, a conventional mortgage) through double-sale *murabaha* financing facility, the ingredients of the financial transaction are the same as those for conventional mortgage (cost of funds, credit risk, collateral property risk, etc.), and the output is the same (a debt on the customer equal to the sum of money he needed to purchase the property plus finance charges exceeding the bank's cost of funds).

In this regard, whether a double-sale procedure is followed, or a simpler single sale takes place via an uncommissioned agent (*bay' al-fuduli*), as suggested earlier in the chapter, the financial provider still converts funds now into funds in the future and compares his future cost of funds (the interest rate he has to pay to fund providers, whether they are depositors, *sukuk* holders, etc.) to the rate of return that he collects. It is in this spirit that we have argued that the "*murabaha*" disclosure rules – when applied to finance – dictate that the Islamic financier should report his cost of funds and interest-rate mark-up to its customers.

Opportunity Cost for Conventional Fund Providers

It is not surprising that LIBOR is the benchmark of choice for Islamic bankers and financiers. That interbank rate represents the opportunity cost for bankers who are operating or were trained in the United Kingdom, as most Islamic bankers have been. If the bank is left with idle funds, LIBOR represents the rate of return it can obtain by lending those funds to other banks. Hence, other borrowers/finance customers must pay the bank a rate of return equal to LIBOR plus a mark-up commensurate with the level of credit risk to which the bank is exposed by lending to them, rather than lending to other banks. Thus, LIBOR has been

the appropriate benchmark for London bankers to use, and the historical precedent for the majority of Islamic bankers who started their careers in U.K.-based
conventional banking.

In contrast, the Islamic financial customer has no access to funds at LIBOR,
and any familiarity he may have with interbank rates would merely result from his
education and level of familiarity with various financial publications. Bankers will
naturally demand at least LIBOR plus the appropriate spread, and competition
will naturally drive implicit interest rates on Islamic financing closer to that benchmark rate (as Shariʿa-arbitrage rents vanish). However, bankers do their customers
a disservice by limiting the process of Islamic financing to explicit benchmarking
of interest rates to LIBOR or any other market rate, and implicitly to rates that
competitors would charge (as dictated by truth-in-lending provisions in various
Western countries).

Indeed, the customer should also consider his own opportunity cost to involvement in a financing contract with any particular financial services provider. In
this regard, the asset-based nature of Islamic finance, if taken seriously, can provide the customer with another economic comparison to determine whether or
not he should engage in any particular financial transaction. Within the context
of our mortgage example, an appropriate Islamic model (whether it is a buy-sell-
back *murabaha* transaction, or a buy-lease-back *ijara* transaction, etc.) should do
more than merely camouflage a conventional mortgage loan through sales, leases,
and the like. It should provide the customer with appropriate tools for determining whether or not the purchase of a particular property at a particular price and
financing that purchase at a particular interest rate constitute a good investment
or financial decision. Islamic financial providers should be equally interested in
looking beyond the quality of collateral and borrower in terms of the credit risk
associated with an Islamized mortgage loan.

This may be done by disentangling the benefits from owning a property and
benchmarking each component to the appropriate market variable. Thus, capital
gains on the property (at the appropriate level of leverage) should be compared
to capital gains that could be made on other investments. Rental rates (value of
usufruct) of similar properties should be compared to interest paid on the borrowed sum, after factoring in tax advantages of deducting mortgage interest for
income tax purposes, where applicable.

Financially wise customers make such comparisons in conventional as well as
Islamic financial transactions. One difference between conventional bankers and
Islamic bankers should be increased involvement of the banker in the real transaction being undertaken by the customer, even if – in the end – it is only a financial
transaction for the bank, which should be benchmarked to the bank's opportunity
cost as measured by LIBOR or other interest rates. An Islamic banker would thus

use additional benchmarks (which every customer should use, but often many would not without the help of a financial advisor) to decide whether or not the financial transaction is advantageous to the customer.

The explicit mechanics of a real transaction (the bank having actually to get involved in buying and selling the property, or leasing it, etc., even if at arm's length through special purpose vehicles, or ex post through uncommissioned agency) force Islamic financial providers to take their customers through this cold unemotional financial calculus. Although efficiency would dictate performing those calculations only within the context of counterfactual financial scenarios (thus avoiding unnecessary transaction costs), the sad reality is that Islamic finance in the short-to-medium term will likely remain captive to premodern procedures, where the actual trading, leasing, and the like is required. The use of additional benchmarks, as discussed in this section, would – at least – allow the spirit of Islamic jurisprudence to be served through adherence to those premodern forms as adopted by Islamic financial providers.

Viability of Islamic Benchmark Alternatives

In recent years a number of jurists and Islamic bankers have called for the development of "Islamic benchmarks," while maintaining that benchmarking rates of return in sale- and lease-based Islamic financing to conventional interest rates is legitimate. The reason suggested by those Islamic finance practitioners is that *murabaha* financing with a profit rate benchmarked to market interest rates looks suspiciously similar to a conventional loan. Those proponents of an Islamic benchmark have also expressed the ambitious goal of eventually developing an entire Islamic yield curve, to be used for benchmarking rates of return in Islamic finance facilities of varying maturities. The recent growth in Islamic bonds (*sukuk*) issues was thus hailed as a positive step in the direction of developing that Islamic yield curve, which presumably can easily emerge once that market develops sufficient depth and liquidity.

In fact, however, this search for Islamic benchmarks and yield curves is misguided, for a number of good reasons. First, Islamic financial practitioners' discomfort with benchmarking to conventional interest rates seems to be based on continuing misconceptions such as that Islamic finance is "interest free" or that Islamic jurisprudence does not recognize the time value of money. As we have seen in Chapter 3, those views – which were foundational for the Islamic economics literature that predated Islamic finance – are fundamentally flawed. Indeed, Islamic jurisprudence does recognize the time value of money, which is precisely why a seller may charge a higher price for a credit sale than he would for a cash sale of the same property.

In this regard, one must note that the juristic argument that "time value is recognized in sales but not in debts or loans" is at best insufficient, and at worst disingenuous. If the claim is based on the need for pricing time value for each transaction separately (based on credit rating, quality of collateral, etc.), then there is a valid argument to be made (in conventional as well as Islamic finance). However, the mere claim is insufficient in this case, since the manner in which appropriate interest rates are determined in sales, leases, and the like remains unspecified. On the other hand, if interest rates in Islamic finance (including the pure time-value components thereof) are benchmarked to conventional interest rates, it would appear that the general claim is vacuous and disingenuous, since it serves only to create arbitrage opportunities, from which jurists stand to be primary beneficiaries.

Divergence of Rhetoric from Reality

With regard to "interest rate" (or the equivalent Arabic "*si 'r al-fā'ida*"), we have to recognize that although the term may have initially applied only to interest on loans, modern usage applies it to any compensation for time value. In fact, an Islamic financial provider in the United States is required by "truth-in-lending" regulation Z to report the implicit "interest rate" in lease or double-sale financing. The sooner Islamic finance providers can disabuse their customers of those lingering misconceptions about time value and permissibility of charging interest in certain types of transactions, the higher will be the industry's credibility with regulators and customers alike.

A closely related reason why Islamic finance practitioners feel uncomfortable about using conventional interest rates as benchmarks is the Shari'a arbitrage nature of Islamic finance, as illustrated in Chapter 1. In fact, Islamic finance has been, and continues to be, fully dependent on conventional finance for its existence and the nature of its products, as well as its rates of return. If Islamic financial providers continue to market their industry based on the rhetoric that conventional finance is generally forbidden and exploitative, then benchmarking to conventional interest rates will continue to be an embarrassment, prompting skeptical customers to ask: "What is the difference between Islamic and conventional finance?" In contrast, if Islamic financial providers were to focus on the substance of Islamic jurisprudence instead of its forms, they can explain to customers that some – but not all – forms of debt are harmful, and some – but not all – forms of interest are harmful.

Indeed, industry rhetoric needs to change so that a double-sale (*tawarruq* style) at 100 percent interest is recognized as usurious predatory lending rather than legitimate trading. Islamic financial providers need to explain to customers that the purpose of following nominate forms of classical Islamic jurisprudence is to impose discipline and ensure that we select from the wide range of conventional financial products only the ones that are advantageous to particular individuals based on their specific circumstances. Then the fact that credit selected through that methodology costs the same as credit selected through different (conventional) screens would no longer be a source of concern or embarrassment for the industry.

Finally, one of the potential advantages of asset-based Islamic financing is that it can be provided at rates that deviate substantially from a time-value benchmark plus credit-risk premium. For instance, a country or corporation with a poor credit rating may be able to obtain financing at implicit interest rates substantially below those dictated by its credit rating if it genuinely collateralizes its debt with real assets, for example, through the currently popular sale-lease-back *sukuk* structures. At least theoretically, lease-backed *sukuk* with different underlying assets should have different implicit interest rates, depending on the quality of collateral, its depreciation rates, market rent, and the like. Moreover, as we shall argue in Chapter 10, lease *sukuk* built on bona fide sale of government assets can help in restarting stalled privatization programs in various Islamic countries.

Disadvantages of "Islamic Benchmarks"

It is true that if implicit rates in Islamic finance were indeed to vary according to the qualities of underlying assets, then the "Islamic-debt" market would never develop sufficient depth and liquidity to generate a uniform benchmark that can be used to determine implicit rates for other Islamic financial transactions. On the other hand, if – as has indeed been the case – the issued *sukuk* are backed by the full faith and credit of issuing governments and corporations, and thus resulting implicit interest rates are determined solely by the issuing entity's credit rating and a conventional benchmark (typically LIBOR), then referring later to those implicit interest rates is at best cosmetic, and at worst misleading. It would be cosmetic if we first strip the implicit interest rate of its credit-risk premium, essentially to reproduce LIBOR under another name, prior to adding the appropriate credit-risk premium for another Islamic debt instrument. To the extent that reproduction of the underlying measure of time value may be erroneous, benchmarking to such rates may lead to erroneous pricing of other Islamic financial instruments.

Consequently, the development of an "Islamic benchmark" is (1) unnecessary, since there is no reason to be embarrassed about using conventional benchmarks, (2) impractical, since sufficient depth and liquidity of homogeneous Islamic financial assets is unlikely, and (3) superfluous or dangerous, since the only logical or practical approach to developing such an Islamic benchmark would be to try to recover the underlying conventional benchmark, which may be done erroneously.

It would be more advantageous for industry practitioners to explain to customers that the products they offer must meet all conventional product requirements, in addition to Islamic considerations that essentially provide further protection to those customers. Then, if Islamic financial products are more expensive than their conventional counterparts (which they are, almost always), bankers can explain that this additional cost is compensation for the service being provided through adherence to those prudential requirements of Islamic jurisprudence, in analogy to higher fees charged by full-service brokers who provide investment advice to their customers.

Other Conventional Benchmarks

While we are discussing the subject of interest-rate benchmarks, it is worthwhile noting that the use of LIBOR as a benchmark, while reasonable for many bank-type financial instruments, seems less appropriate for sovereign bonds. Benchmarking to LIBOR reflects the industry's dependence on London-based banks, and domination – even after the industry's centers of gravity moved from London, Geneva, and Luxembourg to Kuala Lumpur, Bahrain, and Dubai – by bankers who are based, or used to be based, in London. In this regard, no reasonable person would disagree that LIBOR is perhaps the best measure of an English bank's opportunity cost of funds, and hence benchmarking to that rate makes perfect sense for Islamic financial instruments that are similar to bank loans.

In contrast, many of the countries that continue to issue "Islamic debt" (mainly Bahrain, Qatar, Malaysia, Pakistan, and others likely to join the sovereign *sukuk* movement in part to retire their conventional debt, as in the case of Bahrain), would like to be viewed as "emerging markets." Indeed, Malaysia and Turkey – which is currently contemplating issuing *sukuk* – have been on the radar screens of emerging market debt traders for a number of years. In that market the benchmark most commonly used is the yield on U.S. Treasury bonds – with emerging market bond yield spreads (e.g., on indices such as JP Morgan's EMBI+) over U.S. Treasury yields now serving as the most common measures of global economic risk. Migrating sovereign *sukuk* benchmarking from LIBOR to Treasury yields would be a sign of maturity in the sector, signaling graduation of those *sukuk* from a market-niche curiosity generated by bankers and lawyers.

5
Derivative-Like Sales: *Salam, Istisna*ʿ, and *ʿUrbun*

As we indicated in the previous chapter, existence of some property as the object of sale is generally a condition for contract validity. However, there are two notable exceptions that allow sales of nonexistent objects. The first is an ancient contract that predates Islam, called *salam* in the Hijaz area of western Arabia, wherein the Prophet lived, and *salaf* in Iraq, both terms meaning "prepayment." This contract was primarily used for financing agricultural production and was legalized by the Prophetic traditions cited below. A similar contract, called *istisna*ʿ, meaning "commission to manufacture," was legalized in later centuries, likewise to assist financing of nonagricultural (e.g., manufacturing) production.

In recent years Islamic financial practitioners have adapted the classical forms of *salam* and *istisna*ʿ and combined them with other transactions to generate approximations of conventional financial transactions, including interest-bearing loans, interest-bearing bills and bonds, build-operate-transfer and build-operate-own infrastructure and other project financing, etc. We start this chapter by reviewing the classical rules on *salam* and *istisna*ʿ and the innovative uses of those contracts that have been approved in recent years (not entirely without controversy) by various juristic bodies.

5.1 Prepaid Forward Sale (*Salam*)

All six major compilers of Prophetic tradition narrated on the authority of Ibn ʿAbbas that when the Prophet migrated to Madina (formerly known as the city of Yathrib), he found its inhabitants engaging in one-to-three-year forward sales of fruits, with prices being prepaid at contract inception (which gives *salam* = "prepayment sale" its name). He then narrated that the Prophet said, "Whosoever engages in a *salam* contract, let him specify a volume or weight for the object of sale, and a definitive term of deferment." Thus, jurists of all schools considered the forward sale of fungible commodities (measured by weight, volume, length/size, or number of homogeneous units), with full prepayment of the price, to be a valid contract. As in all forward and futures contracts, jurists stipulated that the object of sale should be specified in genus, type, and quality, as well as quantity, however measured. In this regard, they agreed that the *salam* contract constituted an exception to the general prohibition of sale of nonexistent properties, as well as the prohibition of sale of properties that are not in the seller's possession at the time of sale.[1]

Classical jurists recognized the economic need for this contract primarily to allow farmers access to capital (price of *salam*), with which they can buy seeds, fertilizer, and other materials to grow their crops. However, they also recognized that the contract includes an element of speculation, since the *salam* seller benefits if the spot price at delivery time is lower, and the buyer benefits if it is higher. They also recognized that *salam* includes price discounting for time, that is, an element of interest, since the prepaid salam price will be generally lower than the expected spot price at time of delivery. This recognition prompted classical jurists to stipulate numerous conditions on *salam* contracts, to minimize elements of *gharar* and eliminate elements of *riba* therein.

In their efforts to avoid the abuse of *salam* contracts to synthesize *riba*-like transactions, classical jurists imposed strict conditions on delivery and settlement options for the *salam*-short (seller).[2] On the other hand, it is clear – as we shall argue later – that conditions on immediate or near-immediate delivery of the price, which distinguish *salam* contracts from contemporary forwards, are rendered immaterial if the *salam*-long can simultaneously obtain a credit line (e.g., through *tawarruq* or *murabaha*) for the present value of the desired forward price. Hence, we shall focus on the delivery restrictions, which are generally observed today and which have given rise to legal stratagems such as parallel *salam*.

Revocation and Settlement of Long Position

If the *salam*-long wishes to take part in a *salam* contract for purely financial purposes, without intent of taking delivery of the *salam* object, he can theoretically attempt to achieve his goal in one of two simple ways: (1) settle the position with the *salam*-short in cash or some other commodity (based on spot prices on the delivery date, or some other formula), or (2) sell the *salam*-long position to a third party, which is tantamount to selling the *salam* object prior to receiving it. In their efforts to restrict *salam* contracts to genuinely needed economic activities, such as the original financing of agricultural production, premodern jurists generally forbade both avenues. However, as we shall see in the next two sections, contemporary jurists have utilized some minority opinions, as well as the permissibility of debt transfers for *salam* objects, to synthesize purely monetary financial transactions from the *salam* contract.

A third way to settle a *salam* financially would be to revoke the contract shortly before delivery, whereby the *salam*-long may accept a different price from the one he paid (reflecting the difference between the prepaid price and spot price at time of revocation, known by the Arabic name *iqala*). However, although revocation of *salam* sales is permissible, jurists did not allow settlement in cash either directly or through revocation. In that context, classical jurists, starting with Abu Hanifa and his associates Abu Yusuf and Al-Shaybani, relied on a Prophetic tradition: "Whosoever engages in a *salam* contract, let him not take any replacement for the contract's specified price or object."[3] This Prophetic tradition disallows the long from accepting a replacement for the object of *salam* (e.g., financial equivalent at spot price) or from revoking the contract and receiving a replacement for the price refund reflecting that financial equivalent at spot price. In other words, this canonical text appears directly to address the remaining ways in which financial engineers might try to convert the *salam* contract into a purely financial tool.

However, a minority opinion in the Maliki school allowed sale of the object of *salam* prior to its receipt, provided that the object was not foodstuffs. In this regard, if the object is sold to the original *salam*-short, they allowed the sale subject to the condition that the price does not exceed the initial prepaid price. Indeed, in that case, one could characterize the second sale as a partial revocation of the original sale (which is generally not accepted in the Maliki school, but accepted in other schools),[4] together with an exoneration of the *salam*-short's remaining liability.[5] Moreover, the Malikis permitted sale of the *salam* object prior to its receipt to a third party at any price, provided that the price is paid in a different genus, and the *salam* object was not a foodstuff. Those opinions also meant that Malikis allowed settling the long position with the *salam*-short for an equal or smaller amount.[6]

Parallel Salam

Since the Maliki school of jurisprudence does not have a significant following in the areas where Islamic finance has witnessed its greatest growth, selling *salam* objects to third parties was not the first method contemplated to utilize *salam* as a pure financial tool. However, bankers and jurists found another juristic opening for such utilization based on characterization of the *salam*-short position as debt for the fungible *salam* object. Once it is characterized as debt for fungibles, the short position may thus be forwarded to a third party, possibly within the context of mutual debt clearance (*maqassa*). The most practical procedure devised along those lines by Islamic bankers came to be known as "parallel *salam*."

This structure has allowed banks to use *salam* contracts to synthesize debts with fixed or variable interest rates as follows: Party A wishes to borrow $1,000,000 for three months at LIBOR + 200 basis points, and party B is willing to lend him at that rate. Party A may take a short position to sell platinum, deliverable in six months to party B at a specified location, collecting the prepaid *salam* price of $1,000,000. Three months later, the two parties may engage in a second and opposite *salam* contract, usually through a third-party intermediary to ensure separation from the initial contract (as we have described in the case of *tawarruq*), for delivery of the same amount of platinum at the same location, with the prepaid price being $1,000,000×(1+LIBOR+0.02). Then both parties have liabilities toward one another for delivery of the same amount of platinum at the same location, and the two liabilities may be canceled against one another according to the rules of debt clearance (*maqassa*).

There are two main contemporary *fatawa* that pertain to this practice of parallel *salam*.[7] Notice the wording of requests for *fatwa* in the two cases. The questioner in the first *fatwa* asked directly about the permissibility of using this particular financial transaction (parallel *salam*) essentially as an institutionalized method for conventional banking practice. In this case, jurists ruled that, in fact, while the practice was permissible on an individual basis in their opinion, it is not permissible to turn it into a business mode. However, that prohibition was promptly diluted by the following appeal to considerations of competitiveness tantamount to necessity. Cleverly, the posers of the second *fatwa* question omitted asking about making the practice a business mode. Also, the jurists in that second *fatwa* conveniently did not go out of their way to rule on the issue of systematic use, about which they were not asked.[8]

The first *fatwa* that we quote on parallel *salam* was the second *fatwa* of the second Dalla Al-Baraka Symposium:

Question:
Is it permissible to sell the object of *salam* prior to its receipt?

If that is not allowed, is it permissible for the *salam*-long to take a *salam*-short position in the same genus, based on his long position, but without linking the two contracts for what he is eligible to receive and what he is responsible to deliver?

Is it permissible for the *salam*-long to make this a systematic trade?

Answer:

1. It is not permissible to sell the object of *salam* prior to its receipt.
2. However, it is permissible for the *salam*-long to take a *salam*-short position of the same genus, without tying the first *salam*-long position by virtue of the first contract to the *salam*-short liability of the second contract.
3. It is not permissible to use this type of transaction [which was allowed in the second paragraph of the answer] as a systematic mode of business. This is due to the fact

that *salam* was permitted as an exception to general legal rules, based on the needs of producers that can be met through *salam* in individual cases, without turning the latter into a systematic trade. On the other hand, if economic conditions in some Islamic countries, and major benefit considerations, dictate using this methodology as a systematic business mode in special cases, to minimize the effect of existing injustice, then it may be permitted based on that major benefit, as determined by *fatwa* and Shari'a supervisory boards.

The general prohibition of using this structure to synthesize interest-based debt instruments in paragraph (3) was diluted substantially in the last sentence of that paragraph. A second *fatwa* by the Shari'a Board of Al-Rajhi Investment Corporation (*fatwa* #41) indirectly appealed to that window of opportunity by invoking the need for Islamic banks to be competitive with their conventional counterparts in extending credit and being compensated accordingly. In the text of that Rajhi *fatwa*, given below, the questioners tried to be less specific about their intent, but the Shari'a board in fact addressed the issue of synthesizing conventional bank loans in this manner, by appealing to the aforementioned need:

Question:
Please inform us of the religious legal opinion regarding the Corporation's purchase of commodities (such as crude oil, various metals, etc.) through *salam* contracts, with the price being paid immediately, and delivery scheduled for a future date, knowing that the Corporation may sell that commodity through a *salam* contract, by receiving the price at the time of the [second] sale, with delivery scheduled for a future date.

Answer:
The main characteristic of the *salam* contract is that its object is a fungible liability measured by volume, weight, size, or numbers of homogeneous commodities, including agricultural products such as grains, oils, and milk, industrial products such as iron, cement, automobiles, and airplanes, and raw or semiprocessed materials such as crude and refined petroleum.

It is permissible for the *salam*-long (buyer) after the inception of the contract and prior to the delivery date to act as a *salam*-short (seller) for a similar commodity, with similar conditions to the existing contract, or with different conditions. As described, the *salam* contract is a highly efficient tool to meet the needs of an Islamic bank, recognizing that the main task of a bank is to extend credit, and its revenues rely primarily on the compensation it receives for time value.

. . .

Since dealings in credit markets of advanced countries require facing severe and critical competition, and since those countries provide a great deal of flexibility for competition, but put impediments for other tools of investment, this tool [*salam* contract] is considered a vital and important one to allow safe access to markets with flexible and wide competition, while providing protection against customary risks in those markets, such as political and inflation risks.

The Rajhi Shari'a board then proceeded to list five examples of using *salam* contracts to finance trading in a variety of commodities, in most cases emphasizing the real transaction aspect of *salam*. The Shari'a board also listed the generally accepted Hanbali position to be permission of pawning or use of mortgaged collateral (*rahn*) and guaranty (*kafala*) in lieu of liability for the *salam* objects.

Those provisions allow Islamic financiers to use *salam* contracts to synthesize interest-based debt. In fact, applications of *salam*, for example, by the government of Bahrain in issuing short-term bonds known as *sukuk al-salam*, cut more corners in settling the first *salam* for cash, as we shall see in Chapter 6. Those short-term debt instruments (similar to treasury bills) pay a declared interest rates, and they are backed by the full faith and credit of the issuing government. While those *salam*-based *sukuk* represented debt, and therefore were initially nontradable and meant to be held to maturity, repurchase facilities were recently announced to enhance liquidity management of Islamic banks that are the primary buyers of those instruments. Details on how this repurchase facility worked are not readily available, but it is clear how one could be constructed through the parallel *salam* vehicle described earlier.

Conventional and Synthesized Forwards

Classical jurists of all schools of jurisprudence forbade conventional forward contracts, wherein both price payment and delivery of sale object are stipulated as future liabilities.[9] The primary reason they gave for the prohibition is *gharar*, citing in particular ignorance about the state of the object of sale at the specified future date. Thus, they argued, the price to be paid in the future is known, but the future quality of the specified object of sale is unknown, which is a source of ignorance and uncertainty conducive to disputation. Recently Malaysian jurists, led by Dr. M. Hashim Kamali, have argued that legal and institutional advances, especially in organized futures exchanges, eliminate all excessive *gharar* from futures contracts by specifying in standardized contracts the characteristics of objects of sale, as well as compensation formulas for various delivery options given to the futures-short.[10] Consequently, they have allowed trading in Islamic futures, where the only Islamic constraints pertain to, for example, the objects of sale or margin trading rules.

In contrast, most jurists outside Malaysia remain opposed to forward and futures trading.[11] Some refer to the insistence of classical jurists of all schools that the price of *salam* must be paid in full at contract inception. Classical jurists argued that prepayment of the price (which gives *salam* its name) is the essence of permissibility of the contract, to give farmers access to capital with which to buy necessary inputs and sustain themselves until harvest. In addition, when the price of *salam* is also fungible (e.g., monetary), those classical jurists argued that deferment of the price, while the object of *salam* is obviously deferred, would classify the transaction in an explicitly forbidden category of exchanging one deferred liability for another (called *bayʿ al-kali ʾi bi-l-kali ʾ*).[12] However, Malaysian and some other jurists questioned the authenticity of traditions forbidding this type of trade, many of them citing Al-Shafiʿiʾs report that scholars of tradition considered its chain of narration weak. Nevertheless, most scholars continue to reject forward and futures trading, and many of them continue to quote that tradition as proof – especially those influenced by the Hanbali preference of traditions with weak chains of narration over any reasoning by analogy.

Thus, most jurists and Islamic finance practitioners outside of Malaysia ruled that deferment of the price alone (in credit or installment sale) is permissible, as is deferment of the object of sale alone (in *salam* sale), but deferment of both (conventional forward sale) is not permissible. This collection of rulings creates another Shariʿa arbitrage opportunity for synthesizing forbidden conventional forward contracts from the *salam* and credit sale contracts that jurists permitted.

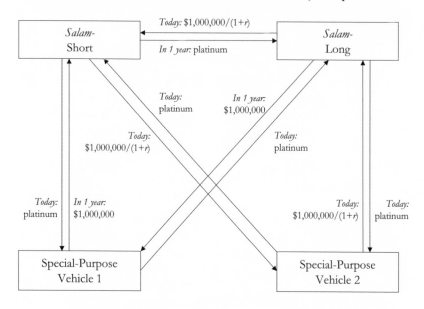

Fig. 5.1. Forward Synthesized from *Salam* and Credit Sales

Figure 5.1 illustrates one possible structure for synthesizing a forward contract from *salam* and a credit facility for its price (characterized variously as *murabaha*, *tawarruq*, etc., depending on banker and jurist preferences). The combination allows the *salam*-long to prepay the present value of the desired forward price.

For instance, if the desired contract was to pay $1,000,000 in one year for some amount of platinum, one could always convert it into a *salam* contract by paying $1,000,000/(1+r)$ at contract inception, where r is the appropriate interest rate. In this regard, the *salam*-short may extend a credit facility to the *salam*-long, perhaps using *tawarruq* with the same platinum serving as the underlying commodity, whereby the *salam*-long will obtain $1,000,000/(1+r)$ today (with which to pay the *salam* price), for which he would have to pay the deferred price of $1,000,000 in one year (at the time he originally desired to make that forward price payment).

The detailed procedure can be implemented as follows, utilizing two special-purpose vehicles, to ensure that no two parties ever engage in more than one trade of platinum with each other – thus minimizing concerns based on the prohibition of *'ina* sales:

1. *Salam*-short sells platinum to SPV1 on credit, for $1,000,000 payable in one year. This is a standard credit sale transaction.

2. SPV1 sells platinum to *Salam*-long on credit, for $1,000,000 payable in one year. This is also a standard credit sale transaction.

3. *Salam*-long sells platinum to SPV2, for a cash price of $1,000,000/(1+r)$. This is a standard spot sale.

4. SPV2 sells platinum to *Salam*-short for a price of $1,000,000/(1+r)$. This is also a standard spot sale.

    The net result of steps 1–4 is a *tawarruq* facility whereby *Salam*-long receives $1,000,000/(1+r)$ today (through SPV1) and owes *Salam*-short $1,000,000 in one year (through SPV2). Finally,

5. *Salam*-long uses the $1,000,000/(1+r)$ as a prepaid *salam* price, which he pays to *Salam*-short.

    As a result of this *salam* contract, *Salam*-short owes *Salam*-long platinum deliverable in one year. In the meantime, *Salam*-long owes *Salam*-short $1,000,000 to be paid in one year. This is the forward contract we wished to synthesize.

This structure ensures that each entity does one and only one transaction with each other entity, hence avoiding any problems with same-item sale-repurchase (*'ina*). This separation also allows the long and short to gain approval from Shari'a boards for all components separately, thus avoiding potential prejudice against synthesizing a forward position. Depending on the Shari'a board or boards of the short and long, transaction costs can be further reduced, according to the *tawarruq* conditions imposed by those boards, which determine transactions costs of that component of our structure. In Chapter 10 we shall discuss the use of similar synthetic forwards to synthesize options, short positions, and the like.

It might appear that this proposed structure merely replicates classical forms of Islamic financial transactions, while adding no contribution to substance. Of course, based on the track record of Islamic finance, that would be the most likely utilization for this and similar contrived structures. In fact, however, the same "marking to market" logic utilized in Chapter 4 can ensure that the suggested structure – at least as a counterfactual that is not in fact implemented – adds substance. In this regard, arbitrage pricing of forwards, as taught in all finance textbooks, will force forward participants who contemplate using the *salam* contract to engage in a beneficial calculation. The arbitrage pricing logic for forwards proceeds as follows:

- Consider two portfolios: (1) a long forward contract plus the present value of the specified forward price (discounted at the riskless interest rate r), and (2) a long position for goods to be delivered at the same future date specified in the forward contract.

- Notice that the second portfolio is precisely the liability on *Salam*-short toward *Salam*-long after full payment of the *salam* price at contract inception.

- Obviously, one can invest the present value of the forward price at the riskless rate (e.g., in treasury bills), thus converting the first portfolio into the second. In other words, if there are no other risks, the two portfolios must have equal values at delivery time.

- Since no risk is being taken between contract inception and delivery time, and since the two portfolios are equal in value at delivery time, they must also be equal in value at contract inception time. In other words, the *salam* price will be correct if and only if it is equal to the present value of the forward price: A higher *salam* price would unjustly favor the seller and vice versa.

Consequently, as we argued in the case of property purchase financing, the calculus imposed by our structure forces the parties through a "marking to market" exercise, which in turn ensures that trading will not take place at unfair prices. Needless to say, performing the calculations to ensure proper pricing does not require actually engaging in multiple inefficient trades. This structure may be used merely as a legal fiction to ensure proper pricing, without actually realizing the efficiency losses associated with multiple trades and corresponding transaction costs.

5.2 Commission to Manufacture (*Istisna'*)

Classical jurists approved another contract to purchase some item that is generally not owned by the seller at contract time, and that may never have existed prior to the contract. Under this contract, generally known as *istisna'* or commission to manufacture, the buyer (known as *mustasni'* or commissioner to manufacture) pays the price either in one or multiple installments, and a liability is established on the worker/seller (known as *sani'* or manufacturer) to deliver the object of sale as described in the contract at some future date.

Thus, *istisna'* shared with *salam* the function of financing the production of nonexistent items, which are established as liabilities on the sellers. However, *istisna'* differed from *salam* in a few main respects: First, jurists did not require price in *istisna'* to be fully paid at contract inception, to facilitate the financing of multistage manufacturing or construction projects, wherein the buyer may pay for each phase separately. Second, the term of deferment in *salam* is prespecified, and the seller must therefore acquire the object of sale at the specified delivery time on the spot market if he fails to produce it – prompting jurists to list a *salam* condition of general availability of the object of sale at delivery time. In contrast, the object of *istisna'* may never come into existence except by virtue of the *istisna'* contract. Hence, the term of deferment in *istisna'* need not be fixed at the inception of the contract.

Third, although the object of a *salam* sale is fungible (e.g., metals or grains), the object of an *istisna'* sale is typically nonfungible (e.g., a freeway or building). Fourth, *salam* contracts are binding on both parties and thus may be voided only by mutual consent. In contrast, *istisna'* contracts were deemed nonbinding on either party by early classical jurists. However, later jurists made the contract binding on both parties, and that opinion was codified in the Hanafi *Majalla* and adopted in the AAOIFI standard.[13] That standard also chose a minority opinion that requires the term of deferment in *istisna'* to be specified, provided that a mutually agreeable term is selected, allowing sufficient time for the necessary work to be done.

Some classical jurists debated whether the object of an *istisna'* contract is the object to be manufactured or the manufacturer's labor/effort. If the contract is merely the sale of an object to be delivered in the future, it would be no different from *salam*. Conversely, if the contract was merely over the manufacturer's labor, it would be an employment or hire contract, as discussed under the rules of *ijara* contracts in Chapter 6. Either characterization by itself would deem the contract impermissible based on analogy, since sales of nonexistent properties are generally forbidden (*salam* being an exception), and hiring contracts require that the employer must provide raw materials.[14]

Jurists of the various schools finally reached a compromise characterization of the contract, stipulating that the object of *istisna'* is the sold object, but that the contract requires the one commissioned to manufacture that object of sale to exert effort in its production. Moreover, contemporary jurists stipulated that if the contract did not require the commissioned party in *istisna'* to do the work himself, he may subcontract the work to another through a second *istisna'* contract. This practice of the commissioned agent engaging in a second *istisna'* contract came to be known as parallel *istisna'*. In parallel *istisna'* there is no direct liability on the final worker toward the initial commissioner/buyer, thus keeping the two contracts separate.[15]

The *istisna'* contract is most commonly used in conjunction with a lease (*ijara*) contract, thus giving rise to a BOT (build, operate, transfer) structure for financing infrastructure development and similar large projects. The Islamic Development Bank has been particularly active in utilizing this contract for financing infrastructure projects in various member countries. Because of the specific nature of this contract, it has not easily lent itself to pure financial applications, thus remaining a tool for real project financing. On the other hand, some advances in securitization have expanded its uses in synthesizing Islamic *sukuk*, as discussed in Chapter 6. In general, project finance structures based on *istisna'* differ very little from their conventional counterparts.

5.3 Down-Payment Sale (*'Urbun*)

In its classical manifestation, *'urbun* was a down payment from a potential buyer to a potential seller toward the purchase of a particular property.[16] If the buyer decided to complete the sale, the *'urbun* counted toward the total price. Otherwise, if the buyer did not execute the sale, he forfeited the down payment, which was thus considered a gift to the seller. Naturally, contemporary jurists and Islamic financial practitioners contemplated the similarity of this arrangement to a call option, which is likewise binding on the seller but not on the buyer. Indeed, some classical Hanbali jurists had even contemplated that the option period should be fixed (making the transaction somewhat similar to an American call option), otherwise the seller may have to wait indefinitely for the potential buyer to decide whether or not to exercise his right.[17]

Classical jurists differed over the legal status of this contract, most of them forbidding it based on a Prophetic tradition (which referred to the transaction under the name *bay' al-'urban*). Although that tradition was deemed nonauthoritative, because of missing links in its chain of narration, most classical jurists still deemed the contract forbidden, because of *gharar*, since the seller does not know whether or not the buyer will conclude the sale. Moreover, they argued, the potential seller gives the potential buyer in this contract an option (in contemporary parlance: a call option), but if the buyer proceeds to exercise that option, the down payment counts toward the price, and the seller would thus not have been compensated for the option.[18]

This argument is particularly interesting, since classical jurists (and most contemporary ones) forbid the sale of naked options (because of *gharar*, according to the same logic as before), and since most of them do not consider mere legal rights (e.g., to exercise an option) to be valid objects of sale. However, those same classical jurists clearly felt that an embedded option (as in the case of '*urbun*) should be properly compensated. It is in this regard that they ruled that the seller is compensated only if the buyer did not exercise his right, and even that may not be sufficient compensation for the time he had to wait, during which he was not able to sell the property and benefit from its price.

In contrast to the majority of jurists of his time, Ahmad ibn Hanbal deemed the practice of down-payment sales permissible. He relied on a Prophetic tradition: "The Messenger of God was asked about down-payment sale (*al-'urban*), and permitted it."[19] Interestingly, scholars of tradition consider this also a tradition with a weak chain of narration. However, this narration was further supported by another weak narration that 'Umar ibn Al-Khattab allowed down payment toward the purchase of a jailhouse. Moreover, classical Hanbali and contemporary jurists of most schools argued that down-payment sales had become very common and provided some compensation to the seller for waiting, in case the buyer decides not to execute the sale. Moreover, contemporary jurists argued, there are weak Prophetic traditions that provide support either for permission or for prohibition. Hence, the Fiqh Academy of the Organization of Islamic Conference (the most prestigious international juristic body) ruled at its eighth session in Brunei in 1993 that down-payment sales are permissible.

'Urbun as Call Option

Most analysts of the differences between the down-payment sale ('*urbun*) and contemporary call options concluded that the latter cannot be synthesized from the former.[20] On the other hand, a number of institutions have been in fact using call options under the name '*urbun*, ignoring some of the finer legal differences between the two contracts. For instance, if a seller wishes to write (sell) a call option to a potential buyer, giving him the right to buy within the specified time window at a strike price of $100, and sell that call option to the potential buyer for c, one may call c a "down payment" and inflate the agreed-upon price in the down-payment sale to $100+c$. Thus, if the option holder decides not to exercise the option, he would have paid the premium c, and if he does exercise it, he would buy at the desired price of $100+c - c$ (the down payment counting toward the price) = $100. Thus, the juristic and legal differences between the classical '*urbun* contract and the contemporary call options are ignored, and the latter is used under the Arabic name of the former.

Case Study 1: Al-Ahli International Secured Fund

In 2000 National Commercial Bank (NCB of Saudi Arabia) launched a protected-principal fund that utilized sophisticated derivative strategies without explicitly trading in options.[21] The declared goal of the fund was to generate capital gains at various participation rates (e.g., 37.5 percent of underlying index, capped at 11 percent, depending on subscription dates) in a weighted basket of global equities that met certain "Shari'a-compliance" criteria (we shall discuss mutual fund screens in Chapter 7). The main marketing feature of the fund was its principal protection (albeit without guarantee from NCB, to avoid giving returns while guaranteeing the principal, which would be deemed *riba* by most jurists).

The fund generated the desired return profile as a two-year process. In the first year, investors received fixed returns from a closed-end *murabaha* fund (see Chapter 6 for further discussion of *murabaha* securitization). In this structure the investor was exposed only to credit risk, but the provider did not directly guarantee the principal. In the second year, the provider kept roughly 95 percent of the original capital in the *murabaha* fund, thus continuing to protect the principal. The remaining 5 percent of the original capital plus profits from the first year were invested in call options, characterized as '*urbun*, as described above. Of course, if the index declined in value, the call options were not exercised. If it increased in value, investors received a gross return equal to the maximum of return based on the promised participation, and the cap rate for their particular subscription date.[22]

An investment bank was selected as an advisor, which managed the indexed portfolio of stocks and structured the product. That advisor was paid a "performance fee" equal to the actual returns on the portfolio above the cap rate. In other words, the advisor's fee was in fact a call option at the appropriate participation rate, with a strike price equal to the index value at the beginning of the year plus cap profits. Of course, the advisor (a conventional investment bank) would turn around and sell that call option to collect a flat fee (shown in the left panel of Figure 5.2). Hence, ignoring NCB's own management fee (then set at 1.5 percent of gross assets), payoffs to fund investors looked like a classical "bullish spread," with principal protected at 100 percent, and participation rate of 37.5 percent in index capital gains, capped at 11 percent (shown in the right panel of Figure 5.2).

A classical bullish spread could normally be structured by buying a call at the desired protection level and selling a call at the cap level. In this case, the long call position at the low end was manufactured through (1) *murabaha* investment for one year, and (2) using the profits from the first year and anticipated profits from the second year to buy call options in the form of '*urbun* (down-payment) purchase of the participation position. The short call position would have been

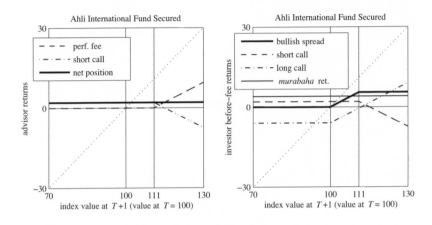

Fig. 5.2. Al-Ahli Secured Fund Returns

more difficult to manufacture, since the investors would own the index participation only if they recognize capital gains and exercise their option. In other words, investors do not own the participation position (even in constructed form) at contract time and thus could not write a call option in the form of down-payment sale of that which they do not own. By constructing the short call position as a gift to the "advisor," the latter can sell the long call he receives thus (to collect his fees), without the Islamic financial provider itself engaging in options trading, which has not (yet) been approved by the Fiqh Academy of the Organization of Islamic Conference or other widely respected juristic councils.

Case Study 2: Al-Rajhi Aman Fund

The direct use of '*urbun* was not necessary for obtaining principal protection. This is illustrated by contrasting the NCB protected fund structure with that of Al-Rajhi's Aman-1 Fund, which was introduced roughly at the same time. Instead of providing complete principal protection, Al-Rajhi chose to provide partial protection, thus alleviating investors' concerns about suspicion of *riba* without resorting to arguments regarding the difference between "guaranteed principal" and "protected principal." In this regard, Al-Rajhi's structure also employed payment with implicit options, which allowed a "partner" to trade those options without implicating the Islamic financial provider.[23] Naturally, the fund was structured with a partner that was in fact an investment bank. The partner was assigned an unspecified share in the fund portfolio, without owning any shares in the actual mutual fund. Thus, that partner was not bound to adhere to Islamic principles as envisioned by Al-Rajhi's Shari'a board.

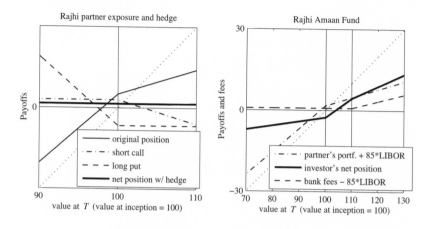

Fig. 5.3. Al-Rajhi Aman 1 Fund Returns

The partner bought 85 percent of the portfolio, at a deferred price equal to the market price at inception. In this way the partner was implicitly paid the interest on that 85 percent share. In return, the partner was entitled to 30 percent of profits, but bore 85 percent of potential losses. This obeys the Islamic rules of partnership (discussed in Chapter 7), whereby profits may be shared according to any agreed-upon percentages, but losses must be borne in proportion to invested capital. Of course, the partner (a conventional investment bank) converted the risky position (30 percent of gains and 85 percent of losses) into a flat fee by selling a call to give up the 30 percent gains, while buying a put to protect it against the 85 percent losses (left panel of Figure 5.3). In the meantime, investors in the fund had the benefit of substantially reduced loss rates without having directly to trade in options (right panel of Figure 5.3).

The use of advisors (in the case of NCB) and partners (in the case of Al-Rajhi) to insulate investors from options trading notwithstanding, Islamic investors have been largely restricted in using derivative-based strategies. In other words, those trading parties or investment advisors served as degrees of separation between the Islamic financial providers and forbidden derivatives trading. One could argue, on the one hand, that making conventional investment banks trade in derivatives in place of the Islamic providers makes economic sense, since those investment bankers have a decided comparative advantage in pricing derivatives and executing trades. On the other hand, the addition of trading parties as buffers between Islamic financial institutions and transactions deemed to be forbidden (interest-based loans, option and future trading, etc.) must be seen fundamentally as a means of exploiting Shari'a arbitrage opportunities.

6

Leasing, Securitization, and *Sukuk*

In recent years leasing has become increasingly popular as a vehicle for financing the purchase of various assets, as well as issuance of various financial instruments, from mortgage-backed securities to bond structures known as *sukuk*. The increased popularity of lease-based financing and securitization stems from the existence of underlying physical assets, the usufruct of which is being transferred under various leases or subleases. Those underlying assets ostensibly allow secondary markets for lease-based debt instruments to emerge, without violating the general prohibition of trading in debts to which most schools of jurisprudence adhere (with the notable exception of Malaysian jurists following a particular opinion within the Shafiʿi school). As we shall see later in the chapter, various jurists apply the physical-asset-backing interpretation of contemporary Islamic financial instruments with varying degrees of strictness.

6.1 General Lease Conditions

Retired Justice M. Taqi Usmani – one of the foremost leaders in Islamic finance, chairing multiple Shariʿa boards – argued that the sale of a lease-backed security transfers material ownership rights and obligations from one lessor to another, and hence the purchaser of such a security is entitled to collect rent thereof. Needless to say, conventional asset-backed securities, whether lease or sale based, are often merely financial claims, with little material distinction between the two. Thus, commenting on common legal structures of lease-backed securities, Justice Usmani wrote:

It should be remembered, however, that the certificate must represent ownership of an undivided part of the asset with all its rights and obligations. Misunderstanding this basic concept, some quarters tried to issue *ijara* certificates representing the holder's right to claim certain amount of the rental only without assigning to him any kind of ownership in the asset. It means that the holder of such a certificate has no relation with the leased

97

asset at all. His only right is to share the rentals received from the lessee. This type of securitization is not allowed in Shari'ah.[1]

Of course, in practical implementations of jurists' restrictions and interpretations, legal and banking experts have a number of degrees of freedom through which they can address jurists' objections to the lack of "any kind of ownership in the asset." In this regard, constructive ownership through shares in bankruptcy-remote special purpose vehicles incorporated for the master lease has become increasingly common (with various additional SPVs put in place to handle repairs and other obligations of the supposed lessors). The aim in constructing those financial structures is simultaneously to satisfy market needs for regular debt instruments and jurists' insistence on material ownership of an underlying asset to justify the collection of coupon payments from the structured instruments. In this chapter we shall discuss the classical lease contract and its various conditions and interpretations in premodern jurisprudence, as well as contemporary jurists' adaptation of those conditions. Then we shall proceed to study contemporary advances in the area of Islamic financial securitization and various *sukuk* structures.

Binding Promises in Leasing

Classical jurists discussed both leasing of assets as well as hiring of workers under the common heading of *ijar* or *ijara*.[2] The object of a lease contract was viewed by the vast majority of classical jurists as a "desirable, known permissible and accessible usufruct," and rent was thus viewed as the price or compensation for that usufruct. However, one major and significant difference between leases and sales is that the majority of classical jurists allowed suspension and deferment of leasing.[3] This allows lease financing to overcome one of the most problematic aspects of double-sale-based financing (*murabaha* or *tawarruq*). In the latter type of financing, most Islamic banks require the customer to make a binding promise that he will purchase the property on credit once the bank buys it. This binding promise clause has been controversial, despite its adoption by most Islamic bank jurists in 1979, based on the minority opinion of the (relatively obscure) Maliki jurist Ibn Shubruma that promises may be made binding.[4]

In lease financing, the bank buys the property and then leases it to the customer, with monthly payments consisting of a rent component and a purchase component, most often reproducing the conventional amortization table that would also be used in *murabaha* financing. The main difference, however, is that it is not controversial to lease the property with a future starting date and prior to obtaining it.[5] Thus, the bank may proceed to acquire the property after having in hand a valid signed lease starting immediately or some time after the property is purchased.

Another interesting application of binding promises in leasing allows jurists to justify lease-to-purchase arrangements. As we have seen in the introduction, most *sukuk* structures involve selling a property to an SPV and then buying it back or receiving it as a gift at lease end. Moreover, many retail Islamic banking customers who wish to finance the purchase of real estate, automobiles, equipment, and the like aim to purchase the property at lease end. Contemporary as well as classical jurists disallowed stipulating in the lease contract that the lessor must sell the property to the lessee at lease end, since that condition negates ownership rights of the lessor and violates the prohibition of "two contracts in one" or "two sales in one contract."[6] However, contemporary jurists allowed lease-to-purchase contracts by arguing that the lessor may make a unilaterally binding promise (which is not part of the lease contract itself) to sell the property, or to give it as a gift at contract end. Moreover, those contemporary jurists have argued that once the promise is made, it becomes binding upon the lessor, in each case using a majority or minority opinion as the need arises.[7]

The only two conditions imposed by those jurists are that the binding promise to sell the property at lease end, if the lessee wishes to do so, must be unilateral, and that it must not be made a condition of the lease (it must be recorded in a separate document). Naturally, if the lessee pays not only the return on capital, but also the return of capital used to purchase the property, as part of lease payments, his own interest will drive him to exercise that option. Similarly, since Islamic banking lessors are primarily financial intermediaries, who are not in the business of owning and leasing properties, exercising the option is in their best interest as well. Moreover, although the option may not be made a condition for the contract, it appears that the separate document obliging the lessor to sell or give the property as a gift at the end of the lease can be signed prior to signing the lease itself. Needless to say, that promise becomes nugatory if the lease is not concluded, but it is binding upon the lessor if the lease is in fact concluded and executed for its full term.

Another note on the issue of binding promises is in order at this stage. Justice Usmani's analysis, as referenced above, implies that a unilateral promise to give the property as a gift at lease end is equally binding to a promise to sell the property at lease end. However, this position seems potentially controversial in light of classical juristic analysis of uncompensated gifts (*hiba*) and offers (*ji'ala*) discussed below.[8] Classical rules in this regard seem to agree with common-law provisions, which lean toward making uncompensated transactions nonbinding.[9] It would thus be more appripriate to use a unilateral promise to sell the property at lease end for some financial consideration, even if minimal or symbolic, and despite concerns regarding same-item sale-repurchase (*bay' al-'ina*), as we shall see later in the chapter.

Flexible-Rate Financing

Contemporary jurists have also found lease contracts to be particularly useful for flexible-rate financing. In this regard, *murabaha* financing requires that the amount of debt established upon the buyer is fixed at contract inception, hence restricting the contract to financing at fixed or predetermined interest-rate schedules. In contrast, with the exception of Shafi'i jurists, most jurists allowed long-term leasing on month-to-month or other periodic bases. In this regard, Shafi'i jurists based their ruling on the conditions of sale, which would require that the entire lease period (during which usufruct, the object of sale, may be consumed) must be specified at contract inception. However, jurists of other schools argued that lessor and lessee can agree to a longer-term periodically renewable lease, whereby the lease is binding on both parties for each period that it is extended with mutual consent.[10]

The mutual consent provision, however, could have been problematic for juristic arguments in the long term, since lessor and lessee have conflicting interests as interest rates rise or fall. To avoid such problems, contemporary jurists took the additional (somewhat heroic) step to link the rent to a flexible-rate benchmark (e.g., LIBOR + spread),[11] ignoring the fact that classical jurists who allowed automatic renewal of lease, possibly at different mutually acceptable rents, did not make the lease binding on any one party. In contrast, Justice Usmani seemed to argue that – in contemporary financial terms – both parties are exposed to interest-rate risk, and hence the demarcation criterion for permissibility may be ex ante acceptance of the benchmark, rather than ex post agreement at each renewal period.

Subleasing, Repairs, and Insurance Costs

The Fiqh Academy of the OIC ruled in 1988 that a lessee is entitled to sell his right to future usufruct either to the lessor or to a third party (sublessee) at any mutually agreed-upon rate. Classical jurists imposed some conditions that limit the lessee's ability to sublease to third parties who may use the property differently, requiring the lessee to obtain the lessor's permission in that case. Conversely, the lessor is allowed to sell the property, provided that the lessee's rights are not compromised. Thus, subleasing and securitization of leases seemed similar in contemporary practice and classical jurisprudence, to an extent that allows leasing to serve multiple functions in Islamic financial structures.

However, as we have already noted, some jurists continued to impose strict conditions to ensure that any party that receives compensation through a lease-based structure has material ownership of the leased property. Thus, Justice Usmani rejected modern financial tools such as head leases and various other forms of financial leases.[12]

In addition, most jurists have insisted that material ownership of the leased property requires assigning all repair costs (beyond routine maintenance and damages caused by lessee abuse or negligence), insurance costs, and the like to the lessor. This is in fact the classical Hanafi opinion,[13] which was codified in the Ottoman *Majalla* and to which most contemporary jurists continue to appeal. It is a very reasonable opinion for simple leases, and it does in fact follow naturally from lessor ownership: Since the lessor suffers losses if the property were to perish, he should bear the cost of insurance, nonroutine maintenance repairs, and so on.

However, as practiced today, most lease financiers are in fact legally constructed (as opposed to natural or human) lessors, with property ownership by SPVs created for the purpose of financing. Those financiers would not have material ownership of the underlying assets were it not for the financing, and they cannot retain ownership thereof past the financing period. Hence, the customer/lessee in fact bears all the costs of repairs, insurance, and the like through carefully calculated increases in rent and side contracts with other SPVs that cover various provisions. This complicated structure increases transaction costs unnecessarily, and the conditions on which jurists insist – and which result in those increased transaction costs – were not derived directly from Islamic canonical texts, but rather from customary practice (*'urf*) in the times and places wherein the classical jurists lived. In fact, classical references are full of statements such as "customary practice (*'urf*) carries substantial weight in determining the conditions of *ijara* and *murabaha*."[14]

However, contemporary jurists seem to insist on costly (and possibly anachronistic) symbols of material ownership of the underlying asset, whether in double-sale (*murabaha*) or lease (*ijara*) financing, to maintain the fiction that interest (collected as price mark-up or rent, respectively) is in fact a return based on risk associated with ownership of a physical asset. This was explicitly the justification given in the 1979 decision in Dubai, which required Islamic banks engaged in *murabaha* financing to obtain full ownership of a property – and the risks associated with it – prior to selling it. The fact that exposure to this risk – to the extent that any remained after insurance – lasted for only a very short period of time was ignored. On the other hand, there is evidence in later juristic opinions, such as the Rajhi Shari'a board ruling on parallel-*salam* financing quoted in the previous chapter, that jurists are progressively recognizing that Islamic banks – like conventional ones – in fact collect interest as compensation for deferment and credit risk. To the extent that transaction costs can be reduced significantly by following contemporary conventions rather than customary practices of premodern times, jurists are likely progressively to abandon some of the current anachronistic conditions, as has been evident in recent *sukuk* issuances.

6.2 Asset-Backed Securities

Contemporary securitization is a decades-old technology in conventional structured finance, which allowed financial institutions to create financial instruments from other financial assets, ranging from mortgage loan to credit card receivables. Its implementations in Islamic finance have been severely limited by jurists' aversion to synthesizing new debt instruments from existing ones, lest one would in fact be selling debt. The sale of debt to third parties has been an active topic of study in classical jurisprudence, and we shall review classical and contemporary juristic views on the topic shortly. First, we provide a very brief review of leasing and securitization for readers who may not be familiar with the topic.

Leasing and Securitization

Securitization methods have come under intense scrutiny in recent years, primarily because of high-profile corporate scandals, but more significantly because of the potential misinformation about corporate assets and liabilities made possible by such securitization methodologies.[15] The very definition of securitization (transforming one type of financial exposure into another) suggests the myriad of ways that it can be abused. A particularly troublesome use of securitization is the procedure of hiding corporate debts by moving them off-balance-sheet, which can also be accomplished through simple leasing. Interestingly for Islamic finance, structured leasing has been a particularly popular way of taking conventional debt off-balance-sheet (in part to show lower debt-to-asset ratios, thus increasing desirability for company stock among investors).

Needless to say, not all off-balance-sheet deals are done to disguise or hide debt. For instance, a company may decide to refinance some of its conventional on-balance-sheet debt by selling some asset (through an SPV) and leasing it back at better interest rates (possibly repurchasing the asset at lease end, as usually done also in the context of *sukuk* structures). However, higher degrees of transparency and disclosure may be required to minimize the possibility of abuse or misinforming investors in such cases.

Since lease-based securitization is the most popular vehicle in Islamic finance, we now focus on that case. In conventional finance there are two types of leases: capital (or financial) leases and operating leases. Under standard accounting rules, a capital or financial lease (where the lessee is the ultimate purchaser) is treated like a purchase, with the leased-to-purchase property appearing on-balance-sheet as an asset and rental payments appearing as liabilities. Interestingly, this type of lease structure (where material ownership of the leased asset passes to the lessee at lease inception) is disallowed by most contemporary Islamic finance jurists.

According to those jurists, material ownership of the asset by the lessor is the only justification for collecting rents, otherwise the lease would be considered a loan contract, and rent/interest would be thus deemed forbidden *riba*.

Financial and Operating Leases

Consequently, securitization of financial leases is also deemed inadmissible by contemporary jurists who have shaped Islamic finance:

> As explained earlier . . . the rent after being due is a debt payable by the lessee. The debt or any security representing debt only is not a negotiable instrument in Shari'ah, because trading in such an instrument amounts to trade in money or in monetary obligation which is not allowed, except on the basis of equality, and if the equality of value is observed while trading in such instruments, the very purpose of securitization is defeated.[16]

We shall review the classical juristic basis of this approach below and discuss the loopholes introduced by contemporary jurists, which allow trading in debt instruments to take place, albeit in a convoluted manner. In other words, the lease conditions imposed by contemporary jurists create yet another Shari'a arbitrage opportunity, from which industry practitioners – including those jurists – are the primary beneficiaries.

First, we turn to the second type of leases, which are allowed by contemporary jurists: operating leases. In that type of lease, the lessor (an SPV or other type of entity) retains ownership of the leased asset. In such cases, the amount of debt for rent typically does not appear on-balance-sheet, since operating lease expenses are generally reported as operating expenses. Keeping the liability for all lease-to-purchase payments (which are naturally larger in sum than the current market asset value of the leased property) off-balance-sheet, the company can show lower debt ratios, higher return on assets, and the like. Interestingly, as we shall argue in the next chapter on Islamic or "Shari'a-compliant" equity investment, a private equity outfit can exploit this Shari'a-arbitrage opportunity by buying companies, "Islamizing" their debts by refinancing them through operating leases, and then selling the companies at a much higher price. This harms investors who do not perform any "before-and-after" analysis to examine the justification of higher market value for the company.[17]

Trying to get the best of both worlds, companies may resort to synthetic leases, which give the lessee some benefits of ownership (e.g., deductibility of interest component of lease payments, property depreciation) while retaining some substantial ownership rights. Technically, a synthetic lease is an operating lease and thus permissible according to contemporary Islamic finance jurists. At the same time it allows the lessee to exercise control over the property without reporting its corresponding assets and liabilities on its balance sheet, the benefits of which we have discussed in the previous paragraph. In Islamic financial practice, bankers and lawyers who are active in structuring such deals negotiate with jurists the (minimum) acceptable level of ownership interest on the part of the lessor, with different jurists and Shariʿa boards applying different standards.

Receivable Securitization and Sale of Debt

The most common types of securitization in conventional finance are applied to receivables (from mortgages, credit card balances, etc.). In this regard, Islamic banks and financial institutions that engage in pure debt financing, such as through *murabaha*, would wish likewise to manage their financial risks by securitizing their receivables. However, we have also seen that contemporary jurists – with the exception of some in Malaysia – have forbidden trading in liabilities and debts. It is worthwhile at this point to review the grounds on which the majority of classical jurists based this general prohibition. This will allow us to develop a better understanding of potential directions that contemporary jurists might take, as well as potential means of synthesizing securitization of *murabaha* receivables and other liabilities generated in Islamic finance.

Classical jurists bundled many different types of liabilities together under the name "*dayn*," including such things as unpaid prices of purchased properties, debts ensuing from loans, due rental payments, and the object of a *salam* sale. All of those liabilities take the form of obligations on the debtor to pay or deliver a monetary or fungible property to the creditor. Jurists considered the sale of such liabilities to the debtor himself or to a third party and for each case considered selling the liability for an immediate or deferred price.[18]

In general, classical jurists forbade the sale of debt either to the debtor or to a third party for any deferred price. They based that prohibition on the same grounds that they used to forbid conventional forward contracts, which are envisioned as trading a liability for the price in exchange for a liability for the object of sale. Both prohibitions are based on a weak tradition: "The Prophet forbade trading one deferred liability for another."[19]

The canonical mode of exchanging one deferred liability for another, which featured prominently in classical jurists' analyses, is the pre-Islamic mode of *riba*, wherein the debtor asked the creditor for further deferment of his debt, in exchange for increasing the amount of the debt. This is contrasted with the case wherein the debtor and creditor agree to settle the debt through some immediate exchange of property, in which case the transaction is valid. On the other hand, classical jurists ruled – subject to appropriate conditions – that it is valid to cancel one debt against another of equal amount and maturity (*maqassa*), as well as to forward a debt to a third party (*hawala*).[20]

The majority of premodern jurists allowed selling a liability to the debtor, as well as forgiving it partially or totally. Interestingly, the price in that case was allowed to be a deferred (albeit briefly) liability in another numeraire. The opinion was based on the Prophetic tradition wherein the Prophet allowed Ibn 'Umar to trade camels in Baqi', with the price denominated in gold and collected in silver or vice versa, provided that the compensation was determined at the spot rate.[21] This permitted practice was seen as trading a liability for the agreed-upon price (denominated in gold) in exchange for another liability denominated in silver.

In this regard, jurists had disallowed general trading of one liability for another because of *gharar*, in the form of uncertainty about delivery of either compensation. However, they argued, when a liability is already established on one party, trading it for another liability implies dropping the original debt, which means that at least one of the compensations has been implicitly delivered. Moreover, since the Prophetic tradition restricted the practice to trading at the spot rate, this ensured that the practice cannot be used as a means of increasing the liability for further deferment. As a consequence, it was deemed permissible to sell a debt to the debtor either at face value (denominated in the same genus, or determined by the spot rate of the genus used as price) or a lower price (the difference being a partial gift or forgiveness of debt). This general analysis culminated in a contemporary ruling by the Fiqh Academy of the OIC at its seventh session in Jeddah (May 9–14, 1992) regarding the practice known as "*ḍaʿ wa taʿajjal*" (reduce the amount of debt for prepayment):

> Reduction of the amount of a deferred liability to facilitate prepayment, whether initiated by the debtor or creditor (*ḍaʿ wa taʿajjal*), is legally permissible, and not considered a form of forbidden *riba*, provided that: (i) it was not stipulated as a prior condition [before initiation of the debt], and (ii) the relationship between the debtor and creditor is binary, otherwise if a third party is involved, the transaction would inherit the ruling for discounting of commercial papers [which is forbidden].

Thus, contemporary jurists restricted the permission to the case of selling the debt at or below its face value to the debtor himself, arguing that a bank or financial institution serving as an intermediary in debt discounting would thus be committing *riba*. However, as we shall see in Chapter 8, some of those intermediation practices were made possible through agency contracts. Also, debt discounting was allowed only as an ex post voluntary practice by the creditor and disallowed as a stipulation in the contract (e.g., in *murabaha*), thus potentially limiting the ability to mimic mortgage and other financial structures completely. Fortunately for Western customers of Islamic banks, secular regulations prevent the Islamic banks from insisting on collecting interest on credit – which is thus characterized as early repayment penalties.

Finally, most classical jurists forbade the sale of liabilities to third parties. Thus, the Hanafis and Zahiris forbade the sale of debt to a third party as a corollary of the general prohibition of sale of undeliverable items. Similarly, classical Hanbali jurists – with the notable exception of Ibn Qayyim – forbade the sale of debts, or offering them as gifts, to any party other than the debtor. In contrast, Maliki jurists and some Shafi'is permitted selling a liability at its face value to a third party subject to strict conditions to exclude the possibility of *riba* and minimize the incidence of *gharar*. That being said, jurists of most schools have been quite lenient on forwarding of debts (*hawala*), which makes practices such as parallel *salam* (executed in collaboration with metal dealers to whom debts are transferred) more practical. The forwarding of debt from one creditor to another, possibly with cancellation of that debt against an existing debt on the first creditor, is in fact tantamount to selling that debt at face value, as allowed by some jurists.

Bundling Asset-Based and Debt-Based Securities: A Paradox

Based on the set of classical opinions summarized in the previous section, contemporary jurists concluded that existing liabilities (debt-based securities) may be sold to the debtor only at or below par value, or forwarded to a third party at face value. This restriction was deemed by Justice Usmani to be the primary reason why purely financial assets were not eligible for securitization from a legal or practical point of view. Thus, *murabaha* certificates were deemed non-negotiable:

> Murabahah is a transaction which cannot be securitized for creating a negotiable instrument to be sold and purchased in a secondary market. ... If the paper is transferred, it must be at par value. However, if there is a mixed portfolio consisting of a number of transactions like musharakah, leasing, and murabahah, then this portfolio may issue negotiable certificates subject to certain conditions.[22]

The concluding part of this quotation introduces an interesting, and paradoxical, twist. The condition imposed on such a negotiable security is that its majority should represent "tangible asset"–based liabilities:

> This may be called a Mixed Islamic Fund. In this case if the tangible assets of the Fund are more than 51% while the liquidity and debts are less than 50% the units of the fund may be negotiable. ... [Otherwise] the Fund must be a closed-end Fund.[23]

We have already addressed contemporary jurists' use of ostensible material ownership of an underlying tangible asset to justify earning a rate of return on lease-based structured securities. Indeed, when HSBC introduced home financing in New York state, initially restricted to *murabaha* financing for practical and legal reasons, its officers stated explicitly that they had hoped eventually to introduce *ijara* financing as well, so that a mixture of *ijara* and *murabaha* receivables may be securitized (with a majority of the former) for secondary market trading.

However, the "majority" rule seems paradoxical. Consider the case wherein an Islamic financial provider wishes to securitize a large portfolio of receivables, of which 36 percent are lease-based and 64 percent are *murabaha*-based. According to the "majority rule" of mixed securitization, one can bundle all of our lease-based receivables with half of the *murabaha*-based receivables and sell the mixed portfolio at a negotiable (market) price. One can then use the same structuring principles to strip the leasing-based component of the portfolio and buy it back at market price, only to bundle with the remaining half of the *murabaha*-based receivables, which can thus be sold at market price. The net result is that the 51 percent rule, articulated above, has been synthetically used to generate a 36 percent rule. With additional steps (and clearly wasteful legal and transaction costs), the rule can be diluted further, bundling a small amount of ostensibly "tangible" – as opposed to financial – assets repeatedly with generic financial assets, with the 51 percent rule satisfied at each step. Hence, the rule serves only the purpose of creating another efficiency-reducing Shari'a-arbitrage opportunity.

6.3 Asset-Backed Leasing Bonds (*Sukuk*)

We now turn to the basic mechanics of a typical lease-backed bond (*sukuk*) issuance. As an example, we shall consider the largest issuance in 2003: that of the seven-year, $700 million Qatar global *sukuk*. The basic structure of that transaction was illustrated in December 2003 by Mr. Robert Gray, chairman of HSBC's (co-lead manager for the issuance) Debt Financing Advisory, as shown in Figure 6.1.[24]

The steps of this transaction are essentially the same as those of the Tabreed structure discussed in the introduction, with the exception that the underlying asset (in this case a parcel of land) is not sold back at lease end, but given back as a gift. In general, the SPV, in this case a trust, utilized for issuing lease-backed securities needs to obtain short-term funding in one of two basic ways: (1) by obtaining a bank loan or some substitute thereof, including the possible deferment of price payment until proceeds are collected from *sukuk* buyers, or (2) by selling the *sukuk* prior to purchasing the property to be leased back. The rest of the transaction is straightforward, with lease payments (in this case covering both principal and interest) passed through to *sukuk* investors. The other potentially thorny issue is the bindingness of a unilateral promise to give the property (land parcel) back as a gift at lease end, which we shall discuss later in greater detail.

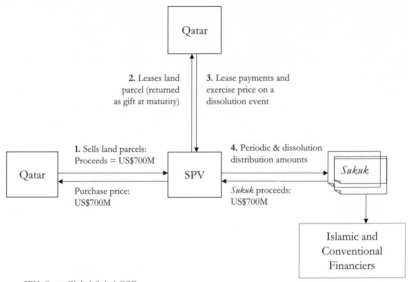

SPV: Qatar Global *Sukuk* QSC
Land Parcel: Land in Doha designated for the development of Hamad Medical City

Fig. 6.1. Structure of Qatar Global *Sukuk*

Credit-Rating Issues

The official offering document for the Qatar Global *Sukuk* issuance stipulated that "It is a condition of the issuance of the Certificates that they be rated 'A+' by Standard & Poor's Ratings Services."[25] On page 9, the *sukuk* rating is linked directly to that of its sovereign issuer: "The ratings of the Certificates will be based primarily on the credit rating of Qatar." In addition, the "ratings" section of the offering listed familiar caveats regarding ratings not being recommendations to buy or sell financial instruments, and lack of guarantees that ratings will remain constant for any period of time.

In Standard and Poor's own publication regarding its rating of the Qatar Global *Sukuk*, the rating agency justified the rating as follows:

The 'A+' rating on QGS's floating rate trust certificates reflects the long-term rating on the State of Qatar for the following reasons:

- All claims due to QGS, including the lease rentals payable by the government of the State of Qatar to QGS under the master 'Ijara' agreement, which will fund the periodic distribution payments on the trust certificates, are a direct, unconditional, unsecured, and general obligation of the government of the State of Qatar and will rank at least pari passu with all other unsecured and unsubordinated obligations of the government of the State of Qatar. The lease rental payments are irrevocable.

- The dissolution amount payable on the trust certificates upon dissolution event is also dependent on an obligation of the government of the State of Qatar. This obligation is the irrevocable undertaking of the government of the State of Qatar to purchase from QGS the land parcel at the agreed exercise price upon a dissolution event occurring, which also represents the dissolution date of the trust. The exercise price will be used to fund the dissolution distribution payment that is payable to certificate holders. The exercise price payable by the government of the State of Qatar will be the purchase price less the aggregate of all amortization payments paid under the master Ijara agreement.

- The issuer, QGS, is a special purpose company with the single objective of participating in this transaction, which should ensure that all payments made by the government of the State of Qatar to QGS would in turn be available to make payments to certificate holders.[26]

This interesting summary analysis was followed by a detailed description of the transaction structure, which concluded the following:

The government of the State of Qatar (the lessee) agrees that it will not claim to be entitled to pay a lesser amount of the rentals provided in the master Ijara agreement by virtue of any circumstance. ... Upon a dissolution event, the lease agreement will be terminated and thereupon, pursuant to a legally robust purchase undertaking, the government of the State of Qatar is required to purchase the land parcel from QGS at the agreed exercise price, the purchase price less the aggregate of all amortization payments paid under the master agreement.[27]

Having established beyond any doubt that the *sukuk* are essentially unsecured debt instruments backed by the full faith and credit of the state of Qatar, in which the leased land plays a ceremonial role, it was clear to the analysts that the credit rating of the *sukuk* should be identical to the credit rating for the country's other sovereign debt. Thus, the remainder of the document concentrated on the analysis of economic prospects for the economy and debt exposure of the government.

Needless to say, that analysis also illustrates that the juristic characterization of *ijara sukuk* structures is questionable. For instance, as the S&P analysis has shown, there are mutually binding conditions that violate the essence of a lease with material lessor ownership of the leased property. In this regard, we have seen that the unilaterally binding condition, which forces the SPV that is totally owned by the government to give the property back as a gift to the government at lease end, is deemed acceptable by contemporary jurists.

However, it is not clear that the SPV (or, by inference, the trust certificate holders) ever owned the property. The fundamental test of ownership in classical and contemporary Islamic jurisprudence is the risk of loss in case of property destruction (hence the various conditions on insurance payment, etc.). In that regard, the master lease agreement for QGS stipulated that on any dissolution event (including destruction of the leased property), the lessee will still be bound to purchase the property at the agreed-upon exercise price. In other words, the sale and lease are merely fiction, and the substance of the structure is that of a conventional bond. Sadly, this is also a very costly fiction, with various legal fees for incorporation of the main trust, as well as all the side contracts on repairs and maintenance, required to exploit the Shariʿa-arbitrage opportunity created by economically incoherent juristic views.

Benchmarking Revisited

Based on the above analysis of credit risk, the variable interest component of rent payable on the Qatar Global *Sukuk* was directly linked to LIBOR:

> The Issuer will make a Periodic Distribution (as defined herein) to Certificate holders (as defined herein) an amount which is calculated on the basis of (i) LIBOR (as defined herein) plus 0.40 per cent. per annum, calculated on the outstanding principal amount of the Certificates as at the beginning of the relevant Return Accumulation Period (as defined herein) on an actual/360 basis plus (ii) beginning with the Periodic Distribution Date falling in April 2006, an Amortization Payment (as defined herein) of one-tenth of the initial principal amount of the Certificates.[28]

Since the issued debt was essentially identical to other unsecured debt by the issuing government, there are no gains to be made from securing the debt with physical assets (by restricting borrowing to the value of the government's assets), or in terms of enhanced ability to borrow at lower interest rates (by marking the implied interest rate on the lease bonds to market rents of the underlying property). Without either of those potential economic advantages, the additional transaction costs of an *ijara sukuk* issuance must be viewed as deadweight efficiency losses from the viewpoint of the issuing entity, were it not for potential buyers who are restricted to this type of debt instrument. One can hope that jurists will eventually realize that the purpose of Islamic jurisprudence should not be the imposition of such inefficiency-inducing transaction costs. However, we have seen that Shariʿa-arbitrage rent-seeking behavior, and general acceptance of form-above-substance in Islamic financial jurisprudence by the public, are likely to continue for the medium term. The best we can hope to accomplish is to introduce some economic substance in the current practice, such as by using *ijara sukuk* structures to revitalize stalled privatization plans in various Islamic countries through bona fide sales of public property, as discussed in Chapter 10.

Reward Pledges and Gifts Revisited

We now turn to the promise to give the property as a gift at lease end, as stipulated in the structure of the Qatar Global *Sukuk* issuance discussed above. This unilaterally binding promise may be analyzed from the point of view of one of two contracts that were studied by classical jurists. The first contract is the gift (*hiba*) contract, and the other is the reward-pledge (*ji ʿala*) contract.[29] Although the first contract appears to be closer to the language used in the *sukuk* structure, in fact, *ji ʿala* (which is usually discussed by jurists as an analog for *ijara*) may be the more appropriate characterization. For both types of contracts, we shall discuss issues like bindingness conditions to determine the ideal means to return the property to its initial and ultimate owner (the lessee under *ijara sukuk*).

Problematic Binding Gift Promise

The first issue we need to consider is the de facto conditionality of the unilaterally binding gift offer in the *sukuk* structure. As we have seen in the previous section, the contract stipulated conditions under which the lease will be dissolved and the lessee will be bound to purchase the property at the properly adjusted exercise price. Consequently, the gift promise is in fact conditional upon completion of the full lease period. The issue of conditional gifts was raised by the earliest classical jurists within the context of a pre-Islamic practice, wherein the owner of some property pledged it as a gift to another in case he (the donor) died first. It is easy to see how this type of conditional gift could have been used as a means of, for example, circumventing inheritance rules or consolidating ownership of partnerships.

Abu Hanifa and his associate Al-Shaybani ruled generally that if a person makes a conditional gift offer, the property is deemed lent to him, and the donee thus may demand it at any time. They based this ruling on a weak Prophetic tradition, but also on the prohibition of substantial uncertainty. More generally, the Hanafi general principle on gifts was codified into Article #837 of the Ottoman *Majallat Al-Ahkam Al-ʿAdliyya*: "A gift contract is concluded through offer and acceptance, and it is executed with receipt." This rule was supported by the Hanafi judge Abu Yusuf as well as Shafiʿi and Hanbali jurists, who ruled that once the potential recipient of the conditional gift takes possession of the gift object, it is considered an immediate and permanent gift. One of the principal textual proofs on which this ruling was based is the Prophetic tradition "There are no temporary or conditional gifts, thus the recipients of such gifts become their owners, alive or dead."[30] The Malikis forbade conditional gifts on similar grounds, concluding similarly that a gift is executed upon receipt.

Although the main context for those canonical texts and juristic analyses pertained primarily to a particular type of conditional gifts, the texts and logic appear much more general. Moreover, the codified legal provision in the *Majalla* is clearly quite general. When applied to the case at hand, once the binding promise to give the land back as a gift to the state of Qatar is made, and once the state of Qatar is in possession of the property by virtue of the lease, it should be automatically declared the recipient of a gift and thus would not be obliged to make any further payments. However, as we have seen in the Standard and Poor's analysis, the legal structure clearly indicates that the state of Qatar must make the payments unconditionally, which is incompatible with the binding promise to give the property back as a gift.

Moreover, the bindingness of a promise to give a gift is itself questionable in light of a Prophetic tradition: "The donor is more worthy of keeping his property, as long as he was not compensated for it."[31] In other words, a gift promise is not binding if the donor had not received compensation, and binding if he had. This can be a source of legal problems, since a group of investors may gain ownership of all the trust certificates and then argue that it is contrary to Shari'a rules to force them to give the gift when the lease expires. In that case, as in the two cases brought before English courts in recent years, the Shari'a provisions are likely to be overruled, undermining the legitimacy of Islamic financial structures. Perhaps that is one of the reasons that this "gift" structure has been quite rare in *sukuk* issuances, with most structures stipulating a sale at lease end. Of course, whether or not the binding promise to return the property is characterized as a sale or a compensated gift, the result would be the same: In both cases, Shari'a and secular legal conditions will be in agreement on bindingness of the promise based on receipt of consideration.

Equally Problematic Binding Reward Pledge

Another form of conditional promise to give a gift or reward that was approved by many classical jurists is known by the Arabic name *ji'ala*. In this contract a donor promises to pay a reward or gift, known as *ju'l*, to anyone who performs a certain task. The most common classical applications included rewards to whoever returned lost property or prizes to winners of various contests, for example. Maliki, Shafi'i, and Hanbali jurists permitted the contract based on the story of Joseph: "They said: we miss the great beaker of the king, and for him who produces it is the reward of a camel load; I will be bound by this promise" [12:72], as well as Prophetic traditions wherein similar promises of rewards were approved.

Although Hanafi jurists deemed the contract impermissible as an *ijara* (hire contract) with substantial *gharar*, they approved it based on juristic approbation in certain circumstances. However, this contract was deemed by Shafi'is and Hanbalis to be nonbinding, and thus they allowed the donor to pay a larger or smaller *ju'l* than specified in the unilateral promise. This gives rise to the same problem we faced in the case of gifts, wherein certificate holders may collectively decide not to fulfill the promise to give the property back. Hence, it appears that compensated resale is the only viable option. However, as we have seen in previous chapters, that approach also raises the very real danger of violating the rules of *'ina* (same-item sale-repurchase).

Two solutions may be provided for this problem. One is to strip ownership of the underlying asset from ownership of the usufruct, structuring the entire transaction on the basis of long-term fixed-rate leases and short-term fixed- or variable-rate subleases. This structure has in fact been used under the name *sukuk al-manfa'a* (usufruct *sukuk*), which we shall discuss in the following section. A second alternative would be to avoid the sale of the property or usufruct by building the entire bond structure on agency contracts similar to the ones discussed in Chapter 8, in the context of financial intermediation.

6.4 Usufruct *Sukuk*

In August 2004 the German state of Saxony Anhalt issued a €100 million five-year bond, which was rated AAA, in line with the state's credit rating. The bonds thus paid a rate of interest equal to EURIBOR. The deal was comanaged by Citigroup and Kuwait Finance House and fully subscribed, with 60 percent of the issue sold to GCC investors in Bahrain and UAE, and the other 40 percent sold in Europe.[32] The structure relied on a trust in the Netherlands, which paid a lump sum (bond price) as rent in a long-term lease of property owned by the Ministry of Finance. Thus, holders of certificates of the trust ostensibly owned the usufruct of those properties for a five-year period. The Ministry of Finance then paid back those certificate holders, through the trust SPV, short-term floating-rate rent benchmarked to Euribor.

This structure avoids the characterization of "head leasing" that was rejected by contemporary jurists:

In [head-leasing], a lessee sub-leases the property to a number of sub-lessees. Then, he invites others to participate in his business by making them share the rentals received by his sub-leases. ... This arrangement is not in accordance with the principles of Shari'ah. ... The lessee does not own the property. He is entitled to benefit from its usufruct only. That usufruct has passed on to his sub-lessees. ... Now he does not own anything, neither the corpus of the property nor its usufruct.[33]

The Saxony Anhalt structure avoids this problem by reversing the order of steps in the transaction. The government first leases property that it owns long term, thus giving ownership of the usufruct to the SPV trust. Only then does it turn around and sublease the property back short term, paying the variable interest rate (benchmarked to EURIBOR) as rent. Hence, at each stage, the party that receives funds receives them in exchange for transferring ownership of well-defined usufruct that it owns.

A second, more straightforward, usufruct certificate structure was imposed by legal constraints, rather than desire to structure conventional bonds in a "Shariʿa-compliant" manner. In the project known as "Manazel Al-Haramain" (housing near the two holy mosques in Makka and Madina), roughly 6,000 housing units were built in towers adjacent to the two holy mosques. Because of religious and legal requirements, ownership of the land had to remain with the state of the Kingdom of Saudi Arabia. Consequently, the state leased the property long term to property developers, who then sold smaller segments of the usufruct (resembling timeshares) to certificate holders, through the usual SPV structures. In principle, those certificates could be treated as financial instruments tradable on a secondary market. However, given the large number of Muslims who each spend at least one week a year on religious tourism, most of those certificates are likely to be held to maturity by their initial or secondary buyers.

Identification of Unidentified Usufruct Shares

When financial assets such as usufruct certificates are converted into physical usufruct, a process of identification of previously unidentified shares in the overall usufruct of the property is required. In this context, the Ottoman *Majallat Al-Ahkam Al-ʿAdliyya*, Article #1114, defined property division (*qisma*) as "specifying portions of a jointly owned property for ownership by each partner, i.e., separating the shares through measurement by size weight, or volume." In this regard, it is easy to define timeshare units in terms of the number of certificates necessary for conversion into weekly usufruct of each specific unit, and then assign the shares on a first-come first-served basis. Since those rules for converting the abstract shares in usufruct represented by *sukuk al-manfaʿa* can be listed in certificate documents, all conversions of certificates into actual usufruct of specific units during specific time periods are deemed to take place by mutual consent of all certificate holders (partners in overall usufruct).

6.5 Sukuk Al-Salam

A number of bond structures could be synthesized from the *salam* contract. The most prolific issuer of *salam* bonds to date has been the Bahrain Monetary Agency, aiming to provide Islamic banks liquidity management tools. At a presentation by Sheikh Salman Bin Ahmed Al Khalifa, director of Banking Services at the BMA, at the International Islamic Finance Forum in Istanbul, Turkey, September 27–29, 2004, the structure of the BMA *sukuk al-salam* structure was illustrated as shown in Figure 6.2. In this structure the government of Bahrain undertakes to sell aluminum on the basis of *salam* (prepaid forward contract) and sells corresponding certificates for receipt of aluminum through Bahrain Islamic Bank, which acts as

1. *At Initiation*

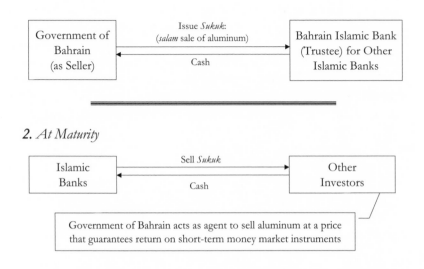

2. *At Maturity*

Fig. 6.2. Structure of BMA *Sukuk Al-Salam*

a trustee. At maturity, the government, which is obligated (as *salam* seller) to deliver aluminum to the certificate holders, acts as a selling agent for those holders, guaranteeing a price equal to the announced principal plus interest. This raises an interesting issue based on the rules of agency: As seller, the government would hold the aluminum in a possession of guaranty, but as an agent for the buyers, it would hold it in a possession of trust. This switch from possession of guaranty to possession of trust is perhaps accomplished through some notification system, but that was not made clear in the disclosed structure.

After receiving the aluminum as the certificate holders' agent, the government of Bahrain promised to sell it at a price equal to the principal paid by the certificate holders plus the return on short-term paper.[34] The full structure can be implemented easily through side agreements with an aluminum dealer, from whom the aluminum will be purchased by the government at maturity, and then to whom the aluminum will be sold again on behalf of the certificate holders.

The actual spot and forward prices of aluminum are quite irrelevant to the transaction. Thus, neither certificate buyers nor the government are exposed to any commodity risk, and the aluminum is used merely as a degree of separation to justify receiving the principal (*salam* price) at initiation, and paying principal plus interest at maturity (ostensibly as an agent-guaranteed spot price for the aluminum). We shall discuss agency conditions in greater detail in Chapter 8, where our focus will be on using agency contracts to allow banks to act as financial intermediaries in financing bona fide deals. Of course, the BMA *salam sukuk* structure described here can be used alternatively to generate any interest-bearing loans, including unsecured ones. In fact, this bond structure looks like a mirror image of *tawarruq*, which we have already identified as one of the most egregious results of rent-seeking Shariʿa arbitrage in Islamic finance.

7

Partnerships and Equity Investment

As one can readily infer from the case studies at the end of Chapter 6, equity investment in the forms of stock- and mutual-fund ownership, as well as index participations with or without principal protection and the like, have been among the more successful areas in Islamic finance. Indeed, it is easier to explain to Muslims and non-Muslims alike the virtues of investing only in certain types of stocks, excluding those of companies that produce, for example, alcoholic beverages or weapons. The links between the "Islamic" brand name, on the one hand, and ethical and economic considerations, on the other, are more direct in those areas.

On the other hand, many Muslims did not accept stock ownership as permissible until recently, and some continue to argue that Islamic jurisprudence recognizes only simple partnership styles, to the exclusion of contemporary corporate structures. At the other extreme, many contemporary jurists have allowed ownership of legal constructs such as stocks, mutual funds, index participations, and the like, albeit under slightly inaccurate legal interpretations of those structures. In this chapter we shall review classical jurisprudence on partnerships of various types, as well as contemporary juristic analyses of limited-liability corporations and corporate stocks.

7.1 Classical Types of Partnership

Simple partnership forms existed in Arabia prior to the advent of Islam and were recognized and legalized both in the Qur'an and in Prophetic traditions.[1] In this regard, a number of simple partnership types were recognized by classical jurists.[2]

The most familiar form of classical partnerships was limited partnerships, which were generally classified under the Arabic name *"sharikat al-'inan."*[3] Limited (*'inan*) partners need not contribute equal amounts of capital to the partnership and consequently may have different degrees of control over partnership assets, even to the extent of giving only one partner exclusive control over capital and assets. Because of those varying degrees of control, each partner is responsible only for dealings that he himself makes. Profits may be distributed according to any agreed-upon formula, but losses must be distributed in proportion to capital contributions, a rule that is extensively applied today in Islamic finance.

Unlimited partnerships were generally known as "*sharikat al-mufawada*" (literally delegated partnerships), wherein each partner allowed the other to deal in his property. Hanafi and Zaydi jurists imposed a peculiar condition that all partners must have equal amounts of wealth to justify this rule of equal and unlimited liability. Of course, this condition was virtually impossible to satisfy and – as Al-Shafi'i correctly pointed out – resulted in considerable *gharar* exposure, since knowledge of another party's net worth is very difficult. Consequently, other schools of jurisprudence allowed partners to contribute only part of their wealth to this type of partnership. However, they maintained that partners must contribute equal amounts to the partnership and thus have equal rights for dealing in the capital they contributed.

A third type of recognized partnerships were so-called credit partnerships, generally known as "*sharikat al-wujuh*" (literally reputation partnerships), wherein a number of partners joined in credit purchases, followed by spot-market sales of the same properties. Profits and losses are distributed among the partners according to their ownership shares in the objects of the initial credit purchases. Jurists of the Hanafi, Hanbali, and Zaydi schools permitted this type of partnership, whereas jurists of the Maliki, Shafi'i, Zahiri, and Imami schools deemed it invalid. Jurists of the latter schools based their objection to this type of partnership on the view that partnership capital must be physical property. Contemporary jurists have argued that following the joint credit purchase of property, property may be established as the partnership capital.

A fourth recognized classical partnership form was called labor partnerships (known variously as *sharikat al-a'mal*, *sharikat al-abdan*, and *sharikat al-sana'i '*), wherein a group of workers collaborated on projects (e.g., building some structure) by contributing labor of various types. The partners thus shared the wages paid for that work. Hanafis, Malikis, Hanbalis, and Zaydis allowed those types of partnerships, although Malikis allowed them only when all workers contributed the same type of work and collected equal profit/wage shares. On the other hand, Shafi'i and Imami jurists, and the Hanafi jurist Zufar, disallowed this type of partnership based on the view that partnership capital must be physical property, and based as well on the perceived difficulty of ensuring that profit shares justly reflect labor contributions of the various partners.

Those classical partnership forms were of very limited use for a number of reasons. First, jurists of most schools deemed partnership contracts nonbinding and thus allowed each partner unilaterally to dissolve a partnership. The Maliki school was an exception, since it deemed partnerships binding and thus allowed their dissolution only by mutual consent of all partners. However, that school has not had a significant following in recent centuries and was superseded by codified Hanafi jurisprudence in regions under Ottoman control. A second and more important reason why classical partnership forms did not thrive in the industrial age is the ruling by jurists of all classical schools that partnerships are automatically dissolved on the death of any partner, whether or not the other partners know of that death.

This made classical partnership forms unreliable and unstable – instability increasing montonically with the number of partners. Hence classical partnership forms were ill-equipped to take advantage of economies of scale in the pre-industrial and industrial ages. Even if heirs to one partner wished to continue the business, the first partnership – in which the deceased took part – was dissolved, and a new partnership needed to be formed. In part building on the seminal historical work of Abraham Udovitch (1970), contemporary economists such as Avner Greif and Timur Kuran have argued that this fundamental characteristic of Islamic partnerships limited them severely, in terms of both size and longevity, in comparison to Western-style limited-liability corporations that retain their own legal personality.[4]

As we shall see later in this chapter, contemporary jurists found little difficulty in adapting classical *'inan* (limited) partnerships and *mudaraba* or *qirad* (silent) partnerships to justify Western corporate structures. Indeed, the basic elements of limited liability and legal personality were already developed in classical jurisprudence, for example, within the contexts of *'inan* partnerships and the legal status of a deceased individual, respectively. Whether or not corporate structures could have evolved indigenously in Islamic jurisprudence is a fascinating topic in institutional economics. Indeed, the institutional limitations imposed by classical partnership forms clearly impeded economic growth in the premodern Islamic world.

A full counterfactual analysis – to understand whether indigenous development of such corporate institutions, or earlier adoption thereof by Muslim jurists in the pre-industrial era, was possible – requires fully understanding the dynamics of juristic institutions, which is beyond the scope of this book. Restricting our attention to the observed historical path of Islamic jurisprudence and finance, we shall proceed to discussing classical views on silent partnerships and then to reviewing contemporary juristic views on, among various topics, corporations, stock ownership, and mutual funds.

Silent Partnership: Theoretical Workhorse of Islamic Finance

The classical partnership form that contemporary Islamic practice has adopted most extensively, albeit in modified form, is the classical silent partnership form known in Iraq as *mudaraba* and in Hijaz (western Arabia) as *qirad*. The model of silent partnership was originally envisioned in Islamic economics and finance as the cornerstone of the prospective Islamic financial industry. In this type of partnership, one party (the silent partner, investor, or *rabb al-mal*) contributes his property as partnership capital, while the other party (entrepreneur or *mudarib*) contributes his labor, expertise, and so on.

One reason that this contract was viewed favorably by Islamic economists and early architects of Islamic finance as a potential building block for the latter is its prominence in medieval Mediterranean trade, in part under the Italian name *commenda*. We shall turn to contemporary utilization of silent partnerships in the next section and later chapters. First, however, we need to summarize the classical conditions of silent partnerships, especially since the contract has significant similarities to labor hiring (*ijara*, wherein the entrepreneur would be characterized as a hired worker) as well as agency (*wakala*, wherein the entrepreneur as agent is paid a flat fee rather than a profit share). Of course, the ruling based on analogy to either of those contracts would have been problematic based on the prohibition of *gharar* (since the profit share characterized as wage or agency fee is uncertain). Thus, classical jurists had to rely on prophetic tradition to legitimize the contract under a separate name (as they had done, for instance, for *salam*) despite that *gharar*. As we shall see in Chapter 8, one of the most significant controversies regarding conventional versus Islamic bank structures revolves around silent partnership conditions related to profit sharing. The agency problem introduced by silent partnership conditions (viewing the silent partner or investor as principal and the entrepreneur as agent) also has significant effects on the regulation of Islamic banking structure as currently envisioned, to which we turn in Chapter 9.

In a classical silent partnership, the investor forwarded his capital to the entrepreneur, most often to trade on his behalf. Profits were shared between the investor and the entrepreneur according to any agreed-upon formula, but all financial losses were borne by the investor. Nevertheless, the silent partnership is still characterized as a profit-and-loss-sharing arrangement, wherein the investor loses his labor and effort if no profits were generated. If, at one extreme, the profit-sharing rule assigned all profits to the investor, then the contract is deemed one of *mubada'a*, wherein the entrepreneur is characterized as a volunteering agent. At the other extreme, if the contract assigns all profits to the entrepreneur, then the contract is characterized as a loan, with significant ramifications for the entrepreneur's liability as a guarantor borrower rather than trustee agent.

Types of Silent Partnership

Silent partnerships were very common in pre-Islamic Arabia. Indeed, the Prophet first met his wife Khadija when he traded with her capital, most likely in a *mudaraba* arrangement. He thus implicitly approved of the contract through both his own actions and by continuing to approve of his companions' utilization of that contract after his Prophetic mission commenced. It appears that the contract may have evolved in Arabia based on sharecropping agreements, wherein those with property and those with labor and skills can collaborate to generate mutually beneficial profits.[5]

Classical jurists recognized two main types of silent partnerships, which gave rise to two types of investment accounts in contemporary Islamic banks. The first type of silent partnerships was restricted. Thus, the entrepreneur's activities were limited to a particular timeframe (starting time as well as duration), location, line of business, and the like. Restricted silent partnerships were permitted by Hanafi and Hanbali jurists. In contrast, Maliki and Shafi'i jurists ruled that all valid *mudarabas* must be fully unrestricted. Unrestricted silent partnerships, which are accepted by all jurists, required only specification of the profit-sharing rule. Otherwise, the entrepreneur receives the investor's capital and is free to invest it in any manner or timeframe that he deems fit.

Jurists of all schools agreed that silent partnerships are not binding on either party as long as the entrepreneur had not commenced working. Moreover, Abu Hanifa, Al-Shafi'i, and Ibn Hanbal ruled that silent partnerships remain non-binding at all times and may thus be dissolved unilaterally by either party. On the other hand, Malik ruled that the contract becomes binding once the entrepreneur begins working. One consequence of this difference in opinion is that the majority opinion does not allow inheritance of rights and responsibilities under silent partnerships, whereas Malik's opinion does allow for such inheritance.

Classical jurists of all schools allowed silent partnerships to be formed with multiple investors and/or multiple entrepreneurs, thus paving the way for reinterpretation of contemporary joint-stock companies. In this context contemporary jurists have approved the practice of mixing attributes of limited partnerships, silent partnerships, and labor hiring conditions to justify various management structures of joint-stock companies. In his seminal work *Al-Sharikat fi Al-Fiqh Al-Islami*, the prominent Azhari jurist and professor Dr. Ali Al-Khafif characterized all limited-liability companies with fewer than fifty partners as silent partnerships, with managers viewed as entrepreneurs. However, the contemporary jurist Dr. Wahba Al-Zuhayli argued that the manager may at times be more appropriately characterized as a hired worker. To the extent that the manager may also own stocks, he may be viewed as one of the silent partners by virtue of owning stocks, and as a hired worker to the extent that he works for the company and collects a fixed wage or fee accordingly.[6]

Valid and Defective Silent Partnerships

Some discussions in Chapter 8 regarding contemporary banking and Islamic banking practices revolve around the nature of the contract if one or more of the silent partnership conditions are violated. Since the majority of jurists viewed silent partnerships as nonbinding, violations of their conditions merely converted them into other contracts. The vast majority of jurists ruled that if conditions of silent partnership are violated, then all profits are assigned to the capitalist, and the entrepreneur should be paid the prevalent market wage for his efforts. The Malikis, on the other hand, developed a complicated "standard silent partnership" format to which the contract reverted if one or more of the contract conditions were violated. We shall revisit the implications of those rules for synthesizing debt instruments directly from defective *mudarabas*.

Conditions on Partnership Capital

The most important silent partnership conditions pertained either to the nature of capital invested in the partnership or to profit-sharing rules. In this regard, most jurists agreed that it is best to invest capital in monetary form, to avoid disputes regarding the value of nonmonetary capital. More recently, AAOIFI standards stipulated that if *mudaraba* capital is provided in nonmonetary form, then it should be booked based on fair market value, whereby any difference between that fair market value and accounting value is considered a profit or loss, depending on sign.[7] Although AAOIFI did not specify the grounds of this rule, it seems to be based on the classical opinions of Abu Hanifa, Malik, and Ibn Hanbal, all of whom permitted listing the prevalent market prices of nonmonetary properties as the capitals of silent partnerships.

Most classical jurists also ruled that silent partnership capital must be present at contract time and thus may not be legally constructed from a liability on the entrepreneur. On the other hand, the majority of jurists also allowed the silent partner or investor to appoint an agent to collect his debts and then invest them on his behalf. Similarly, they allowed an investor to ask a depositary to invest his deposited property on his behalf. Those rulings follow from the rules of trust versus guaranty in possession, which we shall revisit in Chapter 8. Briefly, the entrepreneur's possession is one of trust, as are the possessions of a depositary and an agent (for debt collection or otherwise). In contract, the possession of a debtor is a possession of guaranty, which is stronger. Thus, the majority of jurists require the debtor first to pay off his debt, and only then allow the investor to give the property back to the debtor in trust as a silent partnership investment agent (entrepreneur or *mudarib*). For the same reason, the majority of jurists also required the investor to deliver the partnership capital to the entrepreneur, otherwise the latter's possession of trust would not have been established.

Profit-Sharing Conditions

Most jurists, classical and contemporary, insisted that returns to the investor and entrepreneur must be specified as unidentified shares in profits. Some leniency was allowed if the shares were not known explicitly, in which case most jurists reverted to a default rule of equal sharing in realized profits (recall that all financial losses are borne by the investor). We have also noted that if profit shares were specified, but at extreme values, the contract is deemed a loan if the entire profit was assigned to the entrepreneur, and a voluntary agency if it was all assigned to the investor. On the other hand, the vast majority of classical and contemporary jurists unequivocally rejected silent partnerships wherein one party is promised a fixed amount of money, including as a percentage of provided capital (interest).

The vast majority of classical and contemporary jurists claimed that the rules for profit sharing must be strictly followed in silent partnership. Thus, debtlike instruments such as corporate bonds, which promise a fixed amount of money equal to the invested capital plus interest, were forbidden. Moreover, hybrid equity instruments such as preferred shares were deemed impermissible. However, as we shall see in Chapter 8, some contemporary jurists have argued that classical consensus over the rules of silent partnership may not be very relevant for contemporary practice. They alluded to rules of defective silent partnerships, which entail recharacterization of the contract in terms of other permissible ones. They also argued that contemporary practices need not be limited to classical contract forms, and classical conditions thereof. We shall rejoin this discussion in Chapter 8, within the context of conventional banking practice. However, for the remainder of this chapter, we shall focus on simple common stock equity investments and Islamic finance products that have been structured thereof in recent years.

7.2 Common-Stock Ownership

Equity investments in Islamic finance started with simple mutual funds that applied standard portfolio management techniques to a limited universe of stocks, which excluded, for example, companies with Islamically illegitimate lines of business. In recent years managers have begun to use more advanced trading techniques, including trading on margin and short sales, to boost investor returns in an increasingly competitive Islamic finance market. We begin by listing the most widely held contemporary juristic opinions on equity investment vehicles and trading techniques thereof.

Characterization of Stocks and Mutual Funds

In its seventh session the Fiqh Academy of OIC ruled that the object of sale when a common stock is traded is an unspecified share in the assets of the issuing corporation. In that regard, they ruled that the stock certificate is a documentation of the legal right to that unspecified share. According to that characterization, the academy ruled in the same session that it is not permissible to issue preferred stocks that give their owners priority claims to the company's assets, a guaranteed amount of profit, and the like. Conventional bonds were seen as interest-based loans to corporations and thus impermissible for ownership and trading. However, juristic councils recognized that bonds (characterized as *sukuk* or debt certificates) may in fact be structured from premodern Islamic contractts (e.g., through *ijara* financing or *salam* trading, as discussed in Chapter 6). Legal opinions at Al-Baraka symposia (e.g., *fatwa* #17/2) and other juristic councils regulated the potential convertibility of conventional bonds into common shares and encouraged companies that had issued conventional bonds also to convert them into common shares in the same manner.

Based on this characterization, numerous juristic councils permitted trading common stocks of corporations that have permissible primary businesses. This view followed since ownership of the stock was deemed to imply partial ownership of the company's assets as a silent partner. Under this characterization, a stock owner would be deemed a partner in the company and thus responsible for its operations. Furthermore, mutual funds were allowed by various juristic councils, characterizing the mutual fund provider as an agent for fund shareholders, who were seen as investors in the underlying stocks. In other words, jurists characterized ownership of mutual fund shares as ownership of the underlying stocks, which were in turn characterized as documentations of ownership of unspecified shares in the assets of the various underlying companies.

Needless to say, mutual fund managers in reality promise to pay fund shareholders only the monetary value of the portfolio of underlying stocks but do not promise to deliver the actual stocks to shareholders if they demand that delivery. Indeed, segregated physical storage of stock certificates for mutual fund holders would present substantial logistical difficulties to fund managers and reduce their competitiveness considerably. Fortunately for Islamic finance providers, jurists seem to be satisfied with the fiction of a sequential ownership structure that ultimately leads to ownership of the underlying companies' assets.

Unfortunately for those providers, continuation of that fiction – under which Islamic mutual funds were allowed to be traded – means that index participations have not been generally acceptable in most juristic circles. Most jurists continue to argue that an index is merely a number, which does not represent any real underlying assets. It would seem logical to explain to jurists that in fact an index reflects the value of underlying assets no less (and no more) than the value of a mutual fund reflects the value of the physical assets of its constituent stocks' issuing companies. Nevertheless, as we have seen in the previous chapter, some index participation products have in fact been structured by treating the index as a mutual fund and maintaining the fiction that investors own the underlying companies' physical assets.

"Islamic Screens" and Their Shortcomings

To date, the central "Islamic" focus in Islamic mutual fund management has been on the screening criteria used to exclude certain stocks from the universe of permissibility. Most industry participants have dubbed stocks that survive various screens "Shariʿa compliant," despite the fact that a number of compromises are generally adopted, which result in noncompliance to strict Shariʿa standards. Moreover, Shariʿa compliance would require adherence to positive proscriptions (e.g., "help the poor") as well as negative prohibitions ("do not ferment alcoholic beverages"). In contrast, "Shariʿa-compliance" criteria used by various providers of financial products and services primarily take the form of negative screens.

Line-of-Business Screens

The first set of screens is qualitative, based on the corporation's line of business. Those screens are easier to define in the abstract but more difficult to implement, requiring constant monitoring of company activities by Shariʿa supervisors. For instance, it is easy to say that businesses that serve alcoholic drinks should be excluded (possibly excluding certain hotel chains, airlines, restaurant chains, etc.). However, the issue of degrees of separation, which we have raised repeatedly throughout the book, allows jurists many degrees of freedom.

For instance, *fatwa* #18 by the Shariʿa board of the Dallah Al-Baraka group stipulated that leasing airplanes to airlines that are known to serve alcoholic drinks is permitted. Their reasoning was that the primary business of the airline is transportation of passengers, rather than serving or transportation of alcoholic beverages, and hence any sin for serving those beverages would accrue to the operator of the planes and not to their lessor. The Shariʿa board of Kuwait Finance House issued a similar opinion in their ruling #384, within the context of leasing real estate to embassies of foreign countries, wherein alcoholic beverages will be served.[8] The list of activities that lead to exclusions of various companies vary significantly from one Shariʿa board to another. Some may exclude companies that engage in certain types of genetic research, depending, for instance, on their potential contribution to human-cloning programs, while others may not. The issue in all cases is whether an activity is forbidden and the extent to which it is a primary activity of the company under consideration.[9]

This approach allows for a number of Shari'a-arbitrage opportunities. For instance, instead of purchasing a restaurant chain, one can create an SPV that buys all the assets of the chain, excluding their wine cellars, wine bottles and glasses for serving wine, and the like. Then shares in the newly created company would be permissible, since the primary usage of its capital (e.g., real estate, tables, chairs, kitchens) is serving food rather than alcoholic beverages. With sufficient accounting acumen, one can thus separate ownership of the impermissible part from ownership of the permissible part and sell the latter as "Shari'a-compliant" securities. Later in this chapter we shall discuss in greater detail one particular application of this separation principle to Real Estate Investment Trusts (REITs), which would normally fail the standard financial ratio screens applied in the industry, to which we now turn.

Financial Ratio Screens

In addition to the qualitative screens discussed above, industry practitioners have also developed a set of financial screening rules that exclude companies with excessive debt or excessive interest income. The origins of this idea seem to have germinated at the Al-Baraka Investment and Development Company, which pioneered some of the Islamic mutual fund methodologies later utilized more effectively by the Saudi National Commercial Bank and others. The idea was quite simple: If we exclude all companies that deal in *riba* (viewed excessively generally as any payment or collection of interest), we would be left with a very small universe of permissible equity instruments, leading to massive inefficiency relative to the overall universe of such instruments tapped by conventional fund managers. However, it might be possible to approach the efficiency frontier of risk-return tradeoffs between efficient portfolios, none of which can be dominated by ones that yield the same return with less risk, or higher return with the same risk exposure.

Thus, pioneers of this area sought *fatawa* from jurists, to allow them to include in their portfolios stocks of companies with small or negligible amounts of interest expense or interest income. Early opinions were relatively strict, allowing only for investment in companies with total debts-to-assets ratios of 5 percent, then 10 percent. Over the years those ratios were relaxed, while striving to maintain some notion of retaining only companies with minor debt or interest income. The most common set of financial screens currently used are those of the Dow Jones Islamic Index.[10] Those screens or filters exclude the following:

1. Companies with total debt accounting for 33 percent or more of monthly moving average (over the previous year) of market capitalization.

2. Companies with monetary (cash plus interest-bearing securities) accounting for 33 percent or more of the same monthly moving average (over the previous year) of market capitalization.

3. Companies whose accounts receivables account for 45 percent or more of total assets.

The third screen is interpreted as a yardstick for characterizing the "main business" of companies in question. In this regard, if the majority (more than 50 percent) of a company's assets are financial, rather than real, the main business of the company is deemed to be financial dealings, and it is thus excluded. The basis of this screen is the classical juristic principle that majority determines the genus and characterization of the total.[11] Because of fluctuations in asset values, a cutoff point of 45 percent was selected, instead of 50 percent.

The second screen similarly aims to limit companies that deal in financial instruments or receive substantial amounts of interest income.[12] The one-third rule in the second screen (as well as the first one) is derived from a juristic principle that "one-third is significant," based on a Prophetic tradition restricting voluntary distribution of estate in a will to one-third of the estate. The first screen uses the one-third rule to exclude companies with too much debt and hence significant payment of interest.

Incoherence and Dangers of Financial Ratio Screens

The last two screens create a dilemma for the permissibility of owning shares in Islamic banks, more than 90 percent of whose assets may indeed be in the forms of cash, government and corporate *sukuk*, and accounts receivables from *murabaha* and *ijara*. Similarly, the first screen does not distinguish explicitly between "Islamic debt" (arising from *murabaha* or *ijara*, for instance) and other types of debt. Those two paradoxes have not been discussed widely within the industry for an interesting reason: The bulk of investment of "Shari'a-compliant" funds are in securities listed on the New York Stock Exchange and other major Western exchanges, none of which have listed Islamic banks or companies that seek Islamic financing. This curious fact puts in focus the Shari'a-arbitrage nature of the industry, which has made only symbolic gestures toward investing in compliant shares in Malaysia, Turkey, and other majority Muslim countries. However, even in those few initiatives there has not been to date any serious discussion of the rule in those terms. We shall return to this issue in our case study discussion of REITs below.

Other curious paradoxes pertain to the use of moving averages of market capitalization in the denominator of debt and receivable ratios. Initially, the ratios
used total assets in the denominator. However, it was deemed advantageous to
the size of "Shari'a-compliant" universe of stocks to switch to a restriction on the
ratio of debts to market capitalizations around late 1999, when U.S. stock markets
were in the middle of a speculative bubble that inflated those market capitalizations (especially for information technology stocks, which passed other screens).
Shortly thereafter, when it became clear that market capitalizations were not particularly stable month to month, the standard moved to a ratio of debts to moving
average of market capitalizations, first for three months and then twelve months.

There are in fact two paradoxes in this screening based on ratios of debts to market capitalization. The first paradox comes from the fact that, at any given time,
the same effect of enlarging the permissible universe could have been achieved by
changing the cutoff ratio (currently set at 33 percent), instead of changing the denominator from assets to market capitalization. The second paradox arises from
the use of any fixed ratio, together with a denominator that reflects market capitalization or a moving average thereof. Any such rule is bound to include more
securities as market capitalizations rise, thus potentially including some securities in Islamic fund portfolios when their prices are higher than their long-term
historical averages under similar economic conditions (i.e., when they are overpriced). Conversely, when prices fall, many stocks (including those that were
bought at excessive prices) may be forcibly excluded from the portfolio, because
of failing one or more of the listed financial screens (even if their prices are lower
than long-term averages under similar economic conditions). In other words, any
fixed-ratio screening rule, with market capitalization as the denominator, forces
abnormal purchases at high prices and sales at low prices. Needless to say, such
artificial "buy high, sell low" strategies can have catastrophic consequences.

Combining this analysis with the fact that *riba* is forbidden regardless of amount
or percentage puts in question the wisdom of imposing any fixed financial ratio
screen. Although the rule of one-third has a relatively unrelated origin (in inheritance law), it has indeed been used by jurists in many other contexts. However,
if the rule could be applied to *riba*, then we would in effect be able to impose a
Western-style (post-Calvinist) usury law that limits interest rates to 33 percent or
lower. Moreover, although the rule allows Muslim investors to buy equity shares in
Western companies that have 33 percent or less (interest-bearing) debt-to-market
capitalization, the same jurists who devised that rule forbid Muslim investors to
obtain the same level of interest-based leverage in their own direct investments.
In other words, this rule encourages investment in non-Muslim-based business,
as it discriminates against Muslims by depriving them of leverage opportunities
that make their competitors more profitable.

Finally, if the goal is to meet a particular debt ratio, we have seen in Chapter 6 how debt can easily be taken off-balance-sheet through sale-lease-back transactions. Curiously, the latter procedure has in fact been a popular one in Islamic finance and hailed as converting companies from Shariʿa noncompliance to Shariʿa compliance, when the substance and structure of their financing had hardly changed. Finally, fixing any ratio such as one-third without fixing its numerator and denominator (as evidenced by the switch from assets to market capitalizations) gives the appearance of rigidity of the rule, when in fact the rule is too flexible.

Returning to the historical roots of this one-third rule, we recall that it was justified on the grounds that the universe of permissible securities would be too small if we did not allow any level of debt or interest income. The need (*haja*) to be able to track market averages was viewed as sufficiently acute to invoke the rule of necessity (*darura*), according to which a license is given to the extent of need. In this regard, it would be much more coherent to fix the numerator and denominator of financial ratios (e.g., debt/market capitalizations and receivables/market capitalization) and vary the cutoff ratio rule according to market conditions. When stock prices are generally high, a high degree of efficiency can be obtained with a lower ratio cutoff (e.g., 10 percent), and when they are low, efficiency would dictate using a higher cutoff (e.g., 50 percent). An even better procedure would dictate excluding companies that are, say, in the top 20 percent for those ratios, thus automatically adjusting for overall secular market trends.

In fact, there appears to be a trend toward changing the old Dow Jones Islamic Index ratios. In a recent article on www.zawya.com, Yusuf DeLorenzo stated that five of the six jurists serving on the Dow Jones Islamic Market Indices Shariʿa board have approved different screening rules for Meyer's Shariʿa Funds (an Islamic Hedge Fund pioneer). The new screens remain proprietary, but the characterization given by Mr. DeLorenzo suggests that they are more flexible than their fixed-ratio predecessors. The CEO of Shariʿa Funds, for which those new screens were developed, suggested that they were based on actual interest income and interest expense, rather than levels of debt, but has not given further details.[13]

Case Study on Debt Screens: REITs

In recent years a number of different "Islamic REITs" (Real Estate Investment Trusts) have been marketed to GCC investors, who remain the main source of funds for much of Islamic finance. Indeed, this is not a surprising development, since equity REITs (those that own real estate directly, rather than owning mortgages) fundamentally engage in acceptable business, which is buying, maintain-

ing, and leasing real estate. A typical equity REIT holds the overwhelming majority of its assets in the form of real estate (as shown in Table 7.1) and derives most
of its income from rent.[14]

Table 7.1. *REIT Investments, End of 2001*

REIT Name	Total Assets ($1,000s)	Real Estate Assets ($1,000s)	% Real Estate
AMLI Res. Prop. Tr.	919,002	879,545	95.71
Avalonbay Comm.	4,664,289	4,390,843	94.14
BRE Prop.	1,875,981	1,818,795	96.95
Equity Res. Prop. Tr.	12,235,625	11,300,709	92.36
Essex Prop. Tr.	1,329,458	1,207,647	90.84
Home Prop. of NY	2,063,789	1,933,514	93.69
Archstone Smith Tr.	8,549,915	7,869,220	92.04
Glenborough Re. Tr.	1,388,403	1,289,929	92.91
Camden Prop. Tr.	2,449,665	2,410,299	98.39
Cornerstone Re. Tr.	980,691	942,712	96.13
United Dominion Re.	3,348,091	3,261,301	97.41
Town & Country Tr.	499,370	483,924	96.91
Apartm. Inv. & Man.	8,316,761	8,261,651	99.34

Moreover, REITs are required in the United States to distribute the bulk of
their net income in the form of dividends, and thus they tend to attract long-term
investors who are looking for reliable sources of fixed income. Finally, REITs
have traditionally exhibited low correlations with other asset classes, and thus –
as an asset class – they add a significant diverification opportunity to many stock
investors. However, REITs as an asset class are at a fundamental disadvantage
under Dow Jones Islamic Index and similar screening rules, since the "sweet spot"
or optimal range for the debt-to-assets (leverage) ratio for REITs is considered to
be 40 percent to 60 percent. This range is clearly illustrated in Table 7.2 (second
column from the right), wherein twelve out of thirteen of the largest equity REITs
clearly had debt-to-assets ratios in that range, which exceeds the 33 percent cutoff
rule.

As we see in Table 7.2, all REITs in the sample failed the debt-to-assets 33 percent screen. It is interesting to note in this context that changing the benchmark
to a ratio of debt to floating market capitalization makes the ratios significantly
higher, as shown in Table 7.3 (second column from the right). In this regard, low
growth in market capitalizations of REITs is not viewed negatively by their typical buyers, as we have discussed earlier, since the main attraction for them is
dividend collection, rather than capital gain.

Table 7.2. *Debt-to-Assets Ratios for Various REITs, End of 2001*

REIT Name	Total Debt ($1,000s)	Mortg. Debt ($1,000s)	Total Assets ($1,000s)	Debt/ Assets (%)	% Non-Mortg. Debt/ Assets
AMLI Res. Prop. Tr.	405,126	300,876	919,002	**44.08**	11.34
Avalonbay Comm.	2,082,769	447,769	4,664,289	**44.65**	**35.05**
BRE Prop.	1,008,431	210,431	1,875,981	**53.75**	**42.54**
Equity Res. Prop. Tr.	5,742,758	3,286,814	12,235,625	**46.93**	20.07
Essex Prop. Tr.	638,660	564,201	1,329,458	**48.04**	5.60
Home Prop. of NY	992,858	960,358	2,063,789	**48.11**	1.57
Archstone Smith Tr.	3,853,012	2,330,533	8,549,915	**45.06**	17.81
Glenborough Re. Tr.	653,014	588,420	1,388,403	**47.03**	4.65
		Secured Debt			Non-Secured Debt/ Assets
Camden Prop. Tr.	1,207,047	283,157	2,449,665	**49.27**	**37.71**
Cornerstone Re. Tr.	609,600	554,600	980,691	**62.16**	5.61
United Dominion Re.	2,064,197	974,177	3,348,091	**61.65**	32.56
Town & Country Tr.	475,403	459,403	499,370	**95.20**	3.20
Apartm. Inv. & Man.	4,637,661	3,433,034	8,316,761	**55.76**	14.48

Note: Debt ratios exceeding the commonly used 33% screen shown in bold.

Despite numerous questions by various participants at Islamic finance conferences, providers of Islamic REITs have not to date revealed the methodologies that allow them to include stocks of such companies in their Islamic portfolios. Nonetheless, one can think of two ways to include desirable REITs, such as the ones presented in these tables, in an Islamic portfolio. The first approach is to use the argument provided in the previous section, based on the general principle of need and necessity: that the extent of the license is dictated by the extent of the need. Since the case can be made for REITs as a very useful asset class for investors (especially in light of its low correlations with other classes), the case can also be made – as has been made by Mr. DeLorenzo and others – that as a different asset class, REITs merit a different screening benchmark. As most REITs that are considered good buys on conventional grounds have debt-to-assets ratios around 50 percent, the argument goes, a screening ratio in that neighborhood would be warranted.

An alternative approach is illustrated in the extreme right-hand column of Tables 7.2 and 7.3. In those tables we list the nonmortgage or unsecured (depending on reporting by various REITs) debt-to-assets and debt-to-market capitalization

Table 7.3. *Debt-to-Market Capitalization Ratios for Various REITs, End of 2001*

REIT Name	Debt/Full Mkt. Cap. (%)	Non-Mortg. Debt/Full Mkt.Cap.(%)	Debt/Float Mkt.Cap. (%)	Non-Mortg. Debt/Float Mkt.Cap.(%)
AMLI Res. Prop. Tr.	**90.10**	23.19	**90.10**	23.19
Avalonbay Comm.	**63.26**	**49.66**	**67.01**	**52.60**
BRE Prop.	**71.42**	**56.51**	**71.42**	**56.51**
Equity Res. Prop. Tr.	**73.86**	31.59	**73.86**	31.59
Essex Prop. Tr.	**69.29**	8.08	**76.90**	8.97
Home Prop. of NY	**141.82**	4.64	**172.20**	5.64
Archstone Smith Tr.	**88.49**	**34.97**	**88.49**	**34.97**
Glenborough Re. Tr.	**124.72**	12.34	**134.18**	13.27
		Non-Secured Debt/Full Mkt.Cap.(%)		Non-Secured Debt/Float Mkt.Cap.(%)
Camden Prop. Tr.	**81.03**	**62.02**	**81.03**	**62.02**
Cornerstone Re. Tr.	**113.64**	10.25	**120.18**	10.84
United Dominion Re.	**144.67**	**76.40**	**144.67**	**76.40**
Town & CountryTr.	**142.29**	4.79	**142.29**	4.79
Apartm. Inv. & Man.	**136.53**	**35.46**	**136.53**	**35.46**

Note: Debt ratios exceeding the commonly used 33% screen shown in bold.

ratios. Focusing on the unsecured debt-to-assets ratios, we can see that ten of the thirteen REITs under consideration would pass the traditional 33 percent screen. The logic behind looking at unsecured debt is quite simple: All secured debt, most of which is mortgage debt, can easily be "Islamized," for instance, through sale lease-back. Even if that secured debt is not Islamized, it is still possible to sell shares in the equity component of the REITs' assets, albeit through the utilization of SPVs, possibly including UPREITs or DownREITs, that can strip the equity component from the rest. Of course, Islamizing the debt or isolating it would add unnecessary transactions costs, with no change in the substance of ownership of REIT shares (sharing in the company's equity in real estate).

Consequently, applying the conventional screening ratio rules (taking into account the previous section's arguments for flexibility therein) to unsecured debt rather than total debt seems to be significantly more cost effective. Unfortunately, the Shariʿa-arbitrage approach likely to be followed by Islamic finance jurists and practitioners would be precisely to build the costly structures to Islamize the secured debts of equity REITs, or to separate those debts from the equity portions through various structured products. In fact, the insistence on incurring those transaction costs serves as a barrier to entry, giving the larger financial institutions involved in that field a decided size advantage, because of, for example, economies of scale in creating SPVs and retaining appropriate jurists' services.

Cleansing Returns

For stocks of companies deemed "Shari'a compliant," jurists have imposed a rule that stock returns (theoretically covering both dividends and capital gains) due to company income from unlawful interest should be cleansed. The method of cleansing unlawful gains has been explicitly discussed by classical jurists: The unlawful income must be given to charity.[15] Islamic mutual fund and other financial providers usually provide customers with a list of approved Islamic or other charities to whom unlawful income will be forwarded.

A number of paradoxes arise from return-cleansing rules as currently applied. First, although jurists insist on cleansing the returns caused by interest income, they have not given a rule on how to compute the portion of dividends and capital gains attributed to interest income. For instance, high-interest income indicates that a company has large amounts of cash (e.g., Microsoft) and therefore can move quickly to make profitable acquisitions, engage in research and development, and so on. Investors generally value such flexibility and therefore will bid up the stock price, resulting in capital gains. However, computing the percentage of capital gains due to that psychological effect is virtually impossible.

Another interesting paradox arises from the fact that jurists do not require similar cleansing of returns caused by higher debt ratios. Obviously, a higher level of debt (especially at lower interest rates) can lead to significantly higher returns on equity and consequently higher dividends and/or capital gains. However, those gains caused by interest-based borrowing are not cleansed. Third, while cleansing for interest income is required, cleansing for income from other (secondary) impermissible activities (such as serving alcohol) is not. Finally, it is not clear how "Islamized" interest (e.g., collected or paid through *murabaha* or *ijara* transactions) should be treated.

Some of those concerns can be addressed in the short to medium term by proposing some internally coherent set of rules for cleansing unlawful returns from a variety of sources. The long-term challenge in developing coherent and meaningful cleansing rules is far from minor, however, since designers of those cleansing rules should ensure that they do not introduce unwarranted distortions in optimal portfolio selection rules (comparing precleansing and postcleansing returns). Of course, distortions that serve normative Islamic objectives are welcome, as discussed below in the context of positive screens.

Positive Screens and the Islamic Brand Name

The focus on negative screens reflects the general prohibition-driven nature of Islamic finance more generally. In this regard, providing unequivocally permissible mutual funds was not quite possible, since the universe of companies with, for example, zero interest expense, zero interest income, and no business that is disallowed in Islam would be extremely small. When jurists and financial professionals looked for a compromise, they sought it in the form of screening out companies with significant interest income and interest expense. However, very little effort has been undertaken to apply positive screens as well, such as ones that would favor investment in pollution abatement or community development.

Some positive steps have been taken recently to rectify this situation. For instance, some recent proposals have been made to introduce rating strategies that would combine both negative and positive attributes of a company, as well as measuring the degree of severity of forbidden activity, thus reaching an overall "Islamicity" or "Shari'a-compliance" score. Other recent steps in the right direction include selective regional preference for stocks in countries with significant Muslim populations, such as by issuing region-specific Dow Jones Islamic Indexes. However, the emphasis in selecting stocks in those regions remains a negative one of "avoiding prohibitions."

As we shall argue more generally in Chapter 10, Islamic finance needs to outgrow its current mode of operation, which aims to serve a captive market of customers who are not sufficiently served by conventional finance. In this regard, if the industry is to succeed in reaching the fast-growing educated Muslim middle class, it will have to outgrow this prohibition-driven mentality and demonstrate positive ethical and religious values that it serves. Of course, it is much easier for fund managers simply to work with a smaller universe of permissible securities, within which they can apply their standard portfolio management techniques, rather than incorporate a weighting scheme that trades off risk-return performance, degrees of violation of legalistic Islamic rules, and degrees of serving the ethical goals of Muslims. On the other hand, if and when the industry grows to the point where such tradeoffs are being made in a more sophisticated manner, resulting investment vehicles will be much more appropriately marketed in terms of "Islamic" or ethical investing (where many non-Muslim investors may share the same normative negative and positive screen preferences). In contrast, the ones currently marketed as "Shari'a compliant" can at best be described as "avoiding explicit and major violations of legal prohibitions."

8

Islamic Financial Institutions

Financial institutions, Islamic or otherwise, play two indispensable roles in financial systems. The first role is providing support for various financial markets. For instance, exchanges of various types are institutions that facilitate the functioning of markets, by setting rules of trading and providing clearinghouse and margin logistical support. Those services alleviate many of the information asymmetries between buyers and sellers that might lead to market failures. The second role that financial institutions perform is providing financial solutions where market failures exist despite the existence of market-supporting institutions. For instance, although any company should – in theory – be able to access debt markets by issuing bonds, commercial paper, and the like, transactions costs may be disproportionately high, and investor information may be extremely lacking. In such cases, the terms at which a small investor can borrow from the market may be prohibitive.

In contrast, a bank that retains professional staff specializing in the assessment of loan applications or business plans, for example, can provide loans to investors with limited market experience. The same argument applies even more forcefully to consumer financing, since consumers suffer the additional disadvantage of lacking a legal structure that would allow them to borrow directly from the market. Banks solve the information asymmetries that lead to market failure by capitalizing on economies of scale in processing information on creditworthiness, business plan prospects, and the like. They also rely on economies of scale to enhance their abilities to pool the savings of numerous very small savers and to diversify their investments across the enterprises of numerous very small investors. Thus, specialization together with the unique set of corporate structures and regulatory frameworks for retail and investment banks allow them to fulfill various roles in society for which financial markets fail. Of course, at later stages those financial institutions can tap financial markets to diversify their risks further (e.g., by selling mortgage- and asset-backed securities).

135

Moreover, the theoretical ability of financial markets to provide risk mitigation and transfer mechanisms has its efficiency limits. For instance, it is possible for me to seek the writer of a put option on my car that would specify that the writer will have to buy my car at the strike price, even if it had been damaged in an accident. With millions like me seeking such options, there should be a way to structure the writing of those (insurance) options, circumventing the market failure stemming from information asymmetries. (Am I a crook who will damage his car on purpose? Is my car worth that much? etc.) This informational problem and the associated statistical problem of utilizing sufficient diversification (to ensure that actuarial calculations provide proper pricing formulas for the insurance contract) are again solved through economies of scale. Insurance companies train clerks who specialize in assessing the eligibility of various customers and build statistical models to diversify their risks and price them properly. At a later stage the insurance companies can further mitigate risks by tapping financial markets and wholesale reinsurance companies.

A third group of institutions that we consider in this chapter are venture capital and private equity firms. Those companies specialize in acquisition and control (with various degrees of actual day-to-day management) of prospective or existing companies with financial values that may increase substantially for one reason or another. Venture capital firms typically invest in companies the bulk of whose capital takes the form of human knowledge (engineering specifications, business model, etc.), thus restricting their abilities to access capital in more conventional forms, such as secured borrowing or issuing stock.

The probability of success of the average company at an early stage of development is very small, but the profitability of investing at that stage can be substantial if the company succeeds. This high-risk/high-return profile and lack of sufficient expertise on the part of high-net-worth individuals who may be willing to invest in such companies lead to market failure. By specializing in specific areas, venture capital firms can increase the probability of picking future winners and enhance that probability further by providing advice (sometimes in the form of heavy-handed guidance) to entrepreneurs. They further mitigate risk exposure for investors by pooling the resources of a number of like-minded investors and diversifying their portfolio across a number of investment prospects. Of course, the ultimate success of a venture capitalist is realized when he can take one or more of his investments to market, typically through an initial public offering. Hence, one may think of the venture capital firm as another form of financial intermediary.

Likewise, private equity firms serve a number of investment interests of high-net-worth individuals that are not readily addressed by existing market products. The activities of such firms vary from venture-capital-style investment, to acquisitions and mergers activities typically performed in association with one or more investment bank, to structuring tailor-made fixed-income instruments. Although private equity investments may or may not eventually be taken to market, the various types of institutions involved in this industry (ranging from large investment banks to small financial boutiques and hedge funds) provide valuable financial services that would not otherwise be available because of size and informational-induced market failures.

In this chapter we shall discuss how Islamic versions of commercial banks, insurance companies, and venture capital and private equity firms have evolved over the past few decades. We shall briefly discuss the theoretical "Islamic economics" processes that gave rise to "Islamic financial institutions," the rhetoric of which continues to define that industry to this day. Then we shall discuss in some detail the classical juristic foundations of that rhetoric and continuing debates among contemporary jurists over centuries-old issues. Although Islamic financial practitioners and the contemporary jurists who support them view dissenting juristic voices as a threat to the industry's very existence, we shall argue that, in fact, a synthesis of the different contemporary juristic views (those promoting Islamic finance as it exists today, and those finding conventional finance to be superior and even more Islamic) can help Islamic finance to become more efficient, and to transcend its rent-seeking Shari'a-arbitrage modes of operation.

8.1 Banking and Islamic Banking

Islamic finance was conceived in the 1970s as a practical implementation of contemporary thought in "Islamic economics." The latter field had begun to take shape in the 1950s, based primarily on the writings of Muhammad Iqbal and Abu Al-A'la Al-Maududi in the subcontinent, and Baqir Al-Sadr and Sayyid Qutb in the Arab world.[1] Timur Kuran (2004a) noted the importance for that field of the concurrent emergence of a political independence movement, with accompanying emphasis on national and religious identities. He argued convincingly that the ideology that gave rise to Islamic economics, and sustains it to this day, is socio-politically (and not scientifically or ethically) based on religion. Over the course of three decades, Islamic economics morphed into a subfield of economics as suggested by contemporary leaders of the field:

Islamic economics ... has the advantage of benefiting from the tools of analysis developed by conventional economics. These tools along with a consistent world-view for both microeconomics and macroeconomics, and empirical data about the extent of deviation from [normative] goal realization may help.[2]

[Islamic economics] is the Muslim thinkers' response to the economic challenges of their times. In this endeavor they were aided by the Qur'an and the Sunna as well as by reason and experience.[3]

Therefore, although "Islamic economics" was initially conceived as an independent Islamic social science, it quickly lost that emphasis on independence and redefined its identity in terms of normative ethical and social values. However, once researchers started using conventional economic tools, their discipline was quickly subsumed by the larger field of economics:

[Islamic economic thought] failed to escape the centripetal pull of Western economic thought, and has in many regards been caught in the intellectual web of the very system it set out to replace.[4]

Similar to the convergence of Islamic economics with mainstream economic thought, Islamic finance also quickly turned to mimicking the (interest-based) conventional finance it set out to replace. However, writings in Islamic jurisprudence, Islamic economics, and Islamic finance continued to assert that conventional interest-based banking and finance is the forbidden *riba*. Thus, popular Islamic discourse continues to refer to conventional banks as *"ribawi* banks,"[5] and to assert that the Islamic alternative is "interest free."[6]

Theoretical Structure: Two-Tier Silent Partnership

At its inception, Islamic banking was theoretically conceived based on the principle of profit and loss sharing through two-tier silent partnership (*mudaraba*) in place of the *ribawi* deposit/loan-based commercial banking.[7] Providers of funds would be viewed as principals or silent partners extending their funds to an Islamic bank, who is viewed as an entrepreneur or investment agent. The Islamic bank would thus invest the funds on the principals' behalf, in exchange for a share in profits. If the investments were not profitable, the bank/agent would lose only its effort, and the principals would bear all financial losses. In turn, the bank may invest directly or act as a principal in a second investment agency contract (silent partnership), with its customers seeking funds as limited-liability profit-sharing entrepreneur-agents.[8]

This profit-sharing form of financial intermediation, including legal stratagems or ruses (*hiyal*) to fix profits as a percentage of capital, was hardly new. Indeed, Abraham Udovitch (1981) had dubbed the practitioners of this form of finance in medieval Mediterranean trade, as "bankers without banks."[9] The basic profit-sharing principle also bears very close resemblance to the Jewish legal concept of the *heter isqa* (or *iska*, partnership clause) contract, a silent partnership profit-sharing arrangement, to avoid the Biblical prohibition of *ribit*.[10] Later refinements of the *heter isqa* allowed the profits received by the principal to become a fixed percentage of the partnership's capital, to solve the inherent moral hazard problem in silent partnerships. The fundamental argument underlying the December 2002 ruling of Al-Azhar's Islamic Research Institute revolves around the same issue of fixing the silent partner's profit percentage to solve moral hazard problems.

Two Conflicting Fatawa

Over the past two centuries, there have been two conflicting juristic views of the banking industry: one unfavorable and one favorable. The unfavorable view characterized traditional banking as usury or *riba*-based, both bank deposits and financing being viewed as forbidden interest-based loans. The other view, which originated with the Ottoman Mufti Ebussoud Efendi and continues to this day in various juristic circles, views contemporary banking practice as a new financial technology, which is not intrinsically forbidden, although certain corrections of specific banking behavior may be required to ensure adherence to the percepts of Shari'a. Recently the debate erupted once more with a high-profile *fatwa* from the prestigious Azhar Islamic Research Institute, which deemed the collection of interest on conventional bank deposits permissible (by characterizing it as a fixed profit rate in investment agency). This *fatwa* reiterated an earlier issued *fatwa* in the late 1980s by the current rector of Al-Azhar, Tantawi, who was then the Grand Mufti of Egypt. The logic of that *fatwa*, in turn, was based on the analysis of various earlier Azhar jurists of the twentieth century C.E., as quoted below.

The full text of the Azhar *fatwa* is translated below. Note that the questioner in this *fatwa* characterized conventional bank assets as "permissible investments," thus side-stepping a difficult problem of recharacterization of conventional bank assets, which are mostly loans. Instead, the question set the agenda by focusing the *fatwa*'s language on the liabilities side of banking practice, seeking in effect characterization of funds deposited at the bank in terms of investment agency, a characterization that the Rector of Al-Azhar, to whom the question was sent, had already published. The official issued *fatwa* stated the following:

Office of the Grand Imam, Rector of Al-Azhar

Investing funds with banks that prespecify profits

Dr. Hasan 'Abbas Zaki, Chairman of the Board of Directors of the Arab Banking Corporation, sent a letter dated 22/10/2002 to H.E. the Grand Imam Dr. Muhammad Sayyid Tantawi, Rector of Al-Azhar. Its text follows:

H.E. Dr. Muhammad Sayyid Tantawi, Rector of *Al-Azhar*:

Greetings and prayers for Peace, Mercy, and blessings of God

Customers of the International Arab Banking Corporation forward their funds and savings to the Bank to use and invest them in its permissible dealings, in exchange for profit distributions that are predetermined, and the distribution times are likewise agreed upon with the customer. We respectfully ask you for the [Islamic] legal status of this dealing.

(Signature)

He has also attached a sample documentation of the dealing between an investor and the Bank. The sample reads as follows:

The International Arab Banking Corporation Bank

Date __/ __/ 2002

Mr/_____ Account number _____

Kind Greetings

This is to inform you that your account with us, in the amount of L.E. 100,000 (only one hundred thousand Egyptian Pounds) has been renewed.
For the period 1/1/2002 until 31/12/2002:

Rate of return 10% resulting in a return of L.E. 10,000
Total of deposit + return on distribution date   L.E.110,000

_____
New amount, including return as of 31/12/2002 L.E.110,000

His Excellency, the Grand Imam, has forwarded the letter and its attachment for consideration by the Council of the Islamic Research Institute in its subsequent session.

The Council met on Thursday, 25 Sha'ban, 1423 A.H., corresponding to 31 October, 2002 A.D., at which time the above-mentioned subject was presented. After the members' discussions and analysis, the Council decided to agree that investing funds in banks that prespecify profits is permissible under Islamic Law, and there is no harm therein.

Due to the special importance of this topic for the public, who wish to know the Islamic Legal ruling regarding investing their funds with banks that prespecify profits (as shown by their numerous questions in this matter), the Secretariat General of the Islamic Research Institute decided to prepare an official *fatwa*, supported by the Islamic Legal proofs and a summary of the Institute members' statements. This should give the public a clear understanding of the issue, thus giving them confidence in the opinion.

The General Secretariat presented the full *fatwa* text to the Islamic Research Institute Council during its session on Thursday, 23 Ramadan 1423, corresponding to 28 November 2002 A.D. Following the reading of the *fatwa*, and noting members' comments on its text, they approved it.

This is the text of the *fatwa*:

Those who deal with the International Arab Banking Corporation Bank – or any other bank – forward their funds and savings to the bank as an agent who invests the funds on their behalf in its permissible dealings, in exchange for a profit distribution that is predetermined, and at distribution times that are mutually agreed upon. . . .

This dealing, in this form, is permissible, without any doubt of impermissibility. This follows from the fact that no canonical text in the Qur'an or the Prophetic Sunna forbids this type of transaction within which profits or returns are prespecified, as long as the transaction is concluded with mutual consent. God, transcendent is He, said: "O people of faith, do not devour your properties among yourselves unjustly, the exception being trade conducted by mutual consent . . ." (Al-Nisa':29)

The verse means: O people with true faith, it is not permissible for you, and unseemly, that any of you devour the wealth of another in impermissible ways (e.g., theft, usurpation, or usury, and other forbidden means). In contrast, you are permitted to exchange benefits through dealings conducted by mutual consent, provided that no forbidden transaction is thus made permissible or vice versa. This applies regardless of whether the mutual consent is established verbally, in written form, or in any other form that indicates mutual agreement and acceptance.

There is no doubt that mutual agreement on prespecified profits is Legally and logically permissible, so that each party will know his rights. It is well known that banks only prespecify profits or returns based on precise studies of international and domestic markets, and economic conditions in the society. In addition, returns are customized for each specific transaction type, given its average profitability. Moreover, it is well known that prespecified profits vary from time period to another. For instance, investment certificates initially specified a return of 4%, which increased subsequently to more than 15%, now returning to near 10%. The parties that specify those changing rates of returns are required to obey the regulations issued by the relevant government agencies.

This prespecification of profits is beneficial, especially in this time, when deviations from truth and fair dealing have become rampant. Thus, prespecification of profits provides benefits both to the providers of funds, as well as to the banks that invest those funds. It is beneficial to the provider of funds since it allows him to know his rights without any uncertainty. Thus, he may arrange the affairs of his life accordingly. It is also beneficial to those who manage those banks, since the prespecification of profits gives them the incentive for working hard, as they keep all excess profits above what they promised the provider of funds. This excess profit compensation is justified by their hard work.

It may be said that banks may lose, thus wondering how they can prespecify profits for the investors. In reply, we say that if banks lose on one transaction, they win on many others, thus profits can cover losses. In addition, if losses are indeed incurred, the dispute will have to be resolved in court.

In summary, prespecification of profits to those who forward their funds to banks and similar institutions through an investment agency is Legally permissible. There is no doubt regarding the Islamic Legality of this transaction, since it belongs to the general area judged according to benefits, i.e., wherein there are no explicit texts. In addition, this type of transaction does not belong to the areas of creed and ritual acts of worship, wherein changes and other innovations are not permitted.

Based on the preceding, investing funds with banks that prespecify profits or returns is Islamically Legal, and there is no harm therein, and God knows best,

(signed)
Rector of Al-Azhar
Dr. Muhammad Sayyid Tantawi
27 Ramadan 1423 A.H.
2 December 2002 A.D.

The penultimate paragraph of the *fatwa* hinted at the common objection to fixing profits in the Islamic silent partnership contract (*mudaraba*). As we shall see below, jurists often claim that there is a consensus that the principal's profit share must be specified as a percentage of total profits, rather than a fixed percentage of the capital. The text of the *fatwa* hints at the view that this opinion was merely an artifact of the historical thought of Islamic jurists who developed the principle and does not rely on any direct injunction in canonical Islamic texts.

As we discussed before quoting the *fatwa*, the banker posing the question must have known that the scholar to whom he addressed the question had in fact made a strong argument in favor of characterizing bank deposits in terms of investment agency with profit margins specified as a percentage of capital. In his book on bank operations, Tantawi explicitly focused on moral hazard considerations:

Nonfixity of profits [as a percentage of capital] in this time of corruption, dishonesty and greed would put the principal under the mercy of the agent investing the funds, be it a bank or otherwise.[11]

Tantawi also cited similar opinions by highly respected earlier jurists, including Muhammad 'Abduh, 'Abdul-Wahhab Khallaf, 'Ali Al-Khafif, and others.[12] Most notable among those quotations are the following:

When one gives his money to another for investment and payment of a known profit, this does not constitute the definitively forbidden *riba*, regardless of the prespecified profit rate. This follows from the fact that disagreeing with the juristic rule that forbids prespecification of profits does not constitute the clear type of *riba* which ruins households. This type of transaction is beneficial both to the investor and the entrepreneur. In contrast, *riba* harms one for no fault other than being in need, and benefits another for no reason except greed and hardness of heart. The two types of dealings cannot possibly have the same legal status (*hukm*).[13]

The juristic condition for validity [of *mudaraba*] that profits are not prespecified is a condition without proof (*dalil*). Just as profits may be shared between the two parties, the profits of one party may be prespecified. ... Such a condition may disagree with previous jurists' opinions, but it does not contradict any canonical text in the Qur'an and *Sunna*.[14]

In this regard, the only objection against this dealing is the juristic validity condition for *mudaraba*, which stipulates that profits must be specified as percentage shares, rather than specified amounts or percentages of capital.

I reply to this objection as follows:

First: This condition has no proof (*dalil*) from the Qur'an and *Sunna*. Silent partnerships follow the conditions stipulated by the partners. We now live in a time of great dishonesty, and if we do not specify a fixed profit for the investor, his partner will devour his wealth.

Second: If the *mudaraba* is deemed defective due to violation of one of its conditions, the entrepreneur thus becomes a hired worker, and what he takes is considered wages. Let that be as it may, for there is no difference in calling it a *mudaraba* or an *ijara*: It is a valid transaction that benefits the investor who cannot directly invest his funds, and benefits the entrepreneur who gets capital with which to work. Thus, it is a transaction that benefits both parties, without harming either party or anyone else. Forbidding this beneficial transaction would result in harm, and the Prophet forbade that by saying: "No harm is allowed."[15]

We now note again that this *fatwa* is focused on the liabilities side of banking and even then addresses the issue only from the point of view of depositors. Tantawi (2001) argued that the depositor-bank relationship should be viewed as neither one of depositor-depositary nor one of lender-borrower. Either characterization of the relationship, he admitted, would render any interest payment to be forbidden *riba*. In contrast, he argued, savers forward their funds to banks to invest on their behalf. Therefore, he argued, the relationship is one of principal-agent in an investment agency, and the juristic problem discussed above is only regarding the permissibility of fixing profits as a percentage of capital in such investment agency.

This *fatwa*, and its foundation, clearly contradicted prior *fatawa*, for example, by the Shari'a Appellate Bench of the Supreme Court of Pakistan (on December 12, 1999, containing six hundred pages of rebuttals of arguments similar to those forwarded by various Azhari jurists over the past century).[16] The history of Pakistani rulings unequivocally declared that all forms of interest are forbidden *riba* and urged the government to purge all forms of interest from the economy. Unfortunately, although the Pakistani judgment purported to address the economic concerns (e.g., regarding moral hazard problems), it just made ideological claims and purported that moral hazard problems (characterized as dishonesty) exist in all systems and should be fought separately – thus avoiding honest argument on economic grounds. Given the continued lack of juristic appreciation for the economic viewpoints regarding information asymmetry (let alone the view that finance without "interest" generally defined is impossible), we shall instead look at the counter-*fatwa* issued by an Islamic jurisprudence council shortly after the Azhar *fatwa* was issued, explicitly focusing on juristic grounds for prohibition of interest on bank deposits.

Deposits vs. Loans: Trust and Guaranty

Although Dr. Tantawi argued that the term "deposit" in "bank deposit" is misleading, since the relationship is in fact one of investment agency, the majority of jurists chose to characterize "deposit" (or *wadi ʿa*) in terms of the premodern contract of fiduciary deposit (*idaʿ*), as discussed in classical jurisprudence texts. Within that fiduciary deposit contract, the depositary holds deposited property in a possession of trust. Once the depositary uses the funds deposited therein, however, classical jurisprudence stipulates that the depositary would have thus violated the simple safekeeping duties of fiduciary deposit and must thus guarantee the funds for the depositor.[17] Therefore, the classical juristic argument concludes, the contract can no longer be viewed as a fiduciary deposit (*idaʿ*), and they concluded that the closest contract of guaranty – and hence the one they assign to the transaction – is the loan contract (*qard*).[18]

In the conclusions of the Fourteenth Session of Majlis Majmaʿ Al-Fiqh Al-Islami in Duha, Qatar, January 11–16, 2003, the Azhar IRI's characterization of dealings with conventional banks as a legitimate investment agency was thus rejected. The following lengthy quotation from the official conclusions of the meeting summarizes the contemporary majority view on conventional banking among jurists who support an Islamic banking alternative (including Arab as well as Pakistani and other jurists). Note that – like the Pakistani rulings – the *fatwa* presumes that the alternative to *riba* (viewed as all forms of interest) is "profit and loss sharing," as in *mudaraba* and *musharaka* partnership forms, stipulated in the Islamic economics literature to be the correct Islamic modes of finance that achieve the Islamic ideal:

A. Conventional Bank functions:

Banking laws forbid banks from dealing through profit and loss-sharing investment. Banks receive loans from the public in the form of deposits, and restrict their activities – according to lawyers and economists – to lending and borrowing with interest, thus creating credit through lending deposited funds with interest.

B. Conventional Bank relationship with depositors:

Religious-law (*shar'i*) and secular-law characterizations of the relationship between depositors and banks is one of loans, not agency. This is how general and banking laws characterize the relationship. In contrast, investment agency is a contract according to which an agent invests funds on behalf of a principal, in exchange for a fixed wage or a share in profits. In this regard, there is a consensus [of religious scholars] that the principal owns the invested funds and is therefore entitled to the profits of investment and liable for its losses, while the agent is entitled to a fixed wage if the agency stipulated that. Consequently, conventional banks are not investment agents for depositors. Banks receive funds from depositors and use them, thus guaranteeing said funds and rendering the contract a loan. In this regard, loans must be repaid at face value, with no stipulated increase.

C. Conventional Bank interest is a form of forbidden *riba*

Banks' interest on deposits is a form of *riba* that is forbidden in Qur'an and *Sunna*, as previous decisions and *fatawa* have concurred since the second meeting of the Islamic Research Institute in Cairo, Muharram 1385 A.H., May 1965 A.D., attended by eighty-five of the greatest Muslim scholars and representatives of thirty-five Islamic countries. The first decision of that conference stated: "Interest on any type of loan is forbidden *riba*." The same decision was affirmed by later decisions of numerous conferences, including:

... [List of conferences and Institute opinions prohibiting bank interest]

D. Prespecification of investment profits in amount, or as a percentage of the invested capital

It is generally accepted that interest-bearing loans differ from legal silent partnership (*mudaraba*). In loans, the borrower is entitled to profits and bears all losses. In contrast, *mudaraba* is a partnership in profits, and the principal bears financial losses if they occur, as per the Prophet's saying: "profits are justified for the one bearing liability for losses."
[19]
...

Thus, jurists of all schools have reached a consensus over the centuries that prespecification of investment profits in any form of partnership is not allowed, be it prespecified in amount, or as a percentage of the capital. This ruling is based on the view that such prespecification guarantees the principal capital, thus violating the essence of partnerships (silent or otherwise), which is sharing in profits and losses. This consensus is well established, and no dissent has been reported. In this regard, Ibn Qudama wrote in *Al-Mughni* (vol. 3, p. 34): "All scholars whose opinions were preserved are in consensus that silent partnership (*qirad* or *mudaraba*) is invalidated if one or both partners stipulate a known amount of money as profit."

In this regard, consensus of religious scholars is a legal proof in its own right [elevated to the level of the canon].

As it declares this unanimous decision, the Council urges Muslims to earn money only through permissible means, and to avoid forbidden sources of income in obedience to God and His Messenger.[20]

This opinion contains four main arguments against the correctness and relevance of the IRI *fatwa*: (1) The *fatwa* refers to banks with permissible investments, but banks are forbidden from investing in any instruments other than interest-bearing loans and financial instruments; (2) characterizing the depositor-bank relationship as one of investment agency is incorrect, the correct characterization is one of lender-borrower; (3) there is a consensus that all forms of bank interest are forbidden *riba*; and (4) even if the relationship was to be considered one of investment agency (silent partnership), the prespecification of profits in silent partnerships must be as a percentage of total profits, not as a percentage of capital. The moral hazard argument is ignored, and the principle of return being justified by risk is highlighted. In this regard, it is noteworthy that jurists insist on the financier's bearing risk of property ownership, in essence ignoring credit, interest rate, liquidity, and operational risks to which conventional financial providers are exposed when they extend credit. Paradoxically, as we have seen in Chapter 4, those same jurists have allowed multiple innovations (e.g., through agency in *murabaha*) that practically eliminate risk of ownership and yet continue to justify return based on that cosmetic risk, rather than the true risks of extending credit, Islamically or otherwise.

The first point is clearly valid. One can easily see that by focusing on the liabilities side of banking, the IRI *fatwa*, and its predecessors, ignored the nature of bank assets, which are legally stated as interest-bearing loans and thus forbidden by the overwhelming majority of jurists as *riba*. This renders the IRI *fatwa* irrelevant for conventional banks, as long as interest on loans is deemed to be forbidden *riba*, since the overwhelming majority of conventional bank assets are receivables from loans. On the other hand, given that Islamic banks have been able to replicate debt-based assets of conventional banks, the agency argument utilized in the Azhar *fatwa* seems eminently useful, as we shall argue later in this chapter. At the very least, if jurists continue to support and create Shari'a arbitrage opportunities, they should allow banks to reconstruct their liabilities side using the same arbitrage strategies that they have been allowed to use for reconstructing interest-paying assets (albeit in convoluted forms based on trade, leasing, etc.).

Before proceeding to the discussion of potential reconstructions of Islamic bank liabilities, we further illustrate the Shari'a-arbitrage-inducing economic incoherence of juristic views through the analysis of two other conflicting *fatawa* on insurance. The resolution of the second set of conflicting *fatawa* will also be seen to rest on construction of a proper agency framework for the relevant financial intermediary institutions (banks as intermediaries for credit, insurance companies as intermediaries for risk, avoiding apparent prohibitions of direct trading in credit and risk – *riba* and *gharar*, respectively).

8.2 Insurance and *Takaful*

In the ninth declaration at the second session of the Fiqh Academy of the Organization of Islamic Conference, the academy ruled that conventional insurance is forbidden, with the notable dissent by the late Professor Mustafa Al-Zarqa. Professor Al-Zarqa's opinion, as published in research papers dating back to 1961, had been to permit conventional insurance of all kinds, subject to some conditions on insurance company investment vehicles to avoid *riba*. A number of recent opinions were based on his analysis, which contradicts the Fiqh Academy's. The latter series of opinions culminated in a recent *fatwa* by the Grand Mufti of Egypt, Dr. ʿAli Jumʿa, which deemed conventional insurance permissible, provided that some minor modifications are made to typical insurance contracts used therein.

Two More Conflicting Fatawa

The OIC Fiqh Academy's ruling read as follows:

After reviewing the presentations on insurance and reinsurance by participating scholars in this session of the conference, and after researching the forms, types, principles, and objectives of insurance and reinsurance and the papers presented in that regard, and in light of the issued opinions of juristic councils and research institutes, this academy has reached the following conclusions:

1. The commercial insurance contract, with a fixed insurance premium, as practiced by commercial insurance companies, contains substantial *gharar*, which renders the contract defective. Consequently, it is [religious-]legally forbidden.
2. The alternative contract that respects the principles of Islamic transactions is the cooperative insurance contract, which is built on the principles of voluntary contribution and mutual cooperation. The same applies with regards to reinsurance, which should also be built on principles of mutual cooperation.
3. The academy calls on Islamic countries to exert effort toward establishing mutual cooperative insurance institutions, as well as ones for mutual cooperative reinsurance, so that Islamic economies may be freed from exploitation, and all other violations of the system that God has accepted for this Muslim community.[21]

Likewise, the fifth ruling of the first session of the Fiqh Academy of the Muslim League ruled – with the sole dissenting voice of Dr. Mustafa Al-Zarqa – that commercial insurance is a form of gambling, since the insured pays a premium and either receives no compensation, or a compensation far exceeding what he paid. They also debunked as inapplicable or invalid analogies all the arguments of those permitting insurance based on benefit analysis, general permissibility of transactions unless a prohibition exists, permissibility based on need, and the like. Both juristic councils proposed cooperative insurance (commonly known as *al-takaful al-ta'awuni*) as the viable and Islamically permissible alternative. However, one should not confuse what they mean by the term "cooperative insurance" with mutual insurance as known in the West. In fact, almost all existing *takaful* companies are stockholder owned. The juristic distinction that gives rise to rent-seeking Shari'a-arbitrage opportunities is characterization of the company's obligation to pay for valid claims as a voluntary contribution (*tabarru'*) by the stockholders, thus excluding the contract from the rules of commutative contracts, wherein *gharar* is forbidden. Another problem that operators of *takaful* based on *tabarru'* face is the general rule of nonbindingness of promises to extend gifts or make voluntary contributions, which jurists advising those operators have generally maintained. In addition, *takaful* companies invest in Islamized versions of the debt instruments (mortgage-backed securities, government bonds, etc.) that constitute the bulk of conventional insurance company investments, thus avoiding charges of *riba*.

As we have already stated, a most prominent dissenting voice from that opinion was that of Dr. Mustafa Al-Zarqa, who published two research papers that he had prepared for previous conferences in 1961 and 1976, studying the historical roots, objectives, and mechanics of commercial insurance. He insisted on the following till the end of his life:

I have found no proof in the texts of Islamic Shari'a, or its legal theory, that would forbid insurance itself, in any of its three forms. On the contrary, I found the proofs of Shari'a, and its general objectives, to point jointly toward its permissibility and approbation, as a means of eliminating risk and loss.[22]

Moreover, he condemned those who have

raised doubts in people's minds, and put the public in the dark with regards to the accurate characterization of this topic. ...

Some of those who raise such doubts are driven by obstinate desire to defend earlier opinions that they had issued in haste, and find it psychologically difficult to admit their faults, and others for various other reasons, but without belief in what they say.[23]

A younger student of the same school of thought, Dr. Rafiq Yunus Al-Misri, indicated in a recent publication that he has also reached the same conclusion, that insurance is – in principle – permissible. In the process, he addressed directly the fundamental issue of Shari'a arbitrage (forbidding some transaction, and then permitting it in slightly modified form, with unaltered substance), which we have raised repeatedly:

> By permissibility of mutual cooperative insurance and commercial insurance, we mean permissibility in principle, without necessarily accepting all details. Therefore, I prefer permissibility of insurance, without *hiyal* (legal stratagems, or ruses); for there are jurists who forbid one thing, and then return to permit by various legal stratagems and means of circumvention, without worry or shame. We ask God to protect us from such practices.[24]

In a recent *fatwa* issued in September 2004 by the Grand Mufti of Egypt, Dr. ʿAli Jumʿah, the line of thinking of contemporary jurists who rejected the prohibition of insurance based on *gharar* was summarized, along with opposing views. The Mufti reached the conclusion of permissibility of all types of insurance, with minor recommended corrections, as detailed below in a full translation of the text of the *fatwa*:

Ministry of Justice
Egyptian Dar Al-Iftaʾ

...We have reviewed the question #1139 of 2003, presented by Mr. Tariq Saʿid ʿAli, which included: "What is the Islamic legal status ruling for life insurance?"

Answer:

Since insurance of all kinds is a recent financial practice, on which no explicit legal text ruled regarding permissibility or prohibition – as also in the case of banking operations – its practice has been subject to juristic analysis and research based on general import of legal texts, such as the verse: "Cooperate in righteousness and piety, and cooperate not in sin and transgression, and fear God, for His punishment is strict" [4:2], and the Prophetic tradition: "The example of believers in their mutual love, mercy, and compassion is like the parts of the body, if one part complains, the rest of the body responds with sleeplessness and fever" (reported by Bukhari), and many others.

There are three types of insurance:

1. Mutual insurance, in which a group of individuals or associations organize to compensate themselves if they experience realized losses.
2. Social insurance, in which the state protects workers from dangers to which they are exposed as part of their work, and this is built on the idea of cooperative mutual insurance.
3. Commercial insurance, which is carried out by joint stock companies established for that purpose.

There is near-consensus on permissibility of the first and second types of insurance based on the principles of Islamic Shariʿa, since they are based on voluntary contribution (*tabarruʿ*), and mutual cooperation toward righteousness. Moreover, they are based on the principle of social cooperation and mutual protection between Muslims, without a profit motive, and hence ignorance (*jahala*) and uncertainty (*gharar*) do not render such transactions deffective. Moreover, if collected insurance compensation exceeds the sum of paid premiums, that is not considered *riba*, since those premiums are not paid to grow with time, but rather as voluntary contributions to compensate for losses associated with various risks.

The third type of insurance, commercial insurance – including insurance of individuals – has been the subject of a sharp difference in opinions: While some jurists consider this type of financial practice forbidden based on prohibited *gharar*, gambling, and *riba*, others find it to be permissible and argue that it is built on mutual cooperation and voluntary contribution, and thus it is not a commutative financial contract.

The latter group of jurists (who allowed insurance), also cited as proof general canonical texts from Qur'an and Sunna, as well as logical analysis.

They used proof from the Qur'anic verse: "O people of faith, fulfill your contracts" [4:1], and argued that this applies to all contracts, including insurance. If this contract was forbidden, the Prophet would have clarified that during his speech in Mina, in which he said: "It is not permitted for anyone to take the property of his brother except with his consent." Thus the Prophet made transactions permissible if the one who gives money gives it with mutual consent. In this regard, insurance contracts are built upon mutual consent of the two parties, and are consequently permissible.

Logically, jurists permitted insurance in analogy to silent partnership (*mudaraba*), which is one of the general permissible types of transactions. In this characterization, the insured is considered to be providing capital in the form of insurance premiums, which are forwarded to the insurer to invest. Profits for the insured are the insurance claim payment, and profits for the insurer are the premiums, which he invests profitably. They also relied on customary practice (*'urf*), under which such contracts have become conventional. In this regard, it is well known that *'urf* is a source of legislation, in addition to benefit analysis where legal texts are silent (*masalih mursala*). Moreover, the similarities between commercial insurance and mutual and social alternatives are striking, to the point that permission of those other two types of insurance should be extended to the third.[25]

Life insurance – a type of commercial insurance – is not a type of forbidden *gharar* contracts, since it is a contract of voluntary contribution, rather than financial commutativity [which would have deemed it defective based on *gharar*]. This follows from the fact that *gharar* in such contracts does not lead to disputation between the parties, due to common usage of insurance in all aspects of economic life. In this regard, contracts that have become familiar and accepted, without leading to disputes, are not forbidden.

In fact, *gharar* is deemed to exist in this contract only by considering the contract between one individual and the company.[26] However, since insurance has become part of every economic area, and companies have customarily provided social insurance for their employees, every person now knows beforehand what he pays and what he receives – hence, one cannot characterize this practice as containing the forbidden excessive *gharar*.

Studying the documents of commercial insurance of all kinds, as issued by Al-Sharq Insurance Company and others, shows that the bulk of contract articles are simply regulations predetermined by the insurance company with consent of the customer, who thus becomes bound by those contractual regulations. Moreover, the bulk of those articles do not contradict Islamic Shariʿa. However, some other contract articles must be eliminated or amended to agree with Islamic Shariʿa, based on what was agreed by the leaders of the insurance industry in their meeting with the Mufti of the republic on March 25, 1997, which suggested the following amendments: ... [list of changes to be made in insurance contracts]

The Egyptian Dar Al-Iftaʾ thus finds that there is no Sharʿi objection to allowing any of those three types of insurance. In fact, we hope that insurance coverage will be extended further, to cover currently uninsured individuals. Monthly or annual premiums should be made affordable, and insurance should be made obligatory to get everyone accustomed to saving as well as charitable giving, on condition that their funds are returned to them together with investments that are valuable for them and their nations. Advanced nations and great societies are the ones that inculcate in their citizens the love of saving and working toward what assists them in religion and future life.

God knows best,

The Mufti of Arab Republic of Egypt
Prof. Dr. ʿAli Jumʿah

8.3 Two Sides of the Two Debates

The logic of this recent *fatwa* and the preexisting rejections of its grounds bear striking resemblance to their counterparts in the area of banking. Indeed, Dr. Jumʿa hinted at that similarity in the beginning of his *fatwa* by declaring both insurance (intermediation for risk management) and banking (intermediation for credit extension) as modern financial practices, on which the canonical texts of Islam are silent. While refusing to condemn conventional financial practice as forbidden, progressive jurists argued that they need not accept every detail of industry practice, and indeed proceeded to propose lists of modifications of conventional practice to ensure adherence to the percepts of Shariʿa. We may call their approach the minimalist or reformist approach. The basic tenet of this approach is that there is no need to reinvent conventional financial institutions. Instead, this approach dictates, we should impose the minimal necessary modifications on a functioning system to ensure "Shariʿa compliance." As a consequence, this approach would abolish Shariʿa-arbitrage opportunities and merely add consumer protection and prudential regulations as derived from Islamic canonical texts and premodern juristic derivations therefrom.

In contrast, opponents of conventional financial practice draw analogies to canonical texts, including classical unanimity over the conditions of some classical contracts such as investment agency (*mudaraba*) – consensus being raised to canonical levels in classical legal theory. Thus, while the first approach advocates using the methods and spirit of classical juristic analysis, the second advocates adherence to the specific pronouncements of premodern jurists. Consequently, adherents to the latter view feel that the Islamic financial system needs (at least in form) to be reconstructed from premodern contracts that have been approved by classical jurists: *murabaha*, *ijara*, *mudaraba*, for example, as reviewed in the previous chapters. Of course, we have seen that the contemporary Islamic banking practices, say, of *murabaha*, as approved by the jurists serving on those Fiqh Academies, bear little resemblance to the classical namesake contracts, and much resemblance to conventional banking practice. Nevertheless, jurists who adhere to this point of view, many of whom are actively involved in supporting Islamic finance in various capacities, continue to see Islamic finance as an alternative to conventional finance, rather than a minor modification thereof.

Shari'a Arbitrage vs. Islamic Prudential Regulation

As we have argued, the latter set of jurists, especially those actively involved in developing new products in Islamic finance, are very practical in their approach. They recognize that the functions performed by conventional financial institutions (financial intermediation, amelioration of risk, etc.) are necessary for the functioning of any economy. Hence, while they aim to work from the ground up, as it were, starting from the vantage point of approved contracts in classical jurisprudence, they recognize that the bankers and lawyers with whom they work closely approach the industry from the opposite direction: How can we "Islamize" any given set of financial services or products?

In the final analysis, the two sets of jurists share the same tools (analysis of canonical texts and classical jurisprudence) to reach the same ends (approximation of conventional financial practice in a Shari'a-compliant manner). This coincidence of means and ends is belied by the rhetoric of jurists on both sides of the debate, which often turns vitriolic. The minimalist-approach juristic views are sometimes characterized – quite unfairly – as in opposition to Islamic finance, whereas jurists who support Islamic finance are sometimes characterized – equally unfairly – as cynical in their attack on conventional practices that they actively try to emulate.

In fact, too much effort is wasted on such debates. An objective examination of the two camps would reveal that they have each at times used some aspects of the other camp's approach. For instance, jurists who support Islamic finance have adopted the minimalist approach to stock screening for Islamic mutual funds and other investment vehicles – starting from the existing universe of equity instruments, and devising a set of screens that would not reduce the universe too dramatically. Conversely, most of the minimalist-approach jurists have not (at least not yet) approved various types of derivative securities trading, reasoning – quite correctly, absent appropriate regulatory safeguards – that such trading in risk can be akin to gambling. In the future it is most likely that trading in such derivative securities will be permitted under certain regulatory restrictions, which will be variously proposed by the two sets of jurists approaching the problem from the two opposite extremes.

In part, it has been the objective of this book to reconcile the two views by recognizing classical prohibitions in Islamic jurisprudence as prudential regulatory mechanisms. If we accept this view, then we would recognize that we have a choice whether to start from contracts that are known to have embodied those mechanisms in premodern times (e.g., nominate contracts such as *murabaha* or *ijara*) or to start from conventional practice and impose restrictions that embody the substance of those classical mechanisms. The resulting choice of one approach or the other should be dictated by economic considerations: Which is the path of least resistance for the issue at hand? We shall elaborate on this point in Chapter 10. For now, we turn to the issues of Islamic financial practice in financial intermediation (banking) and risk intermediation (insurance). In this context we shall show that the two contrasting views of jurists supporting the opposing *fatawa* on both issues can be reconciled. The magic solution appears to be viewing financial institutions in terms of general agency contracts, as opposed to specific investment agency (*mudaraba*) contracts, for which too many conditions were stipulated in classical jurisprudence.

8.4 Generic Agency Characterization of Financial Institutions

The proposed use of agency contracts (*wakala*) as an organizing principle for Islamic financial institutions is not new. In the insurance industry, the model of agency has gained popularity in recent years, after having been contemplated (though not yet fully and successfully implemented) in Saudi Arabia by Bank Al-Jazira in their *takaful* (cooperative insurance) model. While maintaining the two main characteristics of other *takaful* companies (stock ownership and characterization of payment of insurance claims on the basis of binding voluntary contribution – *tabarruʿ* – by the *takaful* provider), they charachterized the *takaful* provider as an agent (*wakil*) rather than entrepreneur in silent partnership (*mudarib*). Recognizing difficulties with the voluntary contribution or gift model (wherein bindingness of promises is questionable, as we have seen in Chapter 6), discussions of mutualization have also been ongoing, and there is some likelihood that the *takaful* industry will eventually move to mutual corporate structures.

Agency and Takaful as Mutual Insurance

In the framework of insurance, jurists of the two opposing camps disagreed over the *gharar* issue: Those who based the ruling on the analysis of each individual contract between the insured and the insurer viewed it as a commutative financial contract with *gharar* (premiums are paid, but the insured does not know how much he will get in return). Some other jurists (e.g., in the *fatwa* translated above) argued that – viewed collectively – this is in fact a financial practice built on mutual cooperation rather than commutativity. This argument is unconvincing for conventional stockholder-owned insurance companies. However, it is a legally accurate characterization for conventional mutually owned ones. Another argument, utilized by Professors Mustafa Al-Zarqa, Nejatullah Siddiqi, and others, invokes the law of large numbers to argue that the insurer knows with great accuracy how much it will pay on average (even though it does not know exactly which claims will be filed, etc.). The insured party, on the other hand, is the primary beneficiary from the contract and knows precisely how much he will have to pay in premiums, and how much he will collect in case of damages. Hence, the argument concludes, *gharar* on the insured party's side is not the forbidden kind that can lead to disputation.

The latter argument is convincing, but relies on the reader's judgment regarding the potential for disputation. Therefore, it appears better to eliminate the concern about *gharar* and commutativity of the contract by making *takaful* companies mutually owned. In this context, management of the company will be easily characterized as an agent that collects fixed fees for its agency activities, and the mutual owners of the *takaful* company will be seen quite accurately as a group of individuals engaged in cooperative insurance. In fact, the mutual structure of insurance companies serves other (more direct economic) interests: Managers of a stockholder-owned insurance company answer to the stockholders, and hence aim to maximize profits, which translates into seeking loss ratios that are not advantageous to the insured. In contrast, shareholders of mutual insurance companies are themselves the insured parties, and hence managers will aim to provide them with better insurance value for their premiums. There is indeed a well-documented empirical regularity of mutual insurance companies providing better loss ratios for the insured parties. We shall elaborate further on the call for mutualization and agency in Islamic finance in our analysis of corporate governance and regulation of Islamic financial institutions in Chapter 9.

Of course, there remains the issue of *riba*, which is also cited for the prohibition of conventional insurance. In most countries conventional insurance companies, whether stock or mutually owned, are required to invest in high-quality fixed-income securities such as government bonds and mortgage-backed securities. To the extent that conventional bonds and asset-backed securities are deemed forbidden by jurists supportive of Islamic finance, signing policies with conventional mutual insurance companies may evade *gharar* but would violate the stricter prohibition of *riba*. Consequently, *takaful* companies (or Islamized insurance companies) invest the premiums they collect in Islamic securities. Given the quick growth in issuances of "Islamic" bonds and asset-backed-securities, and given that such securities pay a similar return to their conventional counterparts, this restriction to investing in Islamic securities presents an increasingly diminishing obstacle to providing insurance without violation of Shari'a percepts.

Agency in Banking

As we have seen in previous chapters, Islamic banks have managed to replicate the asset structures of conventional banks quite accurately. However, jurists supporting Islamic finance continue to require Islamic banks to act on the liabilities side in a mutual-fund-like manner. Interestingly, that *mudaraba* structure is in fact one of agency: The bank acts as an entrepreneur, investing the depositors' funds on their behalf. However, in this traditional *mudaraba* structure, classical jurists were indeed in agreement that the entrepreneur or agent may not guarantee a percentage profit/interest rate to the provider of funds. Arguments by Azhar scholars past and present notwithstanding, the above-cited argument that a new type of *mudaraba* should be developed defeats the purpose of using classical nominate contracts, which is to provide continuity and ensure embodiment of the prudential standards imposed by classical jurists.

It is a fact that Islamic banks invest almost exclusively in interest-bearing debt instruments (such as arise from *murabaha* and *ijara* financing, as well as *tawarruq* in recent years). In such investments the only material risks to which Islamic banks are exposed are the same ones to which conventional banks are: credit risks (debtors may default), interest rate risk (the opportunity cost of funds might rise), liquidity risk (too many depositors may demand their funds at the same time), and operational risks (including internal and external fraud, accounting errors leading to penalty payments, etc.). Islamic finance practitioners point to an additional source of risk, called "displaced commercial risk," stemming from the moral hazard problem caused by lack of guarantee of principal to depositors seeking a return on their funds (if depositors suffer a loss relative to conventional bank depositors, they may withdraw their funds from the Islamic bank). We shall discuss this risk in greater detail within the context of corporate governance of Islamic banks in Chapter 9. It would be ideal for Islamic banks to remove that additional source of risk, by providing their investment account depositors a structure similar to familiar conventional deposits.

Note that a simple structure such as closed-end *murabaha* funds as well as open-end *ijara* funds are quite feasible and utilized in various contexts, as we have shown in previous chapters. However, such structures lack the guarantee of the offering financial institutions. To the extent that conventional banks also bolster their own guarantees with access to central banks that act as lenders of last resort, as well as various deposit insurance schemes, such funds fail to mimic the level of safety given to conventional bank depositors.

The clue to making Islamic bank investment deposits similar to conventional bank deposits is to maintain the agency characterization of the bank's role, without resorting to the specific "investment-agency" (*mudaraba*) characterization that ignores the debt-instrument nature of bank investments. In fact, hints at the appropriate agency structure can be already seen in the Bahrain Monetary Agency *salam-sukuk* structure reviewed in the Chapter 6. We have seen that the government in that structure acts as an agent that guarantees a fixed-percentage return to the *sukuk* holders. In fact, we have seen that the same is true for *ijara-sukuk* structures, including the Qatar Global *Sukuk* structure reviewed in Chapter 6. All such *sukuk* structures guarantee a fixed-percentage return to *sukuk* holders, thus fetching the same credit rating and interest rate as conventional bonds issued by the same governments.

On the other hand, juristic analyses of such *sukuk* structures have not been readily accessible, and the structures themselves are too cumbersome for seamless replication of conventional banking practice for Islamic banks that invest in permissible instruments. We have already discussed in previous chapters the economic substance of restrictions imposed on Islamic bank assets, and the potential for squandering said substance. We have also highlighted the fact that the Azhar *fatwa*'s implicit claim that conventional banks' investments are permissible is inaccurate according to its own declared scope of *riba*, and their characterization of bank activities as investment agency (*mudaraba*) is juristically troublesome. Instead, our objective is to find a pure agency model for passing through the debt structure of Islamic bank assets, together with the bank's own guarantee, bolstered by deposit insurance and central bank backing.

Toward that end, we shall consider a particularly interesting pair of *fatawa* regarding Islamic banks acting as agents, without themselves offering financing to the customers viewed as principals. Our objective in analyzing those *fatawa* is the following: Instead of viewing Islamic banks traditionally as investment agents for depositors and then as investors through financing various customers (the double-tier *mudaraba* model envisioned in the fifties and surviving to this day), consider the depositors themselves as investors who finance the various activities of bank customers, the bank itself acting merely as an intermediary agent and guarantor of the financed parties. It is in this regard that the following *fatawa* can be instrumental to setting the appropriate precedents.

The two *fatawa* appear at the end of Ahmad and Abu Ghuddah (1998, *fatawa* 16-13 and 16-14, pp. 365–72). We now provide translations of the most important segments:

16-13 Collection of Certificate Receivables

Question (1):

Please indicate the Shar'i opinion regarding the following operations, which are considered customary banking operations on behalf of bank customers. This class of bank services is different from bank investments, since it does not involve any financing for the customer, with or without deferment. Banks perform such operations using their back offices, seeking – when needed – the assistance of other (corresponding) domestic or foreign banks. This type of cooperation between banks takes place based on prior agreements, wherein each party agrees to perform the banking operations for which the other asks, based on pre-specified conditions and compensations. One of the financial services that banks perform on behalf of their customers, based on instructions issued by those customers, is collection of the values of IOUs, checks, and other certificates that stipulate payment of certain amounts. The steps taken for those financial activities are as follows:

First, the customer gives Faisal Islamic Bank of Egypt one or more certificates (*sukuk*) as described previously, which certificates stipulate that the customer is entitled to a sum of money owed to them by one or more other individuals.

Second, the customer asks the bank to collect the amount owed to him by the debtors, as specified in the certificates, and the amount of money thus collected from the debtor is put at the customer's disposal, either to receive in cash, or to be deposited in a current account at the bank, under his name.

Third, it is customary in such practices that the customer asks the bank to take all necessary legal steps against the debtor if the latter is delinquent, so that the customer may benefit from the legal papers thus produced if he needs to resort to court in order to collect his right from the delinquent debtor.

Fourth, the bank performs the same function regardless of whether the certificates are forwarded to the bank directly by the customer, or through other corresponding domestic or foreign banks, since the bank also relies on other banks in collecting the funds of its own customers, especially if the debtors reside in a different country, wherein the bank has no branches or agents.

Answer:

Agency from the Shar'i point of view is assigning another in place of oneself to perform a known and permissible action that he can perform during his lifetime. Consequently, every action that the individual may perform himself, he may assign to another as an agent in his place. Consequently, the above-mentioned operations, wherein the bank is assigned by its customers to collect the values of debt certificates (*sukuk*) owed by others, are valid agency operations, in which the debtor's consent is not required. It is permissible for Faisal Islamic Bank of Egypt to conduct such operations, provided that the certificates are not documentations of debts based on forbidden activities such as gambling, trading in forbidden goods, etc. In this regard, it does not much matter whether the bank collects the values of certificates itself, or through appointing another bank as its agent, which usually happens when the bank has no branch or agent in the city wherein the debtor resides. If the debtor resides abroad, the corresponding foreign banks may collect the value from the debtor, and then perform a currency exchange to determine the amount in domestic currency, to be paid to Faisal Islamic Bank of Egypt. ...It is noteworthy that Faisal Islamic Bank of Egypt does not, in the course of such operations, perform any financing or pay any amount to the customer prior to collecting them from the debtor, or receiving notification from a corresponding bank that it had collected the amount and put it under the disposal of Faisal Islamic Bank of Egypt.[27]

The nature of receivables that banks can collect on behalf of their corporate customers was more explicitly discussed in the next *fatwa*:

16-14 Collection of installment payments of deferred sale prices

Question:

Deferred price sales constitute a large portion of the balance sheets of companies that sell used cars. Collection of the installment payments for those sales is difficult for such companies, but easy for banks. In this regard, some automobile companies have suggested that we collect the installments that their customers owe them, by deducting those installments from the customers' current accounts, after the latter arrange for automatic deposits of their salaries at Kuwait Finance House. Please tell us if it is permissible to perform the following operations:

First: Opening a current account for the customer wishing to purchase a car (if he does not already have one).

Second: Directly depositing his salary, together with a certification from Kuwait Finance House that his salary is forwarded to us.

Third: Receiving monthly bills for each buyer, specifying the dates for collection, so that we may deduct the same amount out of his account.

Fourth: Deducting the values of installments at the appropriate dates, and providing the automobile merchant company with notifications that the installments were deposited in its account with us.

Fifth: Notifying the automobile merchant companies with the names of customers whose accounts were not debited for the installments, and the reasons for that.

Sixth: Calculating a commission (e.g., 100 monthly) to be collected from the auto merchant. Note that we are not bound to transfer the installments if the customer asks us not to, and the customer is not forced to deposit his salary directly with us.

Answer:

First: I needed to ask about the issue of installment sales, whether they contain interest payments, and whether the contract between the car merchant company and the customer stipulates conditions of increasing the payments for late payment, or reduction for prepayment. This question was answered stating that the customer signed obligations for monthly payments, and no interest is collected in the case of late payment. Moreover, the answer said, the cash price of the car is listed, and expenses for deferment are specified. In response, it was stated that this is not permissible, but rather a single deferred price should be mentioned in the contract, and copies of the contract and bills were requested for study.

Second: Explanation of the steps was requested, and answered as follows – an account is opened for the customer who purchased a car, and then monthly installments were deducted from his account, and Kuwait Finance House takes a commission in exchange for performing this service to the creditor Toyota, which the creditor deducts from the profits he made from his dealing with the customer.[28]

What is most interesting in the second *fatwa* is that most of the probing questions pertained to the mechanics of *murabaha* transactions. However, the collection itself and the mechanics of automatic deductions from the customer's account and crediting of the car dealer's account were not subjects of contention. Assuming that the contract was in fact structured by Kuwait Finance House (as a legal agent) on behalf of the Toyota dealership, there would be no issues about the legality of price specification and other issues. In fact, Kuwait Finance House could also have acted as the dealership's agent in finding appropriate customers with current accounts (to which salaries are automatically deposited or otherwise). The *murabaha* contract would still be between the Toyota dealership and the customer, with Kuwait Finance House fulfilling multiple agency roles. If Kuwait Finance House further certifies to the Toyota dealership that it has sufficient funds in the customer's account to make the payments, then it could in essence guarantee payment of the monthly installments.

The above-mentioned procedure would fully complete the financial intermediation task of Kuwait Finance House on behalf of its corporate customer (the Toyota dealership). However, the same principle could be carried over to funds in a pool of investment accounts (restricted or unrestricted). The Islamic bank need not engage in *murabahas* and *ijaras* directly as the financier. Instead, the Islamic bank can stipulate that it merely facilitates the *murabaha, ijara,* or even *tawarruq* transactions as an agent of the investment depositors, who are themselves the financiers. Thus, the investment account holders would become like closed-end *murabaha* or *ijara* fund owners, with capital and interest payments guaranteed by the financed parties. Hence, their only exposure is to credit risk arising from the possibility of defaults of their debtors.

Now, since the bank is merely an agent for both parties (depositors as financiers, and customers as debtors to those financiers), it can provide third-party guaranty for the debtor-customers' liabilities. One might think that a problem may arise based on the distinction between agent possession of trust and guarantor possession of guaranty. However, the combination of agency (*wakala*) and third-party guaranty (*kafala*) is not problematic in principle. For instance, it has been discussed by contemporary jurists in the context of letters of credit for importers (who possibly have import expenses deposited with the bank as their agent), wherein the bank may be purely a guarantor, purely an agent, or any combination thereof. The important provision in this case is to ensure that the guarantor may not collect fees for offering guaranty, although it is allowed to collect enough fees to cover clerical costs associated with it. As for agency, the collection of agency fees is accepted unequivocally.[29] Unfortunately, contemporary jurists who are active in Islamic finance have rejected this combination of agency and guaranty.[30]

One can hope that Islamic bank jurists will reconsider this prohibition of the combination of guaranty and agency. However, if they do not, then costlier Shari'a arbitrage may still be utilized to generate debt instruments as Islamic banks' liabilities. Instead of treating depositors as investors who share in profits and losses, Islamic banks can provide reverse *murabaha*, *ijara*, or *tawarruq* facilities to depositors – much like governments that issue *sukuk* guarantee principal plus interest to their bondholders. Although this increases the transaction costs relative to the simple conjoining of agency and guaranty, it would allow Islamic banks fully to mimic the liabilities of conventional banks, much as they have mimicked their assets. This would complete the replication of conventional bank financial intermediation, while restricting the set of investment vehicles in which an Islamic bank can intermediate to those approved by the appropriate Shari'a boards (e.g., *murabaha*, *ijara*). For regulators, such Islamic banks will look essentially the same as conventional ones, hence removing impediments to licensing them in various countries, since no alternative regulatory framework will be required. In the next chapter we shall argue for an alternative agency model of mutuality, wherein depositors would in fact be shareholders of the Islamic bank.

Agency in Asset Management

In areas of private equity, venture capital, and fund management, managers of high-net-worth individuals' wealth act predominantly as agents for those individuals, any established trusts or foundations, and others. Of course, this exposes investors to a host of adverse selection and moral hazard problems: If agents invest other people's money, and collect a management fee that increases with returns above a certain threshold (as they often do), they will be tempted to take too much risk. Those agency problems are commonly reduced by requiring fund managers to invest a substantial portion of their own net worth in the same portfolios as their principals. Needless to say, this is the same consideration behind capital adequacy requirements for banks, which also ensure that banks do not take excessive risks with other people's money (in this case, depositors).

Of course, the capital adequacy requirements for banks are significantly stronger than for managers of funds for high-net-worth individuals, precisely because of the differential between risk appetites of small depositors of banks versus wealthy individuals who allocate only small portions of their wealth to various high-risk areas. As we have seen in Chapter 7, Islamic fund management for high-net-worth individuals from the GCC region was one of the easiest areas to develop in Islamic finance, because of parallels between the Islamic and conventional structures of agency contracts therein.

Some of the ideas presented in this chapter can assist in bringing the same agency approach to retail banking practices, without need for a different Islamic banking regulatory framework. This ability to reconstruct Islamic banking as a proper subset of conventional banking practices within the existing regulatory framework would, in turn, reduce the apprehension toward that industry in countries where it has not yet witnessed significant growth, while avoiding currently unforeseen risks that a mutual-fund-style Islamic banking industry may pose to financial sectors where it has been operating. In the following chapter, we shall propose an alternative corporate structure for Islamic banks and insurance companies, based on mutuality. The mutuality approach will address a number of heretofore unresolved problems in Islamic finance, without adding Shari'a-arbitrage transactions costs (e.g., in replicating conventional bank liabilities as discussed above), and maintaining regulatory familiarity – since mutual financial institutions have existed in the West for nearly two centuries, and regulatory best practices therein have become well understood. In the meantime, the agency framework for Islamic fund management companies of various types need not be altered, since the Islamic and conventional models in those areas are virtually identical.

9

Governance and Regulatory Solutions in Mutuality

We need to discuss issues of governance, regulation, and enforcement in Islamic finance only to the extent that Islamic financial markets and institutions differ from their conventional counterparts. Wherever substantive differences do in fact exist, reduction of Islamic financial practices to conventional analogs can provide the easiest approach to regulation and governance. In this regard, we have illustrated through numerous examples in previous chapters that Islamic financial market products are substantively identical to their conventional counterparts. Thus, Islamic financial markets and market-supporting institutions require minimal effort to view all products and operations therein in light of their conventional counterparts, and thus conventional governance, regulation, and enforcement best practices may be applied directly.

For instance, many asset-based transactions can be easily converted into conventional loans for regulatory and enforcement purposes, and regulatory capital, reserve ratio, and risk management requirements may be easily applied to Islamic transactions and the institutions that implement them. The only requirement in this regard is to keep track of things like multiple trades and leases in order to report Islamic loan alternatives in the same format used by conventional banks in their reporting to central banks and other regulators.[1]

Regulation and governance of Islamic mutual funds, investment banks, venture capital firms, and the like are even more direct, since their operations are virtually identical with conventional counterparts. The two sets of Islamic financial institutions for which corporate governance and corresponding regulation and enforcement standards need to be developed are in the areas of banking and insurance. We suggested in Chapter 8 an agency framework for those two sets of institutions. In this chapter we shall elaborate on this proposed agency structure, with emphasis on the need for mutualization in Islamic banking and insurance, which would allow us to reduce governance and regulatory problems to ones for which conventional counterparts are well developed, while ensuring avoidance of forbidden *riba* and *gharar*, both formally and substnatively.

9.1 Rent-Seeking Shari'a Arbitrage and Absence of Mutuality

Historical studies of Islamic banking prior and leading to the Mit Ghamr experiment in Egypt in 1963, which was a pivotal point in the history of Islamic banking, point to the strong influence of European mutual banking institutions and cooperatives. This influence applied equally to early-1950s banking experiments in Pakistan, as well as the 1960s Malaysian Tabung Haji, which eventually gave rise to the fast-growing Malaysian Islamic banking sector. Dr. Ahmed Al-Najjar's initiative in Mit Ghamr appears itself to have been equally influenced by the social and economic thought of the Muslim Brotherhood in Egypt and the mutual banking institutions that Dr. Al-Najjar witnessed in West Germany during his years of study there.[2]

The later GCC-based pioneers of Islamic banking in Dubai, Kuwait, and Saudi Arabia capitalized the first group of Islamic banks in the mid-1970s and later lamented the modes of operation adopted by those banks, which mimicked conventional banking practices. Many today criticize Islamic banks for failing to deliver economic and social development to Muslim populations that remain among the poorest and least educated in the world. Indeed, Dr. Al-Najjar, Sheikh Saleh Kamel, and most of the early pioneers of Islamic banking expressed their displeasure with the industry's modes of operation on the assets side and predicted that foreign banks would soon be able to capture significant market share in an Islamic banking industry built on synthesizing loans and bonds from sales and leases.[3]

On the liabilities side, there is great disparity between the rhetoric and practice of Islamic banking. For instance, Sheikh Saleh Kamel made the suggestion in a recent interview that Islamic bank "depositors" were in fact "partners" who thrived when Islamic banks did, thus assuming a mutuality structure, which is not in fact how Islamic banks are structured today.[4] Some mutuality initiatives in Islamic finance exist in Canada, the United States, Trinidad, and other countries in the forms of housing cooperatives and credit unions, but those are very few to alter the fundamentally Shari'a-arbitrage profit-driven nature of the industry.[5]

Mutuality in Islamic insurance would have also been a natural development, given that jurists sought solutions to the problem of *gharar* inherent in the risk-trading business of insurance through noncommutativity of the relationship between insurer and insured in *takaful*. However, they sought this solution only by making the insurer (still a stock-holder company) pay valid claims as an act of voluntary contribution (*tabarru'*), rather than commutative trade. We have outlined the problems with this model of *tabarru'* in Chapters 6 and 8, especially given the general nonbindingness of gift promises in classical jurisprudence. Interestingly, jurists who approved conventional insurance, as well as jurists who preferred the Islamic *takaful* alternative, were in agreement that the essence of any permissible Islamic insurance scheme lies in its fundamental characterization in terms of mutual cooperation. Thus, mutuality in Islamic insurance would have been natural. However, in insurance as in banking, financial professionals and jurists have approached the industry from the vantage point of exploiting profitable Shariʿa arbitrage opportunities.

Prohibitions as Means of Risk Mitigation

More generally, mutuality in banking and insurance would provide natural solutions to the problems of *riba* and *gharar* associated with intermediation of credit and risk, respectively. In this regard, we have argued in previous chapters that the prohibitions of *riba* and *gharar*, and associated conditions imposed by classical jurists on contracts that allow transfer of credit and risk without violating those prohibitions, are in essence forms of prudential regulation and risk management. Although secular regulators have put in place regulatory requirements that limit systemic risks posed by joint-stock financial companies, mutuality appears to fill a needed regulatory gap for protecting individuals from their own tendencies to undertake excessive risk that may prove personally ruinous. Interestingly, the rise of mutual savings banks and mutual insurance companies appears to have occurred in the West precisely to meet the demands of farmers and other risk-averse groups, who built such institutions to gain access to credit and risk mitigation without necessarily having their financial interests governed by profit motives.[6] It is this similarity of motives and substance that made mutuality a natural idea in the early days of Islamic banking, and in the early literature on Islamic insurance.

    Later in this chapter we shall summarize theoretical results and empirical evidence indicating that mutual financial institutions tend to provide their owners with lower risk and return profiles, and to offer their customers (who are often shareholders as well) better service, compared to joint-stock banking and insurance companies. In other words, mutual financial institutions provide the same financial (credit and risk) intermediation services and products, which are necessary for economic well-being, but do so in a manner that does not increase risks unnecessarily. This lower risk profile also makes mutual financial institutions more resilient, especially during periods of financial panic, such as during the Great Depression of the early twentieth century. It is interesting in this regard to note that the prohibitions of *riba* and *gharar* are precisely restrictions on means of trading in risk (the extension of credit exposes the creditor to potential borrower default or bankruptcy, and leverage increases the borrower's own risk thereof). Thus, the spirit of Islamic jurisprudence allows transfer of credit and risk only if bundled within a financial transaction such as sales, leases, and partnerships.[7] Such bundling regulates the riskiness of financial transactions, thus allowing for necessary risk taking to encourage investment and economic growth, while minimizing individual and systemic risks of bankruptcy and wild fluctuations in economic values.

Rent-Seeking Shari'a Arbitrage Encourages Risk Taking

The lack of mutuality in Islamic banking and insurance is not surprising when we consider the motivation behind their growth in the past two decades, as discussed in the previous chapters: abnormal profit or rent seeking. The bulk of growth in Islamic finance has come from multinational financial conglomerates and conventional banks that were attracted to Islamic finance by lucrative profit opportunities. As we have argued in earlier chapters, the very nature of Shari'a arbitrage – which increases transaction costs – has justified charging higher fees or interest rates for Islamic financial services and products, while competitive pressures have simultaneously limited new entry to the industry mainly to the more efficient multinational rent-seeking financial providers.

In this regard, it is useful to note that demutualization in conventional banking and insurance during the past two decades was driven by the same profit/rent-seeking incentive of Shari'a arbitrageurs. As Gron and Lucas (1997) have argued, demutualization was driven by the stock market boom of the 1980s and 1990s, which strengthened the incentive to seek additional capital from equity markets, as it promised mutual owners fast riches. In this regard, it is generally accepted that demutualization of credit unions and other mutual financial institutions mainly enriched managers and large stockholders, in many instances at the expense of smaller shareholders.

Of course, seeking higher returns – through demutualization or avoidance of mutuality in the first place – can be achieved only through increased risk exposure. To the extent that shareholders in mutual banks and mutual insurance companies selected that ownership structure to avoid excessive risk, yielding to the temptation to pursue investments with higher risks and higher returns appears to contradict the initial incentive to shun risk, at least for the part of their portfolio held with mutuals. In the area of Islamic finance, one could argue that the unique power of religious injunctions (especially against *riba* and *gharar*) is that they protect individuals from temporary greed-driven heightening of their appetites for risk. Alas, by shunning mutuality and adopting some of the most transparent forms of Shari'a arbitrage, the regulatory substance of the Shari'a has been squandered, while adherence to its forms has continued tragically in the shallowest way.

Potential for Mutuality in Islamic Banking

Replacement of conventional bank savings accounts with investment accounts based on profit and loss sharing continues to be the main distinctive feature of Islamic banks, to which much of the work of AAOIFI (Accounting and Auditing Organization for Islamic Financial Institutions, in Bahrain) and IFSB (Islamic Financial Services Board) is devoted. Of particular concern in this context is the fact that Islamic bank managers answer to shareholders, whose risk preferences (associated with equity investment) are typically quite different from those of investment account depositors (conventionally associated with debt investments that seek low risk and low return). The problem is exacerbated by investment account holders' lack of control over bank decisions, which exposes them to substantial moral hazard compared to bank shareholders. Investment account holders are also disadvantaged relative to conventional depositors who are deemed creditors of the bank, and thus have first claims to its assets in case of bankruptcy.

A natural solution to this problem is for Islamic banks to adopt a mutual corporate structure. Of course, as we shall argue below, the mutual corporate form does not eliminate moral hazard entirely, since shareholder/depositors are typically too small individually to control bank operation. Indeed, the literature on mutual banks often identifies each shareholder's ability to withdraw his deposit from the bank as the only means of punishing its managers – a prospect called "displaced commercial risk" in the literature on Islamic banking. However, by eliminating the separate group of profit-oriented shareholders from the formula, or putting them on par with investment account holders in the corporate structure, managers' incentive for excessive risk taking is largely eliminated, resulting in lower risk taking that reflects depositors' preferences.

In later sections I shall argue that mutuality in Islamic banking can in fact bring to the industry large numbers of depositor/investors as well as managers who are committed to Islamic ideals of social and economic development, as opposed to profit- and fee-oriented Shari'a arbitrageurs. A by-product of identification of Islamic banking with mutualization would be to give indigenous Islamic banks a much-needed comparative advantage vis-à-vis international financial behemoths that have been able to attract the most respected Shari'a advisors and law firms, thus capturing fast-increasing market shares in today's Islamic finance industry that is built on rent-seeking Shari'a arbitrage. Unfortunately the Islamic banking industry originally envisioned replacing conventional banks with a mutual-fund model of two-tier *mudaraba*, as discussed in Chapter 8, which created a curious liability structure with full equity shareholders and quasi-equity investment account holders with little protection against moral hazard.

Debt and Equity Structures for Assets and Liabilities

On both sides of financial intermediation, banks can use either equity or debt instruments. In the early literature on Islamic economics and finance, Islamic banks were envisioned to use equity or quasi-equity instruments on both asset and liability sides. In that regard, they would have become the polar opposite of commercial banking practice (wherein debt instruments dominate both the asset and liability sides) in most countries that do not allow German-style universal banking. In general, it has been well known that debt contracts are superior in dealing with information asymmetries of the type discussed above, especially when monitoring is costly.[8] It is not surprising, therefore, that Islamic bankers have discovered at an early stage that the moral hazard problem made equity investment on the assets side of Islamic banking prohibitively risky. Thus, Islamic banks have switched the bulk of their assets to debt instruments as discussed above. On the other hand, Islamic banks chose a peculiar structure on the liabilities side: with some equity holders and some quasi-equity holders. Before turning to that particular structure, we should consider the four possible combinations of debt and equity on the assets and liabilities sides.

The first combination, corresponding to conventional commercial bank structure, matches debt-instrument assets with debt-instrument liabilities. In Chapter 8 we have argued that Islamic banks may indeed replicate the liabilities structure of conventional banks, for example, either by using combinations of agency and guaranty or by synthesizing debt liabilities through reverse *murabahas*. This structure has the advantage that all corporate governance and regulatory issues will be handled in the same manner used for conventional banking. However, as Saeed (1999) has argued convincingly, adopting this structure may undercut the very rationale for the existence of Islamic banks and hence would be an unlikely candidate for Islamic banking in the near future.

At the other extreme, we have a model of equity-instrument assets and equity-instrument liabilities (two-tier *mudaraba*), which was envisioned historically as the Islamic alternative to conventional banking. Of course, this equity-based structure is a very meaningful and successful model for mutual funds, private equity, and venture capital, which have gained substantial market shares worldwide. This class of models plays an important financial intermediation role, through aggregation of savings on the liabilities side, and diversification of investments, with various levels of risk, on the assets side. It must thus play an important part in any financial system, Islamic or otherwise.

However, this structure is not an appropriate model of banking, as Islamic banks discovered quickly from practice. In this regard, the pure equity structure does not provide the appropriate solution for information asymmetries that require financial intermediation in the form of banking, wherein loan officers can specialize in credit risk analysis and utilize economies of scale to reduce moral hazard and adverse selection problems economically.[9] Indeed, the great amplification of moral hazard under that structure is illustrated by the discussion of *mudaraba* conditions in Islamic banking in AAOIFI standards:

> One of the basic characteristics that distinguish Islamic banks from conventional banks is that the contractual relationship of Islamic banks with investment account holders does not specify that holders of these account [sic] are entitled to a predetermined return in the form of a percentage of their investment as this is strictly prohibited by Shari'a. Rather, the contractual relationship is based on the *mudaraba* conract which stipulates that profit realized from investing the *mudaraba* fund is shared between investment account holders – as *rab-al-mal* – and the Islamic bank – as a *mudarib*.[10]

> The basis for considering the *mudarib* as a trustee with respect to the *mudaraba* funds is that the *mudarib* is using another person's money with his consent and the *mudarib* and the owner of the funds share the benefits from the use of the funds. In principle, a trustee should not be held liable for losses sustained by the funds. Rather, the risks of such losses must be borne by the *mudaraba* funds.[11]

> The accounting treatments of the equity or profits of investment account holders differ greatly from one Islamic bank to another. This has prompted AAOIFI, as a first step, to promulgate Financial Accounting Standard No. 5: Disclosure of Bases for Profit Allocation Between Owners' Equity and Investment Account Holders in order to provide users of the financial statements of Islamic banks with information on the bases which Islamic banks adopted in allocation profit [sic] between owners' equity and investment account holders.[12]

Thus, AAOIFI has restricted its role in protecting investment account holders to maximizing transparency and uniformity of reporting standards. The only recourse for investment account holders, assuming that the Islamic bank does not engage in negligence or fraudulent activities, is to withdraw their funds from that bank. This gives rise to what AAOIFI research and later analysts called "displaced commercial risk." That threat of fund withdrawal drives Islamic banks to use their loan-loss reserve accounts to smooth rates of return paid to investment account holders, ensuring their competitiveness against rates paid by other Islamic and conventional financial service providers. This complex set of competing incentives has made the issue of corporate governance of Islamic banks one of the most difficult.

As of the writing of this chapter, the publication of a consultation paper on the subject was promised by the Islamic Financial Services Board for early 2006. All indications at this time point to maintaining the "mutual fund" model, whereby investment account holders continue to lack the protection of board representation as equity holders, or the protection of principal guarantee as depositors.

Under the mutual fund model, all that is required of Islamic banks – as de facto collective investment schemes, even if not labeled as such – is to provide consistent and transparent distribution rules for profits and losses between the competing interest groups (equity-holding owners and quasi-equity investment account holders). This solution appears vastly inferior to the solution in mutuality, which aligns the incentives of shareholders and depositors.

A third alternative would be to use debt instruments on the liabilities side, guaranteeing principal and interest for depositors, while investing the funds using equity contracts. This appears to be the model underlying the *fatwa* issued by Al-Azhar's Islamic Research Institute (discussed in Chapter 8), wherein the payment of interest on deposits was justified as fixed-profit rates on funds forwarded to banks to "invest in permissible ventures." This closely approximates the model of universal banking, wherein savers deposit their funds with the bank on a debt basis, usually with an added deposit insurance scheme, while banks can take equity positions in various companies. Under this structure, Boyd, Chang, and Smith (1998) have shown that moral hazard problems between the bank and the deposit insurance company is increased substantially, especially when banks can benefit from diversion of funds ostensibly being invested (a very real threat in the developing Islamic world where similar abuses exist even within a debt-based bank asset structure). Thus, the model implicitly envisioned by Al-Azhar's *fatwa* – with equity-based bank investments being funded by guaranteed bank deposits – seems to be a very poor candidate for further examination.

This leaves us with the fourth potential combination of debt and equity structures on the asset and liability sides, which is the mutuality structure of thrift institutions such as mutual savings banks and credit unions. Under this model, Islamic banks would – as they do currently – build the bulk of their assets in the form of debt-based instruments, through *murabaha*, *ijara*, and various *sukuk* structures. The finance (loan) officers at those Islamic banks would – as they do currently – rely on the same criteria used by their conventional bank counterparts (prospective debtors' earnings before interest, taxes and depreciation, credit risk scores, etc.). In the meantime the liabilities side of the bank will consist mainly of shares (after excluding various owed debts, e.g., for leased bank buildings), whereby shareholders and investment account holders will be put on par. Of course, this does not eliminate information asymmetry problems. However, it does eliminate the substantial short-term conflict of interest that currently exists between Islamic bank shareholders and investment account holders, which has been a main feature of Islamic banking literature. In other words, this would reduce the corporate governance and regulatory issues for Islamic banks to their well-studied counterparts for mutual thrift institutions such as mutual savings banks and credit unions. Moreover, regulating Islamic finance from a religious point of view should also focus on corporate forms of Islamic financial institutions. In this regard the focus on contract forms only may be sufficient for regulation of Islamic financial markets, but analysis of corporate forms and incentives must play an important role in regulation of financial institutions.

Need for Mutuality in Takaful

As we have argued earlier, the absence of mutuality is even more surprising in the Islamic insurance industry, known generally by its Arabic name *takaful* (mutual guaranty). It is interesting that even companies that use the term *takaful taʿawuni* (cooperative mutual guaranty or insurance) have not adopted mutuality structures. This is particularly astonishing given the classical ruling 9/2 of the Fiqh Academy of the Organization of Islamic Conference (OIC), which distinguished commercial insurance from what it called "cooperative insurance ... built on the principles of voluntary contribution (*tabarruʿ*) and mutual cooperation." In fact, as we have seen in Chapter 8, contemporary jurists have enumerated three types of insurance, which they called mutual insurance, social insurance, and commercial insurance. The first form was envisioned along the lines of Western mutual insurance companies (where policyholders are themselves the stockholders), the second form encompasses state-sponsored pension and health insurance plans, and the third is the familiar type conducted by profit-oriented joint-stock companies. As we have seen in Chapter 8, Dr. Mustafa Al-Zarqa, Dr. ʿAli Jumʿa, and other scholars have also recognized that the mutual insurance version was the least controversial, and unanimously accepted, alternative.

Unfortunately the contemporary Islamic insurance industry has adopted a superficial mutuality notion in its name (*takaful*), but not in substance. Thus, most Islamic insurance providers are structured with stockholder rather than policyholder ownership. Insurance claims are paid by shareholders through the *takaful* provider on the basis of *tabarruʿ* (voluntary contribution, as opposed to contractual obligation). This model based on voluntary contribution, replacing commutative contractual obligations with legally binding unilateral promises, raises a host of legal and juristic problems that have not yet been resolved fully. While insurance providers are typically characterized as investment agents of the stockholders, Bank Al-Jazira in Saudi Arabia has pioneered a characterization of insurance provider as pure agent (*wakil*, rather than *mudarib*). This can be a step toward eventual mutualization, where the insurance provider can act as a pure agent for shareholders who are themselves the policyholders. This would satisfy the most widely accepted means of eliminating *gharar* from insurance, by negating the commutative financial nature of the transaction through mutuality. However, there seems to be precious little initiative for mutualization in the Islamic insurance industry today.

9.2 A Call for Mutuality in Banking and Insurance

Islamic banks have not been allowed to act directly – through agency and guaranty – as financial intermediaries that insulate their investment account holders from the credit risk associated with the bank's own debtors. Saeed (1999) sympathized with arguments by Sami Humud, Baqir Al-Sadr, and others, who aimed to find alternatives within the *mudaraba* context to allow the Islamic bank to guarantee investment account holders' principal. He justified that position based on the view, reported by Ibn Rushd in *Bidayat Al-Mujtahid wa Nihayat Al-Muqtasid*, that an entrepreneur (*mudarib*) who forwards an investor's funds to another entrepreneur thus guarantees the invested principal for that original investor. However, he noted correctly that most Islamic economists and bankers feared that this approach would remove the most important perceived substantive distinctions between Islamic and conventional banking. In particular, he argued that the Hanafi view that depositors can be entitled to a return based on provision of money, rather than liability for risk, "could shatter the foundations of *riba* theory as it is accepted in Islamic banking." Besides, he pointed out correctly, Islamic banks benefited from the provision that investment account holders (as investors) bear the financial risk.

Hence, the best Islamic alternative for conventional commercial banking may in fact be adopting mutual banking structures that have been in existence in the west for well over a century, and for which corporate governance and regulatory issues and methods have become well understood. Hence, Western governance and regulatory frameworks for mutual banks may be adopted to this version of Islamic finance with relative ease. In this regard, while there are a number of different secular models of corporate governance in the world, the Anglo-American model is the one of greatest relevance for Islamic finance, since most countries with fast-growing Islamic financial sectors were previously under various types of British control and continue to have strong links with English and U.S. banks and law firms. In this regard, it is important to note that the bulk of academic and practical advances in corporate governance in the Anglo-American world have the objective of aligning manager interests with those of shareholders. This is accomplished through a variety of mechanisms ranging from shareholder representation on the board of directors to external market discipline and manager compensation schemes.[13]

Allen and Gale (2000) have argued persuasively that the emphasis in theory and practice of corporate governance on making managers pursue exclusively the interests of shareholders is too restrictive. However, the focus in countries where other stakeholders of the firm are considered in corporate governance is often restricted to firm employees (especially in the traditional Japanese context). Within the context of the banking firm, the interests of depositors are not included within the scope of corporate governance, since depositors are considered creditors and first claimants on the banks' assets. Thus, the interests of depositors in the commercial banking setup are guarded by regulators, including deposit insurance corporations, who impose restrictions such as reserve ratios and capital adequacy to reduce the probability of bank failure and potential depositor losses in case of such failure.

The phenomenal growth of Islamic finance at the hands of large multinational banks, such as HSBC and Citi. will no doubt continue in various areas of investment banking and fund management. Needless to say, those activities do not fall within the scope of banking proper, where assets are financed primarily by deposits. Those nonbanking segments of Islamic finance can continue to grow – as they have to date – within the same corporate governance and regulatory frameworks for conventional financial markets and institutions. In the meantime, mutualization can help to bring Islamic banking proper (focusing on the depositary function of banks) within the familiar governance and regulatory framework of thrift institutions.

Mutuality in Banking

In mutually owned banks, shareholders and depositors are one and the same, which resolves the fundamental corporate governance problem in Islamic banking. However, since mutual bank shares are nontradable, one of the main mechanisms of corporate governance through external market discipline – linking managers' compensation to stock prices – is missing. Of course, tying manager compensation to internal accounting entries (profits, volume of transactions, risk adjusted rates of return, etc.) is possible, but it lacks the external discipline and objectivity commonly associated with capital market pricing of stocks. This concern is somewhat ameliorated by the likely high concentration of shareholdings by current owners of Islamic banks, who will continue to have a strong incentive for internal monitoring of bank manager performance and risk taking.[14]

In fact, the very lack of linkage of mutual bank managers' compensations to profitability appears to align their interests with those of the mutual bank shareholders, who generally do not buy mutual bank shares seeking a high-risk, high-return profile. This is in contrast to investors in commercial banks, stocks of which may in fact be bought as part of the riskier components of their shareholders' portfolios. Consequently, mutual bank managers recognize that their potential gains from taking higher risk are bounded, while their potential losses are substantial, since they may lose their jobs.[15]

As long as managers of mutuals avoid excessively risky investment opportunities, managers of mutual banks tend to keep their positions for long periods of time, receiving higher compensations in nonpecuniary forms, including more leisure, better office furniture, and business automobiles.[16] The advantage of longer and more comfortable job tenure increases the mutual bank manager's incentive to shun risks, thus providing shareholder depositors with the types of low-risk, low-return investments that they desire. Research has shown that mutual banks have in fact chosen less risky investment portfolios, thus providing excellent low-risk investment opportunities to uninformed depositor shareholders who have no resources for monitoring bank manager performance.[17] In addition, empirical research has shown that mutual banks are no less efficient in their operations than their stockholder-owned counterparts, even though there is no theoretical reason to think that mutual bank managers would be interested in cost minimization.[18]

Thus there appears to be no secular reason to question the economic merits of mutualization of Islamic banks. On the contrary, there is evidence that mutual banking institutions have played a very important role in the development of the U.S. financial system during the nineteenth century, when they were every bit as competitive as stockholder-owned banks.[19] Many, if not most, mutuals are also structured as nonprofit organizations, which ensures that customers who obtain financing from such mutual organizations have access to credit at lower rates than those generally offered by profit-oriented banks. In this regard, the nonprofit approach to credit extension may bring financial practice closer to the Islamic ideal enshrined in the prohibition of *riba*. Indeed, it is not surprising that early credit unions and mutual savings banks in Europe and North America were closely associated with churches and other religious institutions that sought to avoid usury by providing credit at affordable rates to community members, and to avoid profiting from the extension of such credit. Of course, one cannot make a general claim that all for-profit financial intermediaries would engage in usurious lending if they could. However, recent evidence suggests that the profit motive may indeed drive financial providers in the direction of discriminatory and predatory lending practices, especially when it is difficult legally to prove such accusations.[20]

Mutuality in Insurance

In the area of insurance, it is worthwhile noting that mutual insurance companies have played a major role in many insurance lines in the United States during the

1990s, even gaining market share in some property and casualty insurance lines.[21] Empirical evidence suggests that stock insurance companies bore more risk and provided higher returns through higher cost efficiency.[22] Those results are consistent with theoretical analyses of agency problems of mutuality in insurance companies.[23] Naturally, those results for mutuality in insurance mirrored those discussed in the previous section for mutuality in banking: Mutual insurance companies provide better insurance value (higher loss ratios) for policy holders, since managers answer to them rather than to separate profit-seeking stockholders. Of course, by choosing portfolios of lower risk, mutual insurance companies generate lower profits than their stock counterparts. However, being themselves insurance policy holders, owners of those mutual insurance companies are perfectly happy to have a lower risk and lower return profile arising from provision of better insurance coverage with advantageous loss ratios.

Mutuality in Islamic banking and insurance can play an important role in redefining the "Islamic" brand name of Islamic finance. In this regard, many areas of Islamic finance (e.g., in investment banking and fund management) differ only very slightly from conventional financial practice. Differences in those fields, where they exist, can be sold on substantive grounds (e.g., lower tolerance for debt and leverage, ethical investment bias), which would widen its potential market. Thus, those areas would be better served by dropping the "Islamic" distinction. In the meantime, Islamic finance in the areas of banking and insurance can benefit significantly from highlighting a social agenda for improving the plight of Muslims, who are among the poorest and least educated people in the world today. In that respect, redefining Islamic banking and insurance in terms of mutual community efforts can integrate those institutions seamlessly with charitable activities of the Muslim community (e.g., *zakah* payments can be utilized to provide microcredit at affordable rates). Thus, "Islamic" finance may focus less on forms of contracts (the primary feature of rent-seeking Shari'a arbitrage discussed in earlier chapters) and turn its focus to substantive developmental and community initiatives in finance. In Chapter 10 we shall argue that this redefinition of Islamic finance is important, since the industry's current Shari'-arbitrage path is both unsustainable and dangerous.

10

Beyond Shariʿa Arbitrage

We have seen a number of examples in the previous chapters illustrating how nominate contracts in classical Islamic jurisprudence can be used to synthesize almost any contemporary financial transaction. The art of Shariʿa arbitrage consists of identifying a captive market, with religious injunctions that forbid a given set of financial products and services, and synthesizing those products and services from variations on those premodern nominate contracts. Indeed, the governor of the Bahrain Monetary Agency admitted this nature of Islamic finance in a recent speech:

> "Islamic banking and other Islamic financial institutions are rapidly approaching a cross-roads," Sheikh Ahmad bin Mohammad Al Khalifa told the opening session of a conference on Islamic Banking and Finance in Manama [in late February 2004]. "Islamic banks have grown primarily by providing services to a captive market, people who will only deal with a financial institution that strictly adheres to Islamic principles."[1]

In this regard, the potential for Shariʿa arbitrage seems unlimited. Conventional financial products and services will continue to grow indefinitely, thus providing the Shariʿa arbitrageur an unlimited scope for synthesizing subsets of the ever-growing set of financial choices available to conventional customers. We shall illustrate briefly in this chapter how some of the financial products previously considered impossible to synthesize have in fact been offered in recent years. Indeed, a moderately lucrative industry may be sustained for the foreseeable future based on such Shariʿa arbitrage methodologies. However, there are a number of considerations that suggest that Islamic finance will be better served by moving beyond the Shariʿa arbitrage mind-set.

We have discussed in the introduction some of the main reasons for inefficiency of any industry built on Shariʿa arbitrage: (1) Such an industry will be – by necessity – chasing past returns, and (2) synthesized products are almost certain to increase transactions costs, legal and juristic fees, and the like. Those issues notwithstanding, perhaps the most compelling reason for Islamic finance to move beyond Shari'a arbitrage is the simple financial objective of reaching a larger customer base and mobilizing the talents of Muslim financial professionals. In this regard, Islamic financial products have to date attracted a surprisingly small percentage of potential Muslim clients. More importantly, the fast-growing educated Muslim middle class, perhaps the most likely customer base for the industry in the long term, has mostly shied away from participation in the industry.

In this regard, it might historically have been more lucrative for the industry to cater to a relatively small number of high-net-worth individuals and a segment of the Muslim population that is satisfied by Shari'a-board certification of various form-oriented replications of conventional products. However, for sustained long-term growth, there appears to be no substitute for reaching the growing group of middle class Muslim investors and customers, as well as poorer Muslims aspiring to that middle-class status. The bulk of this Muslim middle class are not as willing to accept sacred authority arguments. Hence, they tend to consult with multiple jurists within and outside the industry and to form their own opinions regarding the Islamicity or lack thereof of any battery of financial products and services offered at any point in time. To cater to the needs of this middle-class potential customer base, Islamic finance needs to outgrow the current Shari'a-arbitrage mode of operation, and to market its products and services based on economic merit rather than formulaic juristic support.

10.1 Shari'a Arbitrage and Criminal Finance

Another major reason to move beyond Shari'a arbitrage is the danger inherent in its mechanics, especially in today's post-9/11 legal and regulatory environments. For instance, although some jurists might find *tawarruq-* or *murabaha*-style commodity and asset trading to be acceptable substitutes for interest-based lending and insist on separation of the multiple commodity sales with which the synthetic loan is structured, such spurious trading raises multiple flags for government authorities, which are increasingly concerned about money laundering and various other forms of criminal financing. Indeed, the "asset-based" distinction – highlighted by Islamic finance practitioners as a virtue – makes Shari'a-arbitrage methods very similar to money laundering and criminal finance methods that rely on commodity and asset trades – with over- or underinvoicing – to achieve their illicit goals.

Moreover, the "degrees of separation" utilized by Islamic bankers to camouflage an interest-bearing loan as commodity or asset trading bear a striking resemblance to the "layering" techniques used in financial crimes. For instance, *tawarruq* or *murabaha* camouflaging of loans relies on two degrees of separation: the third trading party, and an underlying asset or commodity. Some recent efforts, such as in Saudi Arabia, have moved toward "domestic *tawarruq*," that is, ensuring that the underlying commodity and its traders reside within the country's borders, but those efforts merely address the first-order layering concerns of those fighting money laundering and other criminal financial activities. It is always possible to add more layers through which the domestic commodity dealer trades with foreign counterparties, which international trade at least on the surface would appear to be bona fide commerce.

Finally, the use of offshore special purpose vehicles for structuring Islamic financial products, such as lease-based receivables, raises many issues for authorities involved in combating money laundering and criminal financing. In the meantime, the juristic focus on form rather than substance of financial practice often leads to excessive utilization of degrees of separation such as SPVs, for technical reasons not dissimilar to those motivating financial criminals. Tragically, while Islamic financial providers are for the most part far removed from any interest in committing financial crimes, their utilization of Shari'a-arbitrage methods that resemble those of financial criminals is dangerous nonetheless. Since financial criminals have expertise in utilizing similar methods, it would be easy for them to abuse the mechanics of Islamic financial Shari'a arbitrage to reach their criminal ends (in the process relishing the lack of transparency afforded by multiple degrees of separation and spurious "real transactions").

In this regard, it is important to note that the structured finance methods of Shari' arbitrage – which were copied from Western regulatory arbitrage methods aiming to reduce tax burdens on high-net-worth individuals – have already had a checkered history. Indeed, American regulators and accountants were slow to uncover some of the abuses of those structures, which later featured prominently in corporate scandals, such as Enron's. In this regard, regulators and enforcement officials in the countries wherein Islamic finance has thrived are clearly less sophisticated than their Western counterparts, and hence less likely to uncover devious intentions underneath complicated financial structures. Given the industry's young age and fragility, it would be wise to move to simpler and more transparent modes of operation, to minimize the risks of abuse by criminal elements.[2]

10.2 Shari'a Arbitrage at the Limit

In addition to this existential concern for Islamic finance, based on its possible and potentially ruinous association with criminal financial activity, there are a number of economic concerns regarding the sustainability of its current Shari'a-arbitrage mode of operation. The dangers inherent in the Shari'a-arbitrage mode of operation can be easily recognized once we consider the logical limiting behavior of recent industry trends.

Benchmarking ad Absurdum

The history of Islamic finance has illustrated beyond doubt that any conventional financial product can be synthesized from premodern contracts. This is perhaps best exemplified in the "benchmarking" argument utilized by jurists, including Justice Usmani and many others. Their argument states that if my neighbor brews beer, while I am a carpenter, I may demand to make the same profit rate as the brewer next door, without rendering my business activity impermissible. Of course, this formulaic juristic analysis belies the fact that the purpose of finance is not to brew beer, but to allocate credits and risks in a manner that is likely to generate profits. Needless to say, one can use the economically incoherent juristic benchmarking approach to synthesize instruments that track the return on any investment vehicle, for example, the price of a particular vintage of wine or pork bellies, utilizing structures that avoid actually trading in the underlying impermissible commodities.

For instance, in the Bahrain Monetary Agency *sukuk al-salam* structure discussed in Chapter 6, the structure could have just as easily stipulated that the government will act as the *sukuk* holders' agent and guarantees marketing their commodities (permissible aluminum) at the same price as pork bellies. According to the analysis of Shari'a scholars associated with Islamic finance, such a practice cannot be condemned, since, in fact, the Qur'an and Prophetic traditions reserve the severest prohibitions to interest-bearing usurious loans, whose interest rates are being used as benchmarks in various *sukuk* and other Islamic financial products. Thus, given that structures have been approved with flexible rates of return guaranteed to track LIBOR, returns on all other indices and impermissible investment vehicles can be replicated using *sukuk* structures together with benchmarking arguments.

Savings Accounts via Shari'a Arbitrage

Shari'a-arbitrage methodologies can also be used in the limit to solve many of the heretofore troublesome problems in Islamic finance. For instance, Islamic banks since their inception have adhered to the notion that depositors whose principals are guaranteed by the bank cannot earn a rate of return, while "investment account" holders who share in bank profits must also be exposed to potential loss of principal. This provision dates back to the early days of Islamic economics, when an Islamic bank was envisioned as a mutual-fund-like two-tier *mudaraba*. Of course, Islamic banks – as we have seen in Chapter 8 – have in fact replicated all conventional bank assets through Islamized structures. However, on the Islamic bank liabilities side, Islamic finance jurists and practitioners alike have adhered to the notion that the bank cannot guarantee principal for depositors seeking a rate of return on their savings.

The approach most commonly sought by Western banks in recent years has been securitization based. Under those structures banks aim to offer variable-rate savings accounts, certificate-of-deposit accounts, and other vehicles, based on the actual rate of return made on their portfolios of *murabahas*, *ijaras* and *sukuk*. The idea behind those structures is that investment depositors will be directly exposed to the credit risk and interest-rate risks that the Islamic bank faces, and hence that they could suffer a loss of principal. In the United States and the United Kingdom those efforts have, to date, run against regulatory provisions that require depositary institutions to guarantee the principal for depositors. The surprising solution proposed in the United States and apparently followed at the Islamic Bank of Britain proceeds as follows:[3] The ideal Islamic structure would require exposing the investor to risk of principal loss. However, regulators require guaranteeing the principal, and hence the Islamic bank will adhere to that provision until such a time as regulations allow otherwise.[4] In the meantime, Muslim depositors can voluntarily participate in bank losses if they are sufficiently substantial to exhaust the entire bank reserves held for the purpose of smoothing depositor returns.

Of course, as we have seen in Chapter 8, conventional savings account structures can be quite easily structured by utilizing the same Shari'a-arbitrage methods that Islamic banks have utilized extensively on their assets side. Thus, savings accounts can be structured through synthetic *murabahas* or *ijaras*, wherein the depositor is the seller or lessor, and the Islamic bank is the buyer or lessee, who thus guarantees the principal plus interest rate dictated by the market (rather than tied to the specific bank's portfolio). The customer's ability to withdraw funds can be easily enhanced through unilaterally binding promises on the Islamic bank – also allowed by Islamic finance jurists – to buy the property at any time, based on an agreed-upon formula reflecting interest rates and possible penalties for early withdrawal. Although this solution is inferior to the proposal in Chapter 9, based on combining agency and guaranty, it would – at least – allow Islamic banks to fulfill the intermediation function of depositary institutions, albeit by taking Shari'a arbitrage another step forward.

In fact, that step is very likely to occur in the next few years, driven by increased competition for the funds of skeptical and informed middle-class Muslims. Interestingly, as Saeed (1999) argued, taking that extra step may increase the level of skepticism among educated Muslims, as substantive differences between Islamic and conventional finance are blurred further. This may, in turn, give rise to a new wave of "Islamization," built on attacks of excessive laxity of the existing Islamic finance framework. Thus, the cycle restarts with highly inefficient Shariʻa-arbitrage ruses catering to a small conservative market, then becoming more efficient but, for example, losing credibility as competition intensifies. We shall discuss this loss of credibility problem in greater detail later in this chapter.

Hedge-Fund Instruments – Shariʻa-Arbitrage Style

The search for a hedge-fund structure that would be acceptable to the largest possible set of jurists (as well as other diversification vehicles that may improve returns in bear markets, such as REITs) started circa 2000, following the burst of the tech bubble on U.S. exchanges. In recent years there has been significant chatter in Islamic finance circles about Islamic hedge funds. Some were launched reasonably quickly (e.g., as offered by SEDCO in Saudi Arabia), while others took over three years in development (e.g., Sharia Funds of the United States, which relies on UBS Noriba for fund gathering in the GCC). The two cited examples also represent, respectively, Islamic finance veterans who are regional insiders and multinational newcomers to the industry.

Short Sales

The idea of a classical (long/short) hedge fund seemed somewhat natural within Islamic finance. After all, the *salam* contract reviewed in Chapter 5 has a natural short-sale interpretation, both in terms of selling what one does not own at sale time, as well as profitability when spot prices decline (and one can deliver the object of sale by acquiring it at the lower spot price). At various Islamic finance conferences, groups competing to come to market with the first Islamic hedge fund (potentially with significant funds under management) presented their ideas for short sales, ranging from a simple *salam* sale of stocks (without addressing the details of borrowing stocks to execute short sales) to ideas about recharacterization of the process of borrowing such stocks from a primary broker in terms of lease transactions.

Public literature on the exact mechanics used by recently launched Islamic hedge funds is not readily available. That is hardly surprising, since hedge funds generally are not known for their transparency. In fact, as already noted in Chapter 7, even the new screening methods that those hedge funds will use to determine which stocks can serve as underlying assets remain proprietary and secret. Ideas about synthesizing derivatives such as forwards and options also remain well guarded (we were told in jurists' public statements that elements of conventional options exist in *salam* and *ʻurbun* contracts, but no further details were furnished). Needless to say, derivative-based trading strategies have become

indispensable leverage tools for today's hedge-fund managers, especially those restricted in their borrowing behavior, as Islamic hedge-fund managers are likely
to be. Taking into account the inevitable significant increase in Islamic hedge-
fund transaction costs (even compared to conventional hedge-fund costs, which
are high because of the number of active parties required for a simple short sale
transaction), this increased leverage is necessary to generate any reasonable rate of
return to investors.

Of course, synthesizing short sales is not difficult, at least in principle. The
purpose of a short sale is to sell now, collecting the current price p_t. The collected
price grows at the riskless rate r. Tomorrow the short seller needs to buy the stock
to close the short position, which purchase takes place at p_{t+1}. Thus, the short
seller's profit tomorrow is $p_t(1 + r) - p_{t+1} - costs$, where $costs$ cover the interest and dividends paid to the original stock owner, brokerage fees, and the like.
Obviously, the same effect (with different $costs$) could be achieved by engaging
in a forward contract (synthesized from *salam*, through a square transaction such
as the one illustrated in Figure 5.1) with forward price equal to $p_t(1+r)$. In other
words, there is no conceptual mystery as to how short sales can be structured. The
question merely centers around efficiency of the cost structure.

Synthesized Options

There are no conceptual problems regarding the structuring of options either.
In fact, many active participants in Islamic finance have argued that options are
similar both to *salam* and to ʿ*urbun*, perhaps referring to some of the existing
call options synthesized from ʿ*urbun* (e.g., by National Commercial Bank in their
protected principal funds reviewed in Chapter 5). Just as call options can be
synthesized from ʿ*urbun* (down payment) sales, it is equally easy to synthesize call
options from *salam*-long positions with the right to revoke the contract.

Of course, the most profitable (and riskiest) of hedge fund strategies has been
widely compared to writing puts, which is particularly lucrative when the public
are excessively bearish on asset prices. Since we have shown how to synthesize a
forward contract, we simply need to apply the elementary call-put parity structure,
which describes the payoff from a forward contract as the difference between the
payoff from a put option and the payoff from a call option. This simple formula
is used extensively to hedge complex positions in derivatives, and it will no doubt
play a significant role in Islamic hedge funds as well.

10.3 Self-Destructiveness of Shariʿa Arbitrage

The pursuit of Shariʿa-arbitrage profit opportunities contains within its mechanics hidden ruinous dynamics. As can be gleaned from our reviews of various

financial products and services currently offered in Islamic finance, the reader can readily see that "innovation" in Islamic finance has nearly caught up with the conventional sector. In other words, new Shariʿa-arbitrage opportunities that arise from offering new Islamic financial services and products will shortly be limited by the pace of innovation within the conventional sector itself. Shorter lags in bringing conventional innovations to the Islamic finance sector have the undeniable positive effect of improving overall efficiency in the sector. For instance, although Islamic REITs were generally introduced two to three years after their peak profitability (possibly during the downside of their well-documented secular cycle of that asset class), the successor diversification strategy in a bear market will be introduced within months, potentially bearing fruit for Islamic investors.

Declining Shariʿa-Arbitrage Profit Margins

On the other hand, this enhanced efficiency has its downside for the industry. As the gap between Islamic and conventional financial practices continues to shrink, barriers to entry become much more easily surmountable. Early industry players, most of which were indigenous financial institutions in the Islamic world, have already faced growing fierce competition from multinational behemoths such as HSBC, Citi, and UBS. The indigenous providers have been able to survive because of their advantage at the retail level (e.g., National Commercial Bank in Saudi Arabia) and by forging partnerships with the investment banking arms of the multinationals. This has focused the indigenous providers' role on asset gathering, mainly in the GCC region, and mostly for the purpose of investing in Western markets. Needless to say, this specialization at the retail level exposes indigenous Islamic finance providers to declining "terms of trade" in their dealings and competition with multinationals who specialize in the more lucrative investment banking and structuring operations. As those terms of trade worsen for local Islamic financial providers, the overall rents from Shariʿa arbitrage are expected to dwindle as more competitors try to tap this lucrative market.

As competition drives Shariʿa-arbitrage profit margins down, providers – especially the ones that do not share the economies-of-scale advantages of multinational behemoth financial service providers – are likely to pursue cost-cutting measures to remain competitive. The most likely areas for cost cutting are those associated with Shariʿa-arbitrage layering mechanics: costs for the creation of special purpose vehicles, legal fees, and the like. Although the bulk of Islamic financial practice is likely to remain very conservative in those areas, because of the justifiable fears of further scrutiny by anti-money-laundering and criminal-financing agencies, some providers may be less careful and thus fall prey to criminals.

In this regard, it is obvious that a young and relatively obscure industry such as Islamic finance (with the unfortunate "Islamist" stereotypes attached to it in the minds of many) will be judged in the area of combating financial crimes by the practice of its least prudent participants (the weakest links most likely to be abused by financial criminals). In this regard, the inevitable temptation to cut costs by using less reputable law firms, and incorporating SPVs in less reputable and transparent offshore centers, will drive some industry participants to pursue such strategies. To the extent that such strategies in turn increase the risk of a BCCI-type scandal that can prove ruinous to the industry, it would be advisable for industry participants – especially those that do not have economies-of-scale advantages in Shari'a arbitrage – to pursue different strategies that redefine the "Islamic" brand name in terms of such things as community banking and microfinance, as discussed at the end of the book.

Dilution of the "Islamic" Brand Name

Another major effect of "convergence" of Islamic financial practice to conventional finance is the dilution of the industry's "Islamic" brand name. As we have shown in Chapters 1–3, Islamic jurisprudence is in fact a highly adaptive common-law system, despite its constant reference to the fixed canon of Islamic scriptures. We have already reviewed a number of cycles of juristic adaptation to conventional financial practices (e.g., in the areas of secured-loan financing through *murabaha* and *ijara* and fund management with advanced derivative-based strategies). As previous juristic innovations become commonly accepted, and as competitive pressures mount, jurists are likely to continue offering innovations that lead to convergence of Islamic financial practice with its conventional counterpart. This, in turn, will cause disenchantment among potential new customers and existing customers of Islamic finance, as product differentiation between an Islamic product and its conventional counterpart appears increasingly more contrived.

Similarly, this loss of credibility may be driven by a new wave of highly qualified jurists who have not played any significant part in the industry's development to date. Institutions that retain the services of such highly credible jurists may claim that other Islamic finance institutions have in fact gone too far in their innovation. They may thus capture a significant market share by offering less efficient, but more easily defendable, "Islamic" alternatives to conventional financial products. This approach is in fact superior, from a purely economic viewpoint, to replicating the services and products of existing providers of Islamic finance. By segmenting the market into lower-efficiency/higher-credibility versus higher-efficiency/lower-credibility products, the industry can extract more profits, in a manner analogous to price-discriminating monopoly.[5]

This relatively static analysis of industry profitability notwithstanding, the accusatory rhetoric likely to arise from credible jurists (some of which we have already witnessed in recent years) is likely to undermine the overall credibility of the industry among its existing and potential customer base. This credibility crisis is likely to be strongest among the fast-growing Muslim middle-class populations, which we have identified earlier in this chapter as the most important group for future industry growth. In this regard, the industry would be well served by deemphasizing Shariʿa-arbitrage innovations that are likely to undermine its credibility, and instead focusing on developing a positive image based on ethical and developmental considerations that resonate with this growing Muslim middle class, and poor Muslims aspiring to join that middle class, as discussed in the last section of this book.

10.4 Toward a New Islamic Finance Identity

A brilliant recent study on ethical, developmental, and environmental considerations in finance was endorsed by a number of financial institutions. Those institutions were initially invited by United Nations Secretary General Kofi Annan in January 2004 to participate in his initiative on implementing universal principles in business (originally launched in 2000). The study was labeled "Who Cares Wins: Connecting Financial Markets to a Changing World."[6] It provided "recommendations by the financial industry to better integrate environmental, social, and governance issues in analysis, asset management and securities brokerage." The participating institutions provided the following insights that can provide a general framework for a new "Islamic finance" identity:

The institutions endorsing this report are convinced that in a more globalised, interconnected and competitive world the way that environmental, social, and corporate governance issues are managed is part of companies' overall management quality needed to compete successfully. Companies that perform better with regard to these issues can increase shareholder value by, for example, properly managing risks, anticipating regulatory action or accessing new markets, while at the same time contributing to the sustainable development of the societies in which they operate. Moreover, these issues can have strong impact on reputation and brands, an increasingly important part of company value.[7]

Elaborating on this idea of brand-name value based on social and environmental agendas, the report's authors argued that

ESG [environmental, social, and corporate governance] issues can have a strong impact on reputation and brands, an increasingly important part of company value. It is not uncommon that intangible assets, including reputation and brands, represent over two-thirds of total market value of a listed company. It is likely that ESG issues will have an even greater impact on companies' competitiveness and financial performance in the future.[8]

In all three areas of environmental, social and corporate governance, Islamic finance has golden opportunities to redefine the brand name in a manner that enhances its providers' profitability and market value, increases access to the fast-growing potential market segment of middle-class Muslims, and enhances its ability to recruit top-drawer talent from that same market segment for its products. In what follows, we shall review some of the possible features of Islamic finance that are currently underutilized or unutilized in defining the industry's brand name. However, multinational as well as large indigenous Islamic finance institutions are not directly capable of engaging in the poverty alleviation, microfinance, and other socially beneficial activities that are necessary for establishing this new identity and brand name. A network of mutual financial institutions with close ties to religious establishments can perform the necessary intermediation between those institutions' world of high finance and those required social functions.

Macroeconomic Substance: Privatization Sukuk

We have argued in Chapter 6 that asset-based *sukuk* structures can serve two economic functions: (1) They can limit the issuer's indebtedness to the value of its assets, hence minimizing the probability of default or bankruptcy, and (2) they provide a second benchmark for the interest rate paid on the bonds, through market rents of similar properties, which may enable the issuer to borrow at lower rates. Those two sets of benefits to individual corporate and sovereign issuers may be realized only if all borrowing is limited to secured forms (such as *ijara sukuk*, as opposed to commodity-trading-based structures), and if the sold usufruct of underlying assets is marked to market rents, rather than serving merely as a ruse for charging interest rates based only on the issuer's credit rating.

A third advantage of lease- or asset-based *sukuk al-ijara* can be realized at the macroeconomic level. In this regard, it is noteworthy that many of the most active countries in issuing sovereign *sukuk* (e.g., Bahrain, which has been a pioneer in the area) have had their privatization programs stalled for many years. Interestingly, the asset-leasing approach to *sukuk* issuance can solve many of the economic reasons underlying the slowness of privatization programs in various countries.

There are many economic reasons for slow or stalled privatization processes in various developing Islamic countries, including uncertainty about the potential profitability of state-owned enterprises envisioned for privatization and fear of massive and sudden dismissal of public-sector workers by new management.

Overcoming those problems requires preparation of state-owned enterprises for privatization (e.g., collection and dissemination of more accurate information to potential investors, passing appropriate labor law reforms, and putting in place training programs for workers likely to be dismissed). Those steps are costly and difficult, thus requiring some form of precommitment mechanism for the privatizing government.

To date, those precommitment mechanisms have been mostly proposed and enforced by international financial institutions such as the International Monetary Fund. However, most of the GCC countries that are active issuers of *sukuk* (e.g., Bahrain, Qatar) are likely to remain net creditors of the IMF for the foreseeable future. Hence, pressure by such international financial institutions is unlikely to accelerate the privatization processes in those countries – where they are needed to assist in long-term diversification of their economies away from petrochemicals and related industries.

In this regard, lease-based *sukuk* structures can serve as an alternative precommitment mechanism, while simultaneously avoiding thorny Shari'a issues regarding sale-repurchase (*'ina*) or compulsory gift clauses in *sukuk* issues, discussed in detail in earlier chapters. The issuing government can sell its state-owned property (designated for privatization in the medium to long term) to an SPV, which finances the purchase through *sukuk* issuance as done currently. Those *sukuk* would pay fixed interest designated as rent for a period, say, of five to ten years, thus encouraging purchase despite uncertainty about the profitability of the state enterprise that owns that property.

At maturity, instead of selling or giving the property back to the state, the *sukuk* would be made convertible into private shares in the enterprise that had owned the property. In other words, the SPV that was used for issuing *sukuk al-ijara* is not dissolved at maturity. Instead, it becomes the privately held corporation envisioned in the privatization program. Having committed to a privatization time table (term-to-maturity of the issued *sukuk*), the process of information collection, and various reforms to labor and capital structures of the firm, can take place gradually. Indeed, governance of the eventual private corporation can also be done in a smooth manner by allowing a board of directors consisting of government employees and representatives of the *sukuk* holders to oversee the transition.

Mosque-Based Network of Financial Mutuals

Disappointment at the low levels of economic and social development of Muslims worldwide was highlighted in a recent report by the Organization of Islamic Conference and discussed at the opening session of the Conference's meeting in Turkey in November 2004.[9] The problem in the Islamic world is not lack of funds. In fact, banks in the GCC region, as well as in other majority-Muslim countries, have suffered from excessive liquidity, which has generally led to massive increases in all asset prices in the region. Neither is the problem one of lack of desire on the part of wealthy Muslims (and the world community at large) to help poorer Muslims around the world. Indeed, Muslim charities have been faulted mainly for their means of collection and disbursement of funds, but never for lack of resources. The problem, in fact, is one of financial disintermediation in the Islamic world, in which perception about Islamic permissibility of various credit extension schemes may be to blame.

In this regard, while the success of Grameen Bank's microfinance operations in Bangladesh has given many Westerners cause to celebrate, Islamist groups and Islamic finance providers alike have generally criticized Grameen for its social agenda (especially as it pertains to empowerment of women) as well as the relatively high interest rates that it charges on its conventional loans.[10] Some attempts have been made to provide Islamic alternatives, with assistance of institutions such as cash trusts (*waqf*).[11] Such initiatives would be particularly useful, since trusts (*awqaf*) can serve as ideal vehicles for channeling Muslim charitable contributions to subsidize microfinance operations to some of the poorest Muslims around the world. However, those initiatives, as well as socially focused ones that utilize more traditional "Islamic financing" tools such as *murabaha*, remain very few, and they are largely viewed as being on the fringe of Islamic finance.

For "high finance" (Islamic or otherwise) to reach the masses of poor and undereducated Muslims worldwide, intermediation through a network of smaller financial institutions with close social connections to those populations is required. In this regard, our calls for mutuality in Islamic finance (made in Chapters 8 and 9) can provide the formula. Large multinational and indigenous banks can perform their social function by training religious leaders and community members in various Muslim societies to run small-scale thrift institutions (credit unions or mutual banks) and mutual insurance company offices out of at least one mosque in each community. Thus, the extensive network of mosques in the Islamic world can be used to give poorer Muslims access to credit and risk mitigation vehicles, as well as general training on saving and prudent spending and the like. Moreover, since mosque networks have traditionally had a close connection to networks of charitable trusts (*awqaf*) and *zakah*-disbursement organizations, charitable donations can be channeled to the poorer Muslims in the form of financial training and affordable credit and insurance, for example. The actual mechanics of lending and insurance are no obstacle – as we have seen throughout this book.

Appropriate Shari'a-arbitrage schemes may be employed for each region, as necessary, to enable the most underprivileged Muslims to gain access to credit and risk-mitigation vehicles (rather than rent seeking). Sophisticated Muslims will be less likely to shy away from the industry – despite the inefficiency of using juristic ruses – if it fulfilled a valuable social function along those lines. In the meantime, the large indigenous and multinational Islamic financial institutions can continue to fulfill a useful role beyond training, by pooling credit and insurance instruments from the proposed networks of mosque-based credit unions and mutual insurance offices, for placement with socially conscious investors worldwide. Toward achieving those goals, partnerships can be forged between Islamic financial institutions, large multinationals, international financial institutions such as the World Bank and the Islamic Development Bank, and other entities, each providing value based on their own past experience in economic development. Linking charitable giving through the institutions of *zakah* and *awqaf* with the efforts of those international financial consortiums would also ensure applying the best international accounting, regulatory, and enforcement standards, thus allaying many of the current security fears attached to Islamic financial practices.

Positive Screens, Ethical Investment

One of the easiest ways to introduce value to the Islamic finance brand name is to supplement the obvious negative screens discussed in Chapter 8 with some positive screens that contribute to economic development in the Islamic world. Some recent advances, such as Dow Jones' launching an Islamic Market Index for Turkish companies passing the negative screens, are promising. However, to solidify a positive image of Islamic finance, some methodology for balancing negative and positive screens must be developed, so that companies that serve a developmental, educational, or poverty-alleviation role may be allowed to carry more debt/leverage than ones that do not. Needless to say, the manner and extent to which such social and developmental goals are introduced in positive screening can vary significantly between fund managers, allowing for further within-industry brand-name differentiation, as well as customization of social and economic developmental agendas to investors particularly sensitive to specific issues.

Product differentiation through positive social and developmental marketing can also provide indigenous Islamic finance providers with a competitive advantage against the onslaught of multinational financial providers with decisive superiority in mass production of funds based on negative screens. The advantage of indigenous Islamic world financial institutions can be particularly effective when paired with their existing mechanics for distribution of *zakah* for their own companies as well as their Muslim clients. The competitive advantages of those indigenous institutions in establishing domestic trusts (*awqaf*) for charitable and developmental purposes can further enhance their advantage in capturing market share and moving beyond their "asset-gathering" role. Partnerships with multinational investment banks will no doubt remain profitable, given the vast advantage of the latter in know-how and market access. Both types of Islamic finance providers would be well served to develop a positive brand-defining social role.

Conclusion

Islamic finance as it exists today has been shown to reduce economic efficiency by increasing transaction costs, without providing any substantial economic value to its customers. Many have argued that the industry is actually demand driven, and hence jurists and lawyers engaged in Shariʿa arbitrage provide value, by bringing conventional financial products to a market segment that would not have access otherwise. Thus, proponents of that argument assert, Shariʿa-arbitrage mechanisms should be seen as enabling juristic efforts to recharacterize modern financial transactions (*takhrij fiqhi*), rather than legal stratagems to circumvent prohibitions (*hiyal Sharʿiyya*). Moreover, the argument continues, to the extent that Islamic legal restrictions have economic content, the gradual progress of Islamic finance toward increasingly more efficient and more authentically Islamic products will eventually allow the industry to serve the Islamic ideal.

In fact, however, Islamic finance has been largely a supply-driven industry, with jurists who participate actively in Shariʿa arbitrage helping to expand the industry's customer base through indirect advertisement (at various conferences and publications), as well as religious admonishment that Muslims should avoid conventional finance. The form-above-substance juristic approach to Shariʿa arbitrage has also been shown to squander the prudential regulatory content of premodern Islamic jurisprudence, while reducing economic efficiency for customers through spurious transactions, not to mention legal and jurist fees. In addition, as we have argued in Chapter 10, the mechanisms of Shariʿa arbitrage make the industry vulnerable to abuse by criminal financiers, and competitive pressures force the industry to undercut its own grounds for Islamic legitimacy.

As a step toward charting an alternative course for the industry, we have also shown in Chapters 9 and 10 that most of the shortcomings and inherent dangers of Shariʿa-arbitrage behavior – discussed throughout the book – can be minimized by redefining the brand name of Islamic finance in terms of truly religious social and economic developmental goals. Potential customers and financial professionals, on the one hand, and regulators and international bodies fighting financial crime, on the other, will view the industry much more favorably if it is defined primarily by the social goals that it serves, rather than the mechanics of its operation. True success for active participants in the industry can be measured by the extent to which they can integrate those social goals with the mechanics of financial innovation. That, in turn, requires an understanding of the economic reasoning underlying classical jurisprudence, to ensure that developments in the (common-law-like) body of Islamic financial jurisprudence serve substantive ideals, rather than formulaic mechanics.

Toward that end, I have provided in this book a moderately detailed and relatively accessible review of classical Islamic jurisprudence, as well as contemporary interpretations that have led to the current mode of operation in Islamic finance. I have also attempted to shed some light on the economic substance of the classical jurisprudence, with the hope of explaining not only how the industry exists today, but also how it could develop in the future. To the extent that serving the ethical and prudential regulatory substance of Islamic jurisprudence is in fact aligned with the profit motive – through positive identification of the "Islamic" brand name – I hope that the reader found this book to be satisfactory from both the point of view of selfish profit motives, as well as the ethical point of view of selfless contribution to social and economic development. It is my conviction that this is the proper formula through which "Islamic finance" can reach its potential.

Moreover, the ethical and developmental goals discussed above are shared widely by Muslims and non-Muslims alike. Hence, it is clear that once Islamic finance outgrows its formulaic current mode of operation, and assumes a new identity based on substantive and ethical religious tenets, it will no longer need to hide behind the "Islamic" brand name, just as Luther's cobbler needed only to make a good shoe, and to sell it at a fair price, without the need to make or market a "Christian shoe."

Notes

Chapter 1

1 Fordham University's Modern History Sourcebook at www.fordham.edu/halsall/mod/luther-nobility.html.

2 This is possibly an apocryphal story, but it is illustrative nonetheless. Its popularity is illustrated by the fact that evangelical preachers and musical band leaders cite it with equal facility; cf. www.covchurch.org/cov/news/item3369.html and www.ocweekly.com/ink/02/47/music-kane.php, respectively.

3 "Worship" (*'ibada*) in the limited sense would apply only to ritual acts of worship. However, see Ibn Taymiya (2005) for the all-encompassing definitions of the general Islamic concepts of worship and servitude to God: *'ibada* and *'ubudiyya*. The metaphor of society as a single body is also reminiscent of the Prophetic tradition reported by Al-Bukhari and Muslim: "The example of the faithful and their mutual compassion is like the example of a single body – wherein if one part is afflicted with illness, the rest of the body responds with sleeplessness and fever."

4 See, e.g., the quotes of Luther, Calvin, and other leaders of the Christian Reformation on the issues of legitimate interest, usury, and finance; cf. Kerridge (2002). Curiously the Arabic term for indulgences is *sukuk al-ghufran*, or "forgiveness bonds," using the same Arabic term *sukuk*, meaning bonds or debt certificates, that has been used in recent issuances of "Islamic bonds."

5 Not all jurists agree. See, e.g., the argument made by some jurists from Hayderabad in Rida (1986), which aimed to exclude stipulation of interest at the inception of loans (rather than ex post at the time of debt maturity) from the scope of forbidden *riba*. We shall discuss this topic in greater detail in Chapter 3.

6 Document: "THE PRONOUNCEMENT OF THE SHARIA'A [*sic*] ADVISORS" (Section 1. Structure and Mechanism).

7 Law #30 of 2003, published (with corrections) by the official Kuwaiti government newspaper *Al-Kuwait Al-Yawm* (*Kuwait Today*) on June 8, 2003 (issue #619, 49th year), as an amendment to Law #32 of 1968, which dealt with currency, the Central Bank, and regulation of banking practices.

8 Article #86 of the law. All translations in this book are the author's own.

9 Similar provisions regarding Shari'a supervisory boards are central to regulation of Islamic finance in other countries. See, e.g., the Dubai Financial Services Authority (DFSA) regulation for Islamic banks at www.dfsa.ae, and the Bahrain Monetary Agency's at www.bma.gov.bh.

10 Posner (1992, p. 23).

193

11 Posner (1983, p. 33).
12 Qur'an [4:29].
13 Narrated by Al-Bayhaqi and Ibn Majah, and verified by Ibn Hibban on the authority of Abu Sa'id Al-Khudriy.
14 El-Gamal (2003).
15 Literally, Shari'a means "the way" to a watering hole. The term is used more generally to mean "the way of life," but also specifically to mean application of Islamic legal provisions as spelled out in canonical texts and derived therefrom by jurists. The closest analog to the concept of Shari'a is that of Halakah in Judaism. Arbitrage is the practice of exploiting profitable discrepancies between markets, usually by buying a financial product in one market and selling it at a higher price in another. Regulatory arbitrage is the act of restructuring a financial product that is available in one market to make it tradable in another. Shari'a arbitrage is a form of regulatory arbitrage, where the legal restrictions are those perceived to be part of Islamic law.
16 State Bank of Pakistan's Shari'a-Board-approved "Essentials and Model Agreements for Islamic Modes of Financing" are posted at: www.sbp.org.pk/press/Essentials/Essentials-Mod-Agreement.htm.
17 When Central Bank of Kuwait staff are reported to understand Islamic modes of financing well, as reported, e.g., in the International Monetary Fund's Financial Sector Stability Assessment, it is this standardized type that is usually meant; cf. www.imf.org/external/pubs/ft/scr/2004/cr04151.pdf.
18 In fact, the screens can be claimed at best only to ensure Shari'a toleration, rather than compliance: The rule of necessity is fundamental to many of the screens, especially financial ratio criteria. If we were to insist on Shari'a compliance, no company with interest-bearing debt will be allowed in Islamic portfolios. However, the argument goes, that severely restricts the investment opportunities of Muslims, and thus a compromise is reached in terms of "significant" debt or lack thereof, one-third being a convenient benchmark for determining significance, as discussed in Chapter 7.
19 See, e.g., Usmani (1998, pp. 152–3).
20 Rosen (2000, p. 39).
21 Woodbine (1968).
22 Thomas (1949).
23 Makdisi (1999). For instance, the consideration that properties owed in the action of debt (i.e., established as a liability on another) are owned by the creditor did not exist in Roman law (which required receipt before ownership was established). Makdisi (1999, pp. 1676–96) asserted that this development appeared in England around the time of extensive English-Muslim mercantile activity in the Mediterranean. This development made it possible for ownership transfer to occur at the time a contract is concluded (through offer and acceptance), which is maintained to be the case under Islamic law. Makdisi further argued that King Roger II (ruled 1130–54 C.E.) was influenced by Islamic transactions law during his tenure in Sicily. He argued that this influence continued through the tenure of King Henry II (ruled 1154–89) and was subsequently reflected in Anglo-American common law. The influence of Islamic law on British and U.S. common laws extends beyond the substantive laws adopted by the latter. Makdisi further traced the roots of the British jury system, hailed as one of the greatest achievements of Western law, to the Islamic institution of *lafif*, drawing parallels between selection methods and authority of jury in both systems.
24 Arabi (2001, pp. 21, 39–42, 63–5).
25 Hill, "Al-Sanhuri, 'Abd Al Razzaq," in Bosworth et al. (1997, vol. 9, pp. 18–19).
26 As quoted in Arabi (2001, p. 196).
27 Usmani (1998, p. 237).

28 Al-Shafiʿi (1939, p. 477).
29 See Cooter and Ulen (2004, pp. 60–3) for a discussion of the similarities between U.S. common-law and civil-law systems, especially in areas wherein both systems adhere to specific legal texts (such as the Uniform Commercial Code, which makes commercial laws relatively uniform across states). On the importance of reasoning by analogy and reliance on precedent in Anglo-American common law, see Posner (1990, pp. 86–100). Hallaq (1997) is an excellent source on the evolution of reasoning by analogy as a central methodology of Islamic jurisprudence. Masud, Messick, and Powers (1996, pp. 20–6) provide an excellent summary of the educational process for prospective jurist/muftis, especially with regard to their ability to exercise reasoning by analogy.
30 For instance, see Uzair (1955) and Siddiqi (1983).
31 See www.sistani.org/html/ara/menu/2/books/2/inside/192.htm. *Iqtirad* literally means borrowing. The various *fatawa* on banking are provided at www.sistani.org. The English answer on mortgages only states that the intention should not be borrowing. The Arabic answer goes further, by specifying that the intention should be "*istinqadh*" rather than "*iqtirad.*" The former is a term meaning "deliverance" or "salvaging." It is not clear what that intention should be. Perhaps that is why the English version was left vague.
32 However, this and later *fatawa*, e.g., listed at www.islamonline.net, restrict the permissibility to cases of unavailability of Islamic alternatives synthesized through sales or leases.
33 www.sistani.org/html/ara/menu/3/28.html.
34 The interested reader can follow daily Islamic finance news on sources such as www.zawya.com, which reports daily on new *sukuk* issuance and other activities in a section dedicated to Islamic finance news, www.islamicfi.com, and other portals.
35 In this regard, a brief review of the etymology of "*sukuk*" is illustrative: The singular of *sukuk* is *sakk*, meaning written documentation of financial liability. Most historians maintain that the Arabic term "*sakk*" is the root of the French/English "cheque" or "check"; cf. Ibn Manzur (1992) and Qalʿa-Ji (1996). Indeed, Baʿalbaki and Baʿalbaki (1998), a popular English-Arabic dictionary, translates the English "bond" as both "*sanad*" (the conventional Arabic word for government and corporate bonds, plural "*sanadat*"), as well as "*sakk.*"
36 Interestingly, in two celebrated cases, provisions regarding adherence to Shariʿa clashed with secular legal systems (English law): Islamic Investment Company of the Gulf v. Symphony Gems NV (2002), and Beximco Pharmaceuticals v. Shamil Bank of Bahain EC (2004). In both cases, English law was determined to be relevant and "Shariʿa" issues were considered nugatory, since the provisions did not stipulate applying the law of any recognized sovereign state.
37 See the U.S. Senate on Foreign Relations' task force report on the BCCI affair at www.fas.org/irp/congress/1992_rpt/bcci/. A significant number of BCCI investors were in fact significant contributors to Islamic finance. Reported involvement of Islamic banking luminaries in the "golden chain" that financed terrorist attacks – fair or unfair as they may be – further raise the reputational risk in the industry; cf. schumer.senate.gov/SchumerWebsite/pressroom/press_releases/PR01566.html.

Chapter 2

1 The Qur'an also refers to other scriptures as "The Book," e.g., the expression "*ahl al-kitab*" (People of the Book) refers to Jews, Christians, and Magus-Zaroastrians. Islamic scholars and Islamist groups alike often refer to the Qur'an as "the Islamic

constitution." For instance, Hassan Al-Banna, founder of the earliest contemporary Islamist movement, "the Muslim Brotherhood," expressed the dictum "Islam is creed and worship, fatherland and nationality, religion and state, spirituality and action, Qur'an and sword," in the context of which Islamists maintain to this day that "the Qur'an is our constitution"; cf. Delanoue, G. "Al-Ikhwan Al-Muslimun," in Lewis et al. (1986, vol. 3, pp. 1068–71).

2 In this regard, earlier verses of the Qur'an contained very little legal content, the latter increasing significantly over the last ten years of the Prophet's life, wherein the first Islamic society was formed after the Prophet's migration from Makka to Madina circa 622 C.E.; cf. Hallaq (1997, pp. 3–7).

3 Unfortunately, the rhetoric that gives rise to statements such as "the Qur'an forbids interest" stems from reading Qur'anic translations and/or commentaries that are heavily colored by the authors' own economic analyses. For instance, most translations up to the early twentieth century C.E. translated one of the verses of *riba* as "Allah has permitted trade and forbidden usury," whereas translations post the writings of Abu Al-A'la Al-Mawdudi as "forbidden interest." Exegeses and commentaries similarly impose specific understandings of the general Qur'anic term *riba*, thus giving uninitiated readers the impression that the "prohibition of interest" is very clear and explicit. We shall see in Chapter 3 that, in fact, there are forms of interest that are not considered *riba* (e.g., in credit sales and leases), as well as forms of *riba* that are not considered interest (e.g., so-called *riba al-fadl* in hand-to-hand trade with no time component). Moreover, we shall see that jurists of all major schools of jurisprudence recognized that compensation for time value of money is permitted, and warranted, in contracts such as credit sales and leases. Properly understanding what was forbidden, and why, will take us a long way toward fulfilling our quest for efficiency and logic in Islamic finance.

4 Al-Zarqa (1998, vol. 1, p. 74).

5 Literally, "*Sunna*" means norm, rule, law, custom, practice, usage, convention, tradition; Ba'albaki and Ba'albaki (1996).

6 An expert in one branch of Prophetic *Sunna* may not be an expert in another. Thus, Al-Zarqa (1998, vol. 1, p. 75, footnote) cites statements that establish Sufyan Al-Thawri as an expert on Prophetic sayings but not on Prophetic actions, Al-Awza'i as an expert on the latter but not the former, and Malik as an expert on both.

7 Al-Shafi'i (1939, pp. 32–3, 96–103) argued that Prophetic sayings and actions "illustrate the general principles stated in the Qur'an, explain its difficult passages, restrict the domain of its general legal pronouncements, and provide legislation on issues not mentioned therein." For proof, he referred to many verses in the Qur'an, including: "O people of faith! Obey God, and obey the Messenger" [4:59]; "Obey God, and obey the Messenger" [5:92]; "So establish regular prayer, and give regular charity, and obey the Messenger, that you may receive mercy" [24:56]; "O people of faith! Obey God, and obey the Messenger, and make not vain your deeds" [47:33]; "So obey God, and obey His Messenger: if you turn back, the duty of Our Messenger is but to proclaim [the Message] clearly and openly" [64:12]. Hallaq (1993) challenged the commonly held belief that Al-Shafi'i (1939) ushered the inception of formal Islamic legal theory. He concluded from classical citations that this work was largely ignored for at least a century, and argued that the synthesis between traditionists (who wished to restrict Islamic jurisprudence to interpretation of the canonical texts) and rationalists (who wished to depend on general Qur'anic principles and legislate based on logical inference) was attained only a century later by the next generation of Shafi'i jurists such as Ibn Surayj; cf. Hallaq (1997, pp. 30–5).

8 Al-Shafi'i's (1939, pp. 471–6, 1309–20) proof for the canonization of consensus

relied on two arguments: (1) most rulings on which Muslims reached a consensus were derived from the *Sunna*, directly (through a narrated tradition) or indirectly, and (2) even if there is no underlying support from the *Sunna*, the Prophet ordered Muslims to adhere to the community, and thus "whoever agrees with the Muslim community is among them, and whoever disagrees with them thus disobeys [Divine and Prophetic] commands to adhere to the community." Moreover, verse [4:115] states: "whosoever contends with the Messenger after recognizing guidance, and follows a path other than that of the believers, we shall leave him on that path, and land him in hell, what an evil refuge." Also, Ibn Dawud, Ibn Majah, and Al-Tirmidhi narrated a Prophetic tradition: "My nation [of Muslims] will never reach a wrong consensus." Dr. Mustafa Al-Zarqa (1998, vol. 1, p. 77) also argued that true consensus implies that there must be a canonical textual foundation for the ruling, as "it is unfathomable that all respected scholars of the Muslim community would reach the same conclusion without proof from a canonical text." However, he argued, citation of that underlying canonical text is not required to establish authoritativeness of consensus rulings. For instance, he argued, the commission to manufacture contract (*istisna'*, discussed in later chapters) was legalized only by consensus, without direct reference to canonical texts.

9 Al-Zarqa (1998, vol. 1, p. 77).

10 Al-Zarqa (1998, vol. 1, p. 153); "It is very important to distinguish between what we call "Islamic Law (Shari'a)" and what we call 'Islamic Jurisprudence (*fiqh*)'. The former consists of the texts of the Qur'an, which was revealed to the Prophet Muhammad, and the Prophetic *Sunna*. ... In contrast, jurisprudence (*fiqh*) is what scholars understand of the legal canonical texts, and what they infer thereof. ... It is not appropriate to confuse the two, since Shari'a is immutable, and Islamic creed deems it all good and valid. ... In contrast, *fiqh* is the work of jurists ... one of whom may have a different understanding from the other. ... Thus, the jurist's understanding, even if based on the canonical texts, is open to debate and evaluation."

11 Adherents to his dominant methodology declare that "whoever exercises juristic approbation thus legislates." Within the Islamic context, only God has legislative powers, and thus condemnation of jurists who "legislate" are quire severe.

12 See, e.g., Calder (1980) and the references therein.

13 Al-Zarqa (1998, vol. 1, pp. 88, 90–1, 96).

14 See Ibn Rushd (1997, vol. 2, p. 154). Jurists generally continued to justify the use of juristic approbation and benefit analysis based on Qur'anic verses asserting that the objective of religious Law is to guard benefits and prevent harm. Among those verses: "God intends for you facility and not difficulty" [2:185], and "He has chosen you, and has imposed no difficulties upon you" [22:78]. They also relied on Prophetic tradition that "no individual or mutual harm is allowed" [by Law] ("*La darara wa la dirar*"), narrated by Al-Nawawi, Malik, Ibn Majah, and Al-Daraqutni. Finally, they cited actions by the Prophet's companion and second Caliph 'Umar ibn Al-Khattab wherein he used juristic approbation to overrule explicit Qur'anic rules of inheritance; cf. Al-Zarqa (1998, vol. 1, p. 97).

15 Al-Zarqa (1998, vol. 1, pp. 106–10).

16 See Al-Zarqa (1998, vol. 1, pp. 127–35).

17 For instance, the prominent Hanafi scholar Muhammad Al-Shaybani (d. 189 A.H./804 C.E.) stated that this transaction is "as reprehensible to my heart as mountains are large; it was invented by those who devour *riba*"; cf. Al-Zuhayli (2003, vol. 1, p. 115).

18 Khallaf (1972, p. 141).

19 Al-Zarqa (1998, vol. 1, p. 145), Khallaf (1972, pp. 145–9). Moreover, I have

counted 130 references to rulings justified by '*urf* in the Hanafi Al-Sarakhsi's *Al-Mabsut*, 95 references in the Hanafi Al-Kasani's *Bada'i' Al-Sana'i'*, 237 references in the Hanafi Ibn 'Abidin's *Hashiyat Radd Al-Muhtar* (which is the main source for the Ottoman *Majalla*, and a favorite – often only – reference used by Justice M. Taqi Usmani to justify current practice in Islamic finance), 1,182 references in the Maliki Al-Kharshi's *Sharh Mukhtasar Khalil*, 60 references in the Shafi'i Al-Nawawi's *Al-Majmu'* (completed by Taqiyyuddin Al-Subki), and 102 references in the Hanbali Ibn Qudama's *Al-Mughni*. It is particularly interesting that most of those references to customary practice pertained to rules of credit sales (*murabaha*) and leases (*ijara*), which are the most dominant tools of contemporary Islamic finance.

20 Likewise, Ibn Al-Humam stated in *Fath Al-Qadir* that "customary practice is legally equivalent to juristic consensus in the absence of canonical texts." Moreover, this canonization of customary practice is only temporary, and subject to change when customary practice changes.

21 Al-Zarqa (1998, vol. 2, pp. 884, 903–59, 894–5).

22 See Al-Zarqa (1998, vol. 1, pp. 159–256), Al-Zuhayli (1997, vol. 1, pp. 42–61), or Coulson (1994).

23 For instance, the second Caliph, 'Umar ibn Al-Khattab, issued a number of rulings that apparently suspended the implementation of Qur'anic Law. Prominent examples include the suspension of alms payment to newly converted Muslims and friendly non-Muslims, suspension of amputation of thieves' hands during a famine year, and refusal to distribute conquered farm land as booty, establishing them as public property instead. Those precedents, and others agreed upon by Prophetic companions, became canonized as consensus of the early Muslim community. Note: Jurists and legal theorists are careful to say that 'Umar ruled only that the law did not apply in specific instances. For instance, he reasoned that most thieves during the drought may have been stealing merely to survive. This level of doubt prevented the application of the Qur'anic penalty of amputation, which does not apply to one who stole food to avoid starvation.

24 The eight main schools of jurisprudence are the following:

1. The Hanafi school is named after the Iraqi merchant and jurist Abu Hanifa Al-Nu'man (d. 126 A.H./744 C.E.). Two of his closest students/associates are commonly considered to be cofounders of the school: Abu Yusuf (d. 182 A.H./798 C.E.) and Muhammad Al-Shaybani (d. 189 A.H./804 C.E.). It is known for rigorous analogy, as well as frequent use of juristic approbation. This school remains dominant in India, Pakistan, Afghanistan, and regions that had adopted the Ottoman *Majalla*.

2. The Maliki school is named after the Madina jurist and traditionist Malik ibn Anas (d. 179 A.H./795 C.E.). It is known for emphasis on Prophetic traditions and practice of the early Madina community. Its jurists appealed to consensus, analogy, approbation (esp. to forbid stratagems), and benefit analysis. It continues to dominate in many parts of Africa (including upper Egypt).

3. The Shafi'i school is named after Muhammad ibn Idris Al-Shafi'i (d. 204 A.H./819 C.E.), who studied with Malik and the Hanafi Al-Shaybani. His synthesis subordinated analogical reasoning only to Qur'an and *Sunna*, and rejected juristic approbation and benefit analysis. This school continues to dominate in lower Egypt, the Levant, and Malaysia.

4. The Hanbali school is named after Ahmad ibn Hanbal (d. 241 A.H./855 C.E.), an Iraqi traditionist who studied with Al-Shafi'i. This school emphasized Prophetic tradition more than the Shafi'is, ranking weak traditions above valid analogies. It continues to dominate in GCC countries.

5. The Zahiri school is named after its methodology of following the apparent (*zahir*) meaning of canonical texts, otherwise giving jurists full freedom. Its star was the Andalusian jurist Ibn Hazm (d. 454 A.H./1062 C.E.). The school has few adherents today.

6. The Ja'fari (or Imami) school is named after the Shi'i Imam Ja'far Al-Sadiq (d. 148 A.H./765 C.E.). Its methodology is very similar to that of the Shafi'i school. It dominates today in Iraq, Iran, and most other majority-Shi'i countries.

7. The Zaydi school is named after the Shi'i Imam Zayd ibn 'Ali Zayn-al-'Abidin (d. 122 A.H./740 C.E.), great-grandson of the Prophet. This school values rational analysis highly and variously uses analogy, approbation, and benefit analysis.

8. The Ibadi school is named after 'Abdullah ibn Ibad (d. 80 A.H./699 C.E.). This school also uses all methods of juristic inference, including analogy, approbation, and benefit analysis. It dominates in Oman and some East and North African countries.

25 An abbreviated taxonomy is provided by Zuhayli (1997, vol. 1, pp. 62–4). Hallaq (2001, pp. 1–23) provides a thorough survey of various juristic taxonomies. The main thesis of Hallaq (2001) is that truly independent jurists may never have existed. He argued that their addition to the taxonomy was necessary for authoritativeness of lower-category jurists. Thus, the fiction of independent jurists was created by attributing earlier and later opinions and principles to designated prominent jurists. Hallaq (1984) also questioned the received wisdom that the gates of *ijtihad* were closed after the fourth century A.H.; cf. Abu Zahra (1996, pp. 42–4). Rather, Hallaq argued, jurists adopted only the rhetoric of more dependent jurists, while some continued to exercise relatively independent inference.

26 Al-Zarqa (1998, vol. 1, pp. 225–6, 243).

27 Arabi (2001, p. 195).

28 In addition to the agenda setting questions raised in this section, Hegazy (2005) poses interesting questions regarding conflicts of interest and the legitimacy of eliciting *fatawa* from jurists who receive financial compensation from the elicitor. He also raises questions about the manipulability of the institution of *fatwa* to devise legal stratagems, which are similar to the questions I raise here about agenda setting.

29 'Atiyyah (1986).

30 A number of depositaries of public finance *fatawa* are available; e.g., see www.islamicfi.com/arabic/fatwa/index.asp, or fatawa.al-islam.com.

31 For instance, a number of recent providers of Islamic REITs would not reveal their specific screening rules for debt ratios (it is well known that optimal leverage rates for REITs would dictate roughly 50 percent debt-to-assets ratios, which is significantly higher than allowed debt levels in Islamic mutual funds).

32 In Chapter 9 we shall argue that regulators care about macrostability and bankers care about risk and return, whereas religious law attempts to protect individuals from their own poor decisions.

33 The material in this section is gleaned from three main sources by three of the most eminent jurist-scholars in the area of financial transactions in the current era, who have addressed those topics directly and exhaustively: Professors Muhammad Abu Zahra (1996), Mustafa Al-Zarqa (1998, vol. 1, pp. 333–647), and Wahba Al-Zuhayli (1997, vol. 4, pp. 2875–3271).

34 Corporations were adopted in the Islamic world by Al-Azhar jurists in the mid-twentieth century C.E. Kuran (2003, 2004b,c) identifies limitations on classical Islamic partnerships – which were dissolved, e.g., on the death of any partner – along with inheritance laws that favored partitioning estates as reasons for the Islamic world's relative decline in Mediterranean trade after the thirteenth century.

Corporations allowed for scale economies, persistence, and capital accumulation that traditional partnerships could not.

35 On the other hand, the majority of non-Hanafi jurists accepted certain types of legal rights and services, such as usufruct of a house or machine, as eligible property, thus considering lease in part as sale of usufruct, as we shall note below. The two sets of conditions are not unrelated, as the contract known as *ijar* or *ijara* applied to both hiring workers and leasing property.

36 However, cash *waqf* were established in the late nineteenth century as prototype banks in some Ottoman-ruled areas and have acquired new popularity in Bangladesh and elsewhere as vehicles of Islamic financial intermediation.

37 Ignoring easement rights, preemption rights, etc., which constitute limitations on every ownership.

38 Abu Ghuddah and Khuja (1997a, *fatwa* 6/4, pp. 84–7). Needless to say, the 1990 structure is more efficient, and closer to conventional mortgage practice, with all implied protections of bank-customer interests. Maliki jurists pointed out that ownership of usufruct is more general than a mere right of usage, since the owner of usufruct – if he is not restricted by lease conditions – may be entitled to transfer ownership of the usufruct to a third party, e.g., by subletting the property.

39 Otherwise, classical jurists ruled that if different lessees utilize property differently, then lessor permission should be obtained prior to transferring usufruct rights. Naturally, similarity of usage may be imposed through covenants in the initial lease, thus making it impossible for a blacksmith, e.g., to use one of the Makka residential units as a metalwork shop. However, the requirement does limit the scope of utilization of this structure, e.g., for industrial parks, where different lessees may produce different amounts of pollutants, and so on.

40 Search dictionary.lp.findlaw.com for the noun "mortgage."

41 Many Prophetic traditions emphasize this condition, including "I shall meet God before I give anyone something owned by another without his consent, for trade requires mutual consent" (narrated by Al-Bayhaqi and Ibn Majah, and verified by Ibn Hibban, on the authority of Abu Sa'id Al-Khudriy); "Trade, and options thereof, require mutual consent" (narrated by 'Abdal-Razzaq in *Al-Jami'* on the authority of 'Abdullah ibn Abi Awfa); "No two should part [after a trade] without mutual agreement" (narrated by Abu Dawud and Al-Tirmidhi on the authority of Abu Hurayrah).

42 The term *qard*, derived from the past tense *qarada*, means cut-off piece, since the lender (*muqrid*) cuts off a piece of his property and gives it to the borrower (*muqtarid*). It is a contract of exchange: The Hanafis define it as an exchange of a certain amount of fungible property now for an equal amount of fungible property in the future. The other schools define it as an exchange of a certain amount of fungible property now in exchange for a liability (debt) established on the borrower. Abu Hanifa and Muhammad Al-Shaybani ruled that ownership of lent property is transferred from lender to borrower on receipt, whereas Abu Yusuf held the minority opinion that the lender retains ownership as long as the lent property is not consumed. Most Shafi'is and Hanbalis agreed with the majority Hanafi view that ownership is transferred from lender to borrower on receipt. The Malikis ruled that ownership of lent property is transferred to the borrower through the contract, i.e., before receipt. They used this ruling to conclude that returning the exact borrowed property may not be allowed if the property had changed – since it was exchanged for a liability for equal amount. See Al-Zuhayli (2003, vol. 1, pp. 373–4).

43 As quoted and analyzed by Al-Raysuni (1997, p. 129).

44 To the extent that two legitimate sales are concluded to circumvent the prohibition of

riba, Shafiʿi and Zahiri jurists reasoned, that is a matter of intention, and they could not rule on validity based on perceived intention. This analysis would suggest that classical nominate contracts should play a minor role in contemporary Islamic jurisprudence. In contrast, Maliki jurists, in addition to acceptance of canonical prohibition of same-item sale-repurchase, relied on their juristic principle of considering components of the exchange, rather than contract names. If the transaction resulted in the same economic substance of an interest-based loan, they argued, it must have the same legal status of prohibition.

45 Ibn Taymiyya (1998, vol. 3).

Chapter 3

1 This fundamental benefit-oriented view of divine legislation is central to the Islamic legal theory, e.g., of Al-Ghazali and Al-Shatibi; cf. Al-Raysuni (1997).

2 This prohibition is based on one interpretation of the Prophetic tradition that forbids conjoining the "two sales in one." This tradition is cited and discussed in greater detail in Chapter 4.

3 The term is also synonymous with the Hebrew name for forbidden usury: *ribit* or *ribis*; cf. Stern (1982), Reisman (1995).

4 Al-Jaziri (1986). We shall argue in this chapter that the forbidden *riba* is not the same as interest. Biblical scholars have also recognized the difference between legitimate interest, which is proper compensation for time, etc., and usury, which is profit made for the sheer act of credit extension; cf. Kerridge (2002).

5 The first study in Rida (1986) was a letter sent to Rashid Rida, soliciting his opinion on a *fatwa* by unnamed jurists from Hayderabad, stipulating that the forbidden *riba* is mentioned in the Qurʾan only in abstract form, requiring explanation from Prophetic traditions. The jurists' analysis then concluded that the forbidden *riba* does not apply to interest stipulated at the inception of loans – which Abu Hanifa deemed only reprehensible, and thus could not have considered a form of the forbidden *riba*. Rida's own analysis stops short of declaring such interest as non-*riba*. However, he did make it clear that the definitively forbidden *riba* was interest on matured debts, especially interest on interest.

6 The etymological root of *nasiʾa* is the three-letter past-tense verb *nasiya*, which means to defer (also to forget), implying that this type of *riba* occurs in time, i.e., through deferment of payments.

7 See Al-Qurtubi (1996, vol. 3, p. 235), exegesis of verse [2:364]. The Qurʾan recognized this prohibition as Biblical, chastising Jews who devoured *riba* (Hebrew: *ribit*) despite that prohibition in verse [4:161]. Muslim writers often emphasized the Biblical prohibition of *riba* /*ribit*, especially in [Exodus 22:25], [Leviticus 25:34–46], [Deutronomy 23:19–20], and [Luke 6:27–36]. Talmudic Rabbinic literature, as well as Catholic councils elaborated on this prohibition. Talmudic literature restricted the prohibition to intrafaith interest-based lending (cf. *Bava Metzia* 70b–71a), but Maimonides (*Laws of Loans*, ch. 5, Law 2) further restricted interest-based lending to non-Jews to the extent dictated by necessity. Catholic doctrine also upheld the prohibition starting with the First Council of Carthage (345 C.E.) until the Fourth Lateran Council (1215 C.E.), during which Jews were allowed to charge interest at nonexorbitant (usurious) levels. Post-Calvin developments redefined "usury" in terms of interest-rate ceilings. This prohibition of usury as exorbitant interest predates Mosaic Law. The code of Hammurabi (circa 2100 B.C.E.) set interest-rate ceilings of 33 percent and 20 percent on in-kind loans. Ancient Indian law allowed interest charges to accumulate only up to the point of doubling the principal.

8 Qurtubi (1996, vol. 4, p. 130).

9 Al-Zuhayli (1997, vol. 5, p. 3713).

10 See, e.g., the lengthy list of quotations from prominent jurists of all major schools in Al-Misri (1997, pp. 39–48).

11 Reported by Muslim on the authority of Abu Sa'id Al-Khudriy.

12 See De Roover (1999).

13 Narrated by Al-Bukhari and Muslim on the authority of Usama.

14 Al-Zuhayli (1997, vol. 5, p. 3703).

15 Al-Zuhayli (1997, vol. 5, pp. 3708, 3724–5, 3737–9).

16 Ibn Rushd (1997, vol. 3, p. 184).

17 Of course, lacking the tools of calculus, which were only developed six centuries later, he could not speak of marginal utilities and hence spoke only of "benefits." However, the economic idea is still the same: Equity dictates equality of amount when trading fungibles of the same genus, and equality of value when trading nonfungibles or goods of different genera.

18 Reported by Al-Bukhari. In variants of this tradition, reported by Muslim and Al-Nasa'i, Abu Sa'id Al-Kudriy narrated that it was Bilal who traded two volumes of lower-quality dates for one volume of higher-quality ones, which he gave to the Prophet.

19 For a lengthy list of references on this literature, and a mathematical model of harmful borrowing behavior based on the empirical facts therein, see El-Gamal (2000).

20 That is the meaning of the phrase *qard hasan* (a goodly or beautiful loan), which is the only form of loan discussed in the Qur'an. In Qur'anic verses [2:245], [5:12], [57:11], [57:18], [64:17], and [73:20] dealing with loans, the indicated "borrower" in charitable and goodly works (characterized as loans) is God, who multiplies the loan value manifold.

21 For this and many classical definitions of *gharar* that highlight variously types of deception, random events, and incompleteness of contract language, see Al-Zuhayli (1997, vol. 5, pp. 2408–3411).

22 Those examples include pebble sales, as well as sales of the catch of a diver, fish in the sea, birds in the sky, the sperm and unfertilized eggs of camels, an unborn calf in its mother's womb, etc.

23 Al-Darir (1997), Al-Zuhayli (1997, vol. 5, pp. 3415–31), and El-Gamal (2001).

24 Instead of selling the catch of a diver, which is not known, the potential buyer can simply hire the diver for the period of time of one catch, thus buying a known amount of labor and avoiding the violation of rules of *gharar* sales.

25 Al-Baji Al-Andalusi (n.d.).

26 Al-Subki, continuation of Al-Nawawi (n.d., vol. 9).

27 Ibn Taymiyya (1998, vol. 4).

28 The literal meaning of the term *gharar* according to Qadi 'Iyad is "That which has a pleasant appearance and a hated essence"; cf. Al-Qarafi (n.d., vol. 3, p. 266). The origin of the term is the three-letter past-tense verb "*gharra*," meaning "to deceive."

29 Kuwait Awqaf Ministry (1995, vol. 21, "*gharar*"). Other special cases include sale of possibly undeliverable goods (e.g., birds in the sky) or goods that may not exist at delivery time (e.g., unborn calf).

30 For a formal mathematical illustration of the argument in this section, and references to the underlying literature on boundedly rational decision making under risk and uncertainty, see El-Gamal (2001). Likewise, the companion paper El-Gamal (2000) develops a formal model for dynamic inconsistency in borrowing, and the usefulness of Shari'a constraints as potential precommitment mechanisms.

31 A survey is provided in Camerer (1998).

32 For instance, Fox, Rogers, and Tversky (1996) showed that professional options traders exhibit the same type of behavior as students recruited as subjects in laboratory experiments. However, results in List (2004) suggest that subjects with extensive market experience may in fact learn to act in accordance with neoclassical economic theory.

33 Dr. Yusuf Al-Qaradawi, who described himself as one of the early supporters of Islamic banking, recently criticized many developments in the industry quite harshly. He was particularly critical of *tawarruq*, which is a natural extension of traditional *murabaha* financing; cf. http://www.qaradawi.net/site/topics/article.asp? cu_no=2&item_no=4142&version=1&template_id=119&parent_id=13.

Chapter 4

1 Of course, if this behavior becomes prevalent, elimination of transaction costs on multiple trades within a short period of time can encourage "property flipping," which in turn can feed speculative bubbles in real estate.

2 This tradition was reported by Al-Bukhari and Muslim and considered by Ibn Rushd to be one of the most authoritative Prophetic traditions available.

3 For general treatment of conditions in sale, see Al-Zuhayli (2003, vol. 1, ch. 2, pp. 13–50).

4 Notable exceptions are dominance of the Shafi'i school in Malaysia and Shi'i jurisprudence in Iran. However, as we have argued in previous chapters, the dominance of the Hanafi school based on its codification by the Ottomans, and the Hanbali school based on its dominance in the GCC, where most Islamic finance is funded, continues to define the industry. Thus, Vogel and Hayes (1988) appropriately restricted their attention to those two schools.

5 See moamlat.al-islam.com (in Arabic; search for "*bay' al-fuḍūlī*.").

6 For general and school-specific conditions on trust sales, see Al-Zuhayli (2003, vol. 1, ch. 11, pp. 353–66).

7 Reported by Malik in his *Muwatta'* on the authority of 'Abdullah ibn 'Umar ibn Al-Khattab, and by Ahmad, Al-Bukhari, and Muslim on the authority of Abu Sa'id al-Khudriy.

8 See Al-Zuhayli (2003, vol. 1, pp. 287–8).

9 Al-Zuhayli (2003, vol. 1, pp. 290–1).

10 De Roover (1999).

11 Search fatawa.al-islam.com (in Arabic) search for "*platīn*."

12 See Al-Zuhayli (2003, vol. 1, p. 14).

13 The term "*'ina*" literally means "the very same item." For the ensuing discussion of juristic opinions on same-item sale-repurchase, see Al-Zuhayli (2003, vol. 1, pp. 114–17).

14 Ahmad narrated that Al-'Aliyah bint Ayfa' said, "The wife of Zayd, the mother of his child, and I visited 'A'isha. The mother of his child said: "I sold a slave to Zayd ibn Arqam in exchange for 800 Dirhams deferred, then I bought him back for 600 Dirhams in cash." 'A'isha said, "Woe to what you sold and bought. Tell Zayd that he has voided his *jihad* with the Prophet, unless he repents." Other jurists rejected this tradition based on a missing link in its chain of narrators. Ahmad and Abu Dawud narrated on the authority of Ibn 'Umar that the Prophet said, "When people are miserly with their Dinars and Dirhams, trade in *'ina*, follow cows' tails, and leave striving in the cause of God, then God will send unto them a suffering that He will not lift until they rediscover their religion." The authenticity of this tradition is also questioned by other jurists.

15 In this regard, it is noteworthy that reprehension (*karaha*) for Hanafis is much worse than for other schools, since they deem performing reprehensible actions as sufficient grounds for Muslims to be deprived of the Prophet's intercession on the day of judgment.

16 Ibn Qayyim Al-Jawziyya (n.d., vol. 3, p. 135).

17 Ibn Taymiyya (1998, vol. 4, p. 399).

18 Kuwait Awqaf Ministry (ongoing, "*bay' al-wafa'*").

Chapter 5

1 For full lists of classical *salam* conditions in various schools of jurisprudence, see Al-Zuhayli (2003, vol. 1, pp. 239–56).

2 In classical language, the *salam* buyer is called *rabb al-salam* or *al-muslim*, the *salam* seller is called *al-muslam ilayhi*, the object of *salam* is called *al-muslam fihi*, and the price of *salam* is called *ra'su mal al-salam*, or *salam* capital. I shall use more contemporary terminology for forward and futures contracts, calling the salam seller the *salam*-short and the *salam* buyer the *salam*-long.

3 Narrated by Al-Daraqutni on the authority of Ibn 'Umar. Other variations on this narration were reported by Abu Dawud and others.

4 Al-Zuhayli (2003, vol. 1, p. 258).

5 Such exoneration is a dropping of the salam-long's right, which is generally permitted; cf. Al-Zuhayli (2003, vol. 1, pp. 259–60).

6 This opinion was reported, without endorsement, by AAOIFI for its *salam* standard, based on the opinion of Dr. Al-Darir; cf. AAOIFI (2000, p. 287).

7 I utilize the methodology of quoting multiple *fatawa* three times in this book, of which this is the first. This exercise clearly illustrates the manipulative approach to Shari'a arbitrage. To use a humorous analogy: instead of asking if one can smoke while supplicating to God, one may ask if one can pray at all times, even while smoking! Comparing those *fatawa* side by side clearly illustrates the first-mover advantage that bankers enjoy, and their consequent ability to formulate Islamic jurisprudence, as discussed in Chapter 1.

8 See fatawa.al-islam.com (in Arabic; search for "*al-salam al-muwazi*").

9 See Al-Zuhayli (2003, vol. 1, pp. 109–10). They called this type of sale *al-bay' al-mudaf* (appended sale) and gave as an example of such sales the language: "I have sold you this item for so-much at the beginning of the next month."

10 See Kamali (2000).

11 See Kalamli (2000, p. 241) for various classical arguments against deferment of the price.

12 The tradition they quote states that "The Messenger of God forbade *gharar* sales, trading one deferred compensation for another, and the discount repurchase of debts." Reported by Al-Daraqutni in his *Sunan*, as well as in the *Musnad*s of Ibn Abi Shaybah, Ishaq ibn Rahawih, and Al-Bazzar on the authority of Ibn 'Umar. The language translated here is that reported by Al-Bazzar.

13 AAOIFI (2000, pp. 388–9).

14 For conditions of *istisna'* in classical and contemporary jurisprudence, see Al-Zuhayli (2003, vol. 1, ch. 7, pp. 267–80).

15 AAOIFI (2000, p.193).

16 Classical jurists used multiple names for "down-payment sale." Those included "*al-'arabun*" and "*al-'urban*." However, the most common Arabic term, and the one that has dominated discussion in Islamic finance circles, is "*'urbun*," an Arabized term that lexically means "advance payment."

17 See Al-Zuhayli (2003, vol. 1, p. 99).
18 See Al-Zuhayli (2003, vol. 1, pp. 99–100).
19 Reported by 'Abdulrazzaq in his *Musannaf* on the authority of Zayd ibn Aslam.
20 For instance, see the argument in Vogel and Hayes (1998).
21 See www.alahli.com/pb/investing/islamicfunds/securedfunds/iesf.jsp.
22 There was a minimum initial subscription of $25,000, minimum subscription increments were set at $10,000, and investors had to maintain a minimum of $15,000 after the first year. Subscription and redemption dates were fixed annually, and minimum redemption was set at $10,000.
23 Details on the structure were available in October 2002 at www.alrajhibank.com.sa/profitsharingagreement.htm. That link is not currently active.

Chapter 6

1 Usmani (1998, p. 179).
2 The proper Arabic name of the contract is *ijar*. It appears that the popular contemporary variation "*ijara*" was invented to rhyme with other Arabic names of contracts used in Islamic finance, such as *murabaha*, *mudaraba*, and *musharaka*.
3 Al-Zuhayli (2003, vol. 1, pp. 387, 415). In this regard, while Shafi'i jurists strictly applied the rules against sale of nonexistent items in the case of leasing nonfungible properties, non-Shafi'i jurists allowed future leasing (suspended for commencement at a later date) based on the view that the purchase of usufruct is in fact always a gradual process, wherein future usufruct does not exist at time of contract.
4 See Al-Misri (1997). A debate between Dr. Rafiq Al-Misri and Dr. Yusuf Al-Qaradawi centered around the permissibility of this binding promise clause, especially if justified based on concatenation of opinions from different schools (*taqlid*).
5 If the lessor fails to buy the property to be leased starting at a future date, the lease contract is simply voided.
6 The Prophetic tradition forbidding two sales in one was narrated on the authority of Abu Hurayrah in Malik's *Al-Muwatta'*, as well as Al-Tirmidhi, Al-Nasa'i, and Abu Dawud. See discussion of the topic in Al-Zuhayli (2003, vol. 1, pp. 117–19).
7 Usmani (1998, p. 176).
8 See, e.g., the rules of gift in Al-Zuhayli (2003, vol. 1, pp. 539–68).
9 In Islamic jurisprudence, one who recalls his gift is harshly chastised, but generally not forbidden from doing so; see Al-Zuhayli (2003, vol. 1, pp. 539–68).
10 Al-Zuhayli (2003, p. 393).
11 Usmani (1988, pp. 168–71).
12 Usmani (1988, p. 181).
13 Al-Zuhayli (2003, vol. 1, p. 417).
14 See enumeration of references to customary or conventional practice ('*urf*) in this context in Chapter 2, note 19, many of which stipulated that *al-'urfu mu'tabarun fi al-murabaha* and *al-'urfu mu'tabarun fi al-ijara*. In this regard, enforcing nineteenth–century C.E. Damascene conventional practice (codified in Ibn 'Abidin's writings, upon which jurists such as Justice Usmani rely for those conditions) seems to be grossly inappropriate and costly anachronism.
15 For instance, Citigroup and JP Morgan Chase & Co. agreed in 2003 to pay a $300 million settlement on charges related to their involvement in Enron-structured deals that *may* amount to fraud. Of course, proving a fraud charge would have been very difficult, since the district attorney's office would have had to prove intent to commit

fraud. However, the settlement illustrates that the methodology of securitization is easily abused.

16　Usmani (1998, p. 180); this is a continuation of the previous Usmani quotation.

17　One explanation for the increase in price, of course, is the fact that screening rules used to determine if a company is "Shari'a-compliant" commonly allow only investment in companies with sufficiently low debt ratios; this methodology would allow access to a larger set of investors, thus raising prices through increased demand.

18　Information in this section summarized from Al-Zuhayli (2003, vol. 1, pp. 78–82).

19　Narrated by Al-Daraqutni on the authority of Ibn 'Umar and deemed authentic by Al-Hakim. However, as pointed out in the previous chapter, its chain of narration was deemed weak.

20　The classical *hawala* was a contract for transferring existing debts. The term is also used currently by informal money transfer outfits, which assist expatriate Muslim workers in sending money to their families at substantially lower transactions costs than those charged by banks and wire transfer services. Technically, the procedure of money transfer does not constitute a *hawala*, since a debt is created (when the provider of funds forwards them to his local "*hawala*" operator) in order to transfer it to another operator in the destination country. In fact, what is called *hawala* nowadays is much closer to the *suftaja* procedure discussed in the section on currency exchange (*sarf*).

21　Narrated by Ahmad and the four authors of *Sunan*.

22　Usmani (1998, p. 147).

23　Usmani (1998, p. 218).

24　Powerpoint presentation, "Development and the Future of the Sukuk Market," presented December 8, 2003, at the World Islamic Banking Conference, available at www.megaevents.net/wibc/2003/Presentations/.

25　Qatar Global *Sukuk* offering circular dated October 2003, available at lfxsys.lfx.com.my.

26　Document issued September 10, 2003, p. 1, available at "Qatar Global Sukuk QSC–Trust Certificates Due 2010," www2.standardandpoors.com.

27　Ibid., p.2.

28　Ibid., cover page.

29　Conditions of the *hiba* (gift) and *ji'ala* (reward pledge) contracts are covered in Al-Zuhayli (2003, vol. 1, pp. 535–71 and pp. 437–43, respectively). We provide a brief summary of those conditions in this section.

30　Narrated by Al-Nasa'i and Ibn Majah on the authority of Ibn 'Umar. It is also supported by a number of other traditions. See Al-Zuhayli (2003, vol. 1, p. 543, footnote 7).

31　This Prophetic tradition was reported in various forms by Ibn Majah, Al-Daraqutni, Al-Tabarani, Al-Hakim, Al-Bayhaqi, and Ibn Hazm, on the authorities of Abu Hurayrah and Iibn 'Umar. The version on the authority of Ibn 'Umar was deemed valid by the last three listed compilers.

32　According to news story at www.thebanker.com/news. On the other hand, Kuwait Finance House appears to have chosen to underwrite a significant portion of the issuance to ensure its full subscription. In fact, retail markets for Islamic *sukuk*, more generally, remain highly underdeveloped.

33　Usmani (1998, p. 180).

34　Structure illustration taken from speaker slides distributed on CD-ROM by IIFF organizer: IIR. Of course, the price must equal principal plus return, not return as shown in the slide on the CD-ROM. The text in the "agency" box was thus edited to state that the government "guarantees return." The "AGENCY" aspect is highlighted through letter capitalization on the original slide, to avoid prohibition under rules of *'ina* (the government cannot itself be the buyer).

Chapter 7

1 Jurists provide proof of the legality of partnership from the Qur'anic rules of inheritance (e.g., "if more than two [children], then they share in a third [of the estate]" [4:12]), as well as the story of David's ruling on the matter of two sheep-herding brothers: "Truly many partners [in business] betray each other" [38:24]. Moreover, numerous Prophetic pronouncements legalized partnerships, including one that is attributed to God (so-called Hadith Qudsiy): "I am the third of every two partners as long as neither one betrays the other. If one of them betrays the other, I leave that partnership" (narrated by Abu Dawud and Al-Hakim, and deemed valid).

2 See Al-Zuhayli (2003, vol. 1, pp. 448–63).

3 *Sharika* meaning partnership, and *'inan* meaning horse reins, which according to Al-Subki alluded to each partner's control of the other's interest in a manner similar to holding the reins of a horse.

4 For instance, see Greif (2005) and Kuran (2003, 2004b) and references therein.

5 Juristic details in this section are based on Al-Zuhayli (2003, vol. 1, pp. 485–533).

6 Al-Zuhayli (2003, vol. 1, p. 492).

7 AAOIFI (2000, p. 188).

8 For those, and numerous similar *fatawa*, see fatawa.al-islam.com, under the *ijara* tab, and the topic "utilization of leased properties" (in Arabic).

9 One can accumulate degrees of separation in this context as we have done previously in the discussion of direct loans, same-item sale-repurchase, adding a third-party intermediary in same-item sale-repurchase, adding two intermediaries, etc. Serving alcoholic beverages is not permitted, whereas some jurists (e.g., according to one reported opinion of Ahmad ibn Hanbal) allowed transportation of alcohol from one non-Muslim to another, more jurists would allow leasing vehicles that are used for transportation, more still will allow leasing facilities that house such vehicles, etc. In other words, prohibitions that can be avoided in form are easily circumvented by adding sufficient degrees of separation to meet the standards of relevant jurists for any given market segment.

10 Listed at djindexes.com/jsp/imiMethod.jsp.

11 For instance, an alloy of 51 percent gold and 49 percent nickel is still considered gold and, if traded for pure gold, must be traded in equal weight, in accordance with the rules of *sarf* discussed in Chapter 4.

12 Earlier screens excluded companies with interest income exceeding 5 percent or 10 percent of total income, but they seem to have been abandoned in recent years.

13 Y. DeLorenzo "Breakthroughs in Risk Management for Islamic Finance," published in the Islamic finance section of www.zawya.com on October 28, 2004.

14 I am grateful to Rushdi Siddiqui and Vasana Wijentunge of Dow Jones for providing me data from an SEC filing at the end of 2001, which are used in this section.

15 Moreover, the cleansed amount does not count toward the required *zakah*. Obligatory charity, usually computed on stocks as 2.5 percent of market value, although other opinions dictate variously computing it as 10 percent of capital gains and dividends collected, or as 2.5 percent of capital gains and dividends that have been held for a year; cf. Al-Qaradawi (1999). Although the money is unlawful for the Muslim investor, it is in fact deemed by classical and contemporary jurists to be lawful to the recipient in charity. This ruling is based on the general principle codified in the

Hanafi *Majalla*, Article 98, as "change in the cause/means of acquiring a property is legally equivalent to change in the nature of the property itself."

Chapter 8

1 See the survey of Haneef (1995) for summaries of the early Islamic economics writers' views and contributions to the field.
2 Chapra (1996, pp. 53–4).
3 M. N. Siddiqi in Ahmad and Awan (1992, p. 69).
4 Nasr (1991, p. 388).
5 Hence Sadr identified Islamic banking as "no-*riba*" (*la-ribawi*) bank. Interestingly, contemporary financial providers have adopted names such as Lariba and Noriba, playing on that particular characterization of conventional banks as dealers in the forbidden *riba*.
6 See, e.g., Siddiqi (2004).
7 The first reference to suggest this structure is widely referenced as Uzair (1955).
8 This concept of sequential silent partnership, wherein the agent (*mudarib*) in one *mudaraba* acts as the principal in another, was generally approved under the notion of *al-mudarib yudarib*; cf. AAOIFI (2000).
9 Much of Udovitch's analysis is based on his study of the compendium of Hanafi jurisprudence *Al-Mabsut* by Al-Sarakhsi, which listed numerous legal stratagems or ruses that are not dislike those utilized today in Islamic finance to replicate conventional financial practices.
10 Most commonly understood within Jewish Law as a prohibition of charging interest on loans to fellow Jews; cf. Stern (1982). See also Reisman (1995), wherein variations on most of the contemporary practices in Islamic finance were reported as potential solutions to avoid the Biblical and Rabbinic laws of *ribbis*.
11 Tantawi (2001, p. 131).
12 Respectively, Tantawi (2001, pp. 94–104, 165–204, and 204–11).
13 Quoted by Tantawi (2001, p. 95), attributed to Khallaf, who in turn attributed the quote to Muhammad 'Abduh's article in *Al-Manar* (#9, 1906, p. 332). Similar arguments were made by Rashid Rida, Al-Dawalibi, and Al-Sanhuri, in various forms. Their arguments were based, respectively, on restricting the strict Qur'anic prohibition to post hoc charging of interest, charging interest on consumption (as opposed to production) loans, and charging compound interest. The current opinion of Tantawi is quite different, in that it takes the issue away from one of interest-bearing loans to one of investment with prespecified profits.
14 Quoted by Tantawi (2001, p. 95–6), and attributed to Khallaf, *Liwa' Al-Islam* (1951, #4[11]). On the Web site www.islamonline.net, Yusuf Al-Qaradawi cited Prophetic traditions on the authority of Rafi' ibn Khadij that report a Prophetic prohibition of preassignment of part of leased land's produce for the owner, as a form of rent. Al-Qaradawi argued by analogy that silent partnership profits should not be fixed as a percentage of the capital.

I requested a meeting at Al-Azhar in January 2003, in the Saleh Kamel Center for Islamic Economics, at which the Center Director Dr. Muhammad Abdul-Halim 'Umar was present, as well as Dr. Mabid Al-Jarhi (then director of IRTI at the Islamic Development Bank), Dr. Muhammad 'Umar Al-Zubair, and two faculty from Al-Azhar: Dr. 'Abdullah Al-Najjar, who had helped to draft the Azhar IRI *fatwa* text, and Dr. M. Ra'fat 'Uthman, who had dissented from the issued IRI opinion.

The tradition narrated on the authority of Rafi' ibn Khadij was reported by Al-Bukhari: "We used to lease land with produce of one part of the land earmarked for the landlord. Sometimes, one part of the land would yield produce, and the other would not. Thus, the Prophet forbade us from doing so. We never leased land for gold or silver at that time." Other narrations of the tradition report prohibition of any geographical, temporal, or quantitative specification of the return for either party engaged in sharecropping. Classical jurists inferred from that tradition that no party in any form of partnership should have a predetermined rate of return, thus generalizing from sharecropping (*muzara'a*) to silent partnership (*mudaraba*). Ibn Qudama thus reported in *Al-Mughni* that jurists whose opinions counted had reached a consensus on the prohibition of predetermination of profits for either party of a *mudaraba* silent partnership – in part since the total profits may be smaller than the profits promised to one party, which would thus violate the nature of the contract.

Dr. 'Abdullah Al-Najjar wrote a lengthy discussion of the Prophetic traditions on the authority of Rafi' ibn Khadij, arguing – based on the narration and analysis by Al-Shawkani in *Nayl Al-Awtar* – that the classical prohibition of prespecification of profits in *mudaraba* was not based on that canonical tradition, but rather on the resulting *gharar* that may lead to disputation. On the other hand, he argued, Ibn Qudama and other jurists are in agreement that regular sharecropping and silent partnerships (with prespecified profit shares, and unspecified profit amounts) also include substantial *gharar*, since they may be viewed as hiring contracts (*ijara*) with uncertain wages. (Note that Ibn Qayyim had rejected the characterization of silent partnerships as *ijara bi-l-gharar* [hiring with uncertain wages], arguing instead that *mudaraba* should be studied as a separate contract.) Thus, Dr. Al-Najjar argued, sharecropping, silent partnership, and similar contracts belong to the class in which *gharar* is tolerated, provided that it does not lead to legal disputation and animosity. In addition, he argued based on Al-Shawkani's and Ibn Qudama's analyses of the tradition on the authority of Rafi' that the opinion in fact may have been his own, rather than the Prophet's, and thus would not be binding. He also reported that Zayd ibn Thabit disputed the relevance of the tradition of Rafi', arguing that – at most – it was restricted to a specific incident that led to physical violence (as narrated by Abu Dawud). He also reported that Ibn 'Umar rejected the tradition of *Rafi'*, arguing that leasing land for fixed rent was allowed, as did Ibn 'Abbas and others, who generally discarded most of the traditions reported by Rafi', which disagreed with consensus of the early Madina community.

Dr. 'Uthman replied with appeals to the analysis of Al-Nawawi, which stipulated that the tradition was rejected in terms of its application to leasing land for fixed rent. However, he argued, its import was still recognized for the prohibition of fixing profits in *mudaraba*. In this regard, he argued that restriction of the general import of the tradition would constitute an invalid restriction without language that justifies specification of its general language (*takhsis bi-ghayri mukhassis*).

15 Quoted by Tantawi (2001, pp. 95–6), and attributed to Khallaf, *Liwa' Al-Islam* (1951, #4[12]). Dr. Tantawi thus appears to have avoided addressing the debates regarding Rafi''s tradition. Instead, he concentrated on what happens if the *mudaraba* with fixed profits is indeed deemed defective. In that case, he argued based on the analyses of Ibn Al-Humam in *Fath Al-Qadir* and Al-Shafi'i in *Al-Umm* that a defective *mudaraba* is converted into a hiring contract (*ijara*), wherein the entrepreneur is viewed as a worker who should be compensated based on prevailing market wages. Tantawi (2001, p. 133) concluded: "Thus, we say that the bank investing money for a prespecified profit becomes a hired worker for the investors, who thus accept the amount the bank gives them as their profits, and any excess profits (whatever they may be) are deemed the bank's wages. Therefore, this dealing is

devoid of *riba*. In summary: We do not find any canonical text, or convincing analogy, that forbids prespecification of profits, as long as there is mutual consent."

16 A summary of the rebuttal arguments is provided by Dr. Khurshid Ahmad, available at www.eldis.org/fulltext/riba.pdf.

17 Since the deposit contract is one of trust rather than guaranty, the depositary guarantees funds only against its own negligence and transgression, not unconditionally.

18 Tantawi (2001) also explicitly rejected this characterization, declaring that, indeed, interest on loans would be forbidden *riba*, but that there are no valid grounds to convert the deposit contract into the classical loan (*qard*) contract, even if regulators treat it as a debt contract.

19 The text of the tradition is *al-kharaju bi-l-daman*, narrated by Ahmad and the authors of *Sunan*, with a valid chain of narration.

20 *Qararat wa Tawwiyat Al-Dawrah Al-Rabiʿat ʿAshr li-Majlis Al-Fiqh Al- Islami* (Decisions and Conclusions of the Fourteenth Session of the Islamic Jurisprudence Council), Decision #133 (7/14), pp. 20–4.

21 See moamlat.al-islam.com (in Arabic, search for *"al-taʾmin"*).

22 Al-Zarqa (1994, p. 8).

23 Al-Zarqa (1994, p. 9)

24 Al-Misri (2001, p. 6).

25 The Fiqh Academy of the Islamic League rejected those analogies. They argued that the analogy on *mudaraba* is invalid, since the principal retains ownership of the capital in *mudaraba*, while the insured party does not retain ownership of paid premiums. This argument would not apply to mutual insurance, wherein shareholders are stockholders. They also objected to the analogy due to differences in inheritance and profit distribution rules. Moreover, they categorically rejected the argument based on social conventions (*ʿurf*), declaring that it is not a recognized source of legislation – which illustrates their strict adherence to the letter of Islamic legal theory, rather than the actual practice of jurisprudence, as advocated by progressive jurists. Finally, they rejected appeals to benefit analysis, by arguing that benefits are negated by the prohibition – and hence implied harm – caused by ignorance, *gharar*, and *riba*.

26 The Fiqh Academies that found insurance forbidden argued that the assessment of *gharar* or lack thereof must be made at the level of individual contracts, rather than collectively by invoking the law of large numbers.

27 *Fatawa of the Shariʿa Supervisory Board of Faisal Islamic Bank Egypt*, (in Arabic); fatwa # 36.

28 *Sharʿi Fatwas in Economic Matters*, vols. 1–3, (in Arabic); Kuwait Finance House, *fatwa* #317.

29 See Al-Zuhayli (2003, vol. 2, p. 42) and references therein to Dr. ʿAli Al-Khafifʾs book on contemporary applications of guaranty/*kafalah*.

30 See, e.g., *fatwa* 13/1 in Abu Ghuddah and Khujah (1997a, p. 219), and *fatwa* 11/3 in Abu Ghuddah and Khujah (1997b, p. 167).

Chapter 9

1 The bulk of AAOIFI's work has aimed to translate reporting standards of Islamic banks to their conventional on-balance-sheet counterparts, according to generally accepted accounting standards. In some countries, e.g., Turkey, the central bank merely expects Islamic banks operating under the name "Special Finance Houses" to use the same reporting standards as conventional banks. This reduces the difficulty of comparing the performance of Islamic and conventional banks to a minimum, as

shown in El-Gamal and Inanoglu (2004, 2005). Those studies suggested that Islamic banking as practiced in Turkey was not less efficient than its conventional counterpart. In fact, once the accounting entries are converted into conventional terminology (of loans, etc.), the banking technology of Islamic banks was found to be virtually identical to the technologies of other private banks in the country. This is consistent with earlier comparative studies of Islamic and conventional banking in Turkey and elsewhere, e.g., Aggarwal and Yousef (2000), Agagolu (1994), Al-Deehani, Abdelkarim, and Murinde (1999), Iqbal (2001), Samad (1999), and Bashir (1999).

2 See, e.g., Warde (2000, p. 73) and references therein.

3 See, e.g., Saeed (1999, pp. 119–28) and references therein.

4 In the *Daily Star* (Monday, August 15, 2005), Osama Habib reported that Sheikh Kamel does not fancy the word customer or depositor and prefers to use the term "partner." "Those people who place their money in Al-Baraka bank or any other Islamic bank are considered shareholders of these banks. This means if these banks prosper so will they."

5 See, e.g., Siddiqi (2004, p. 107) and the references therein.

6 Of course, informal variations on credit unions have been known in various rural societies under different names; cf. MacPherson (1999). However, mutual corporate structures and corresponding regulatory and legal structures were developed first in Europe, and then in North America, before spreading to the developing world.

7 As we have argued in Chapter 3, this asset-based grounding of financial transactions can reduce risk by providing security, as well as a means of marking prices of credit and risk to market. Of course, as we have seen in later chapters, Islamic finance has – unfortunately – squandered those built-in risk-reduction mechanisms by adhering only to the forms of premodern jurisprudence, while squandering its substantive restrictions.

8 See, e.g., Townsend (1979), Hart and Moore (1994). Similar analysis for Islamic finance was conducted by Humayun Dar and John Preseley (2000), who suggested that equity financing is optimal only for sufficiently small-scale operations, wherein the cost of monitoring is minimal.

9 Even within its natural environment, this pure equity structure has given rise to numerous conflict-of-interest problems in the United States, leading historically to the enactment of the Glass-Steagall Act separating banking and securities dealings, and more recently the Sarbanes-Oxley Act of 2002 addressing more complicated conflicts of interest. See, e.g., Puri (1996) and Micaela and Womack (1999).

10 AAOIFI (2004a, p. 215).

11 AAOIFI (2004b, p. 241).

12 AAOIFI (2004a, p. 215).

13 This literature arose as a response to the realization that managers may pursue their own interests, rather than those of shareholders, following the publication of Berle and Means (1932). For major advances in this field, see Schleifer and Vishny (1997).

14 See Allen and Gale (2000, pp. 95–110) and references therein.

15 Fama (1980), Fama and Jensen (1983a, b).

16 See O'Hara (1981).

17 See Rasmusen (1988).

18 See, e.g., Altunbas, Evans, and Molyneux (2001).

19 See Hansmann (1996).

20 Of course, Western legal and regulatory systems have built-in provisions against predatory lending, especially to minority groups. However, there are difficulties in quantifying the appropriate interest rate to charge debtors with very high levels of credit risk; cf. Hibbard (2005), see also Hagerty and Hallinan (2005). In contrast, the

very reason for existence of mutually owned credit unions is to shun the profit motive in credit extension, and thus extend credit to members at the lowest possible rates; cf. MacPherson (1999).

21 See Born et al. (1998).

22 See Lamm-Tennant and Starks (1993), Gardner and Grace (1993, 1994), Cummins, Weiss, and Zi (1999), and Swiss Re (1999).

23 See, e.g., Mayers and Smith (1977) and Smith and Stutzer (1995).

Chapter 10

1 Opening speech by the governor of the Bahrain Monetary Agency, as reported in *Monday Morning*, February 25, 2004; cf. www.zawya.com/story.cfm?id=ZAWYA20040225134523.

2 For more details of this argument, see my testimony on Islamic financial methods before the U.S. Senate Committee on Banking, Housing and Urban Affairs' hearing on "Money Laundering and Terrorist Financing Issues in the Middle East," available at banking.senate.gov/_files/gamal.pdf.

3 Mr. Nizam Yaqubi, a member of their Shari'a board, described the Islamic Bank of Britain savings account structure thus at the International Islamic Finance Forum, held in Istanbul, Turkey, October 2004, at a session wherein the author also spoke. The U.S. *fatwa* is available at www.shapefinancial.com/ipif/SHAPE_Deposit_2.pdf.

4 Needless to say, the second provision can lead to litigation if the regulatory framework were in fact to change. In this regard, the two English court precedents of the Symphony Gems and Beximco cases – wherein the court ignored provisions regarding Shari'a as insufficiently specific and thus unenforceable – suggest that the provisions may be of little more than psychological benefit.

5 For a model that explains the advantages of this market segmentation, and its effect on the number of jurists likely to participate in the industry, see El-Gamal (2002).

6 United Nations (2004).

7 United Nations (2004, p. i).

8 United Nations (2004, p. 9).

9 Bashir (2004).

10 See www.grameen-info.org. Extensive economic literature on microfinancing has shown that repayment rates on microloans are incredibly high, especially when supported by group-lending technologies such as those pioneered and popularized by Grameen. This makes such lending profitable, especially given new securitization technologies that have allowed microfunds to emerge, again pioneered in Bangladesh through Grameen Foundation USA's first bond issuance of $40 million to support microfinance institutions in nine developing countries. See William Baue, "First and Largest International Microfinance Bond Issued," at www.socialfunds.com/news/article.cgi/article1498.html.

11 Cash *awqaf* were generally accepted under the Ottoman interpretation of Hanafi jurisprudence and allowed by Ebussoud Efendi, Grand Mufti of the Ottoman empire, to give interest-bearing loans.

Bibliography

AAOIFI. (2000). *Ma'ayir Al-Muhasabah w Al-Muraja'a w Al-Dawabit lil-Mu'assasat Al-Maliyyah Al-Islamiyya* (AAOIFI, Bahrain).

AAOIFI. (2004a). *Accounting, Auditing and Governance Standards for Islamic Financial Institutions 2003–4* (AAOIFI, Manama).

AAOIFI. (2004b). *Shari'a Standards* (AAOIFI, Manama).

Abu Ghuddah, A., and E. Khuja (eds.) (1997a). *Fatawa Nadawat Al-Baraka 1981–1997* (Majmu'at Dallah Al-Baraka, fifth printing, Jeddah).

Abu Ghuddah, A., and E. Khuja (eds.) (1997b). *Fatawa Al-Hay'a Al-Shar'iyya lil-Baraka* (Majmu'at Dallah Al-Baraka, Jeddah).

Abu Zahra, M. (1996). *Al-Milkiyyah wa Nazariyyat Al-'Aqd* (Dar Al-Fikr Al-'Arabi, Cairo).

Agaoglu, E. (1994). "A CAMEL-wise Comparative Financial and Market Share Analysis of the Islamic Banks Currently Operating in Turkey," *Middle East Technical University Studies in Development*, 21(4).

Aggarwal, R., and T. Yousef. (2000). "Islamic Banks and Investment Financing," *Journal of Money, Credit and Banking*, 32(1).

Ahmad, A., and A. Abu Ghuddah (1998). *Fatawa Al-Khadamat Al-Masrifiyya* (Al-Baraka Investment and Development Company, Jeddah).

Ahmad, A. and K. R. Awan (eds.) (1992). *Lectures on Islamic Economics* (Islamic Development Bank, Jeddah).

Al-Baji Al-Andalusi. (n.d.). *Al-Muntaqa Sharh Al-Muwatta'* (Dar Al-Kutub Al-Islamiyyah, Beirut).

Al-Darir, M. S. (1997). *Al-Gharar in Contracts and Its Effects on Contemporary Transactions*, IDB Eminent Scholars' Lecture Series, no. 16 (IDB/IRTI, Jeddah).

Al-Deehani T., R. A. Abdelkarim, and V. Murinde. (1999). "The Capital Structure of Islamic Banks under the Contractual Obligation of Profit Sharing," *International Journal of Theoretical and Applied Finance*, 2(3).

Al-Jaziri, A. (1986). *Al-Fiqh 'ala Al-Madhahib Al-Arba'a* (Dar Ihya' Al-Turath Al-'Arabi, Cairo).

Allen, F., and D. Gale. (2000). *Comparing Financial Systems* (MIT Press, Cambridge, MA).

Al-Misri, R. Y. (1997). *Bay' Al-Taqsit: Ta'lil Fiqhi wa Iqtisadi* (Dar Al-Qalam, Damascus).

Al-Misri, R. Y. (2001). *Al-Khatar wa Al-Ta'min: Hal Al-Ta'min Al-Tijari Ja'iz Shar'an?* (Dar Al-Qalam, Damascus).

Al-Misri, R. Y. (2004). "Hal Al-Fa'idah Haram bi-Jami' Ashkaliha?" *Majallat Jami'at Al-Malik 'Abdulaziz lil-Iqtisad Al-Islami*, 17(1).

Al-Qaradawi, Y. (1996). *Al-Ijtihad fi Al-Shari'a Al-Islamiyyah, ma'a Nazarat Tahliliyyah fi Al-Ijtihad Al-Mu'asir* (Dar Al-Qalam, Kuwait).

Al-Qaradawi, Y. (1999). *Fiqh Al-Zakah: A Comparative Study of the Philosophy and Rulings of Zakah according to the Quran and Sunna* (International Institute of Islamic Thought, Herndon, VA).

Al-Qarafi, A. (n.d.) *Al-Furuq* ('Alam Al-Kutub, Beirut).

Al-Qurtubi, M. (1996). *Al-Jami' li-Ahkam Al-Qur'an* (Dar Al-Kutub Al-'Ilmiyyah, Beirut).

Al-Raysuni, A. (1997). *Nazariyyat Al-Maqasid 'inda Al-Imam Al-Shatibi* (Dar Al-Kalimah, Mansoura, Egypt).

Al-Shafi'i, M. (1939). *Al-Risala* (Al-Maktabah Al-'Ilmiyyah, Beirut).

Al-Subki, T. (continuation of Al-Nawawi, A.) (n.d.). *Al-Majmu' Sharh Al-Muhadhdhab* (Matba'at Al-Imam, Egypt).

Altunbas, Y., L. Evans, and P. Molyneux. (2001). "Bank Ownership and Efficiency," *Journal of Money, Credit and Banking*, 33(4).

Al-Zarqa, M. (1994). *Nizam Al-Ta'min: Haqiqatuh, wa Al-Ra'y Al-Shar'i fih* (Mu'assasat Al-Risalah, Beirut).

Al-Zarqa, M. (1998). *Al-Madkhal Al-Fiqhi Al-'Am* (Dar Al-Qalam, Damascus).

Al-Zuhayli, W. (1997). *Al-Fiqh Al-Islami wa Adillatuh* (Dar Al-Fikr, Damascus).

Al-Zuhayli, W. (M. El-Gamal, translator) (2003). *Financial Transactions in Islamic Jurisprudence* (vols. 1 and 2) (Dar Al-Fikr, Damascus).

Arabi, O. (2001). *Studies in Modern Islamic Law and Jurisprudence* (Kluwer Law International, The Hague).

'Atiyyah, J. (1986). *Al-Bunuk Al-Islamiyya Bayna Al-Hurriyya wa Al-Tanzim, Al-Taqlid wa Al-Ijtihad, Al- Nazariyya wa Al-Tatbiq* (Ri'asat Al-Mahakim Al-Shar'iyya wa Al-Shu'un Al-Diniyya bi-Dawlat Qatar, Duha).

Ba'albaki, R., and M. Ba'albaki. (1998). *Al-Mawrid* (Dar Al-'Ilm lil-Malayin, Beirut).

Bashir, A. (1999). "Risk and Profitability Measures in Islamic Banks: The Case of Two Sudanese Banks," *Islamic Economic Studies*, 6(2).

Bashir, A. (2004). "Development Reports Paint Poor Picture of Muslim Socio-economic Status," *Arab News*, November 25.

Berle, A. and G. Means. (1932). *The Modern Corporation and Private Property* (Commerce Clearing House, New York).

Born, P., W. Gentry, W. Viscusi, and R. Zeckhauser. (1998). "Organizational Form and Insurance Company Performance: Stocks vs. Mutuals," in D. Bradford (ed.), *The Economics of Property-Casualty Insurance* (University of Chicago Press, Chicago).

Bosworth, C., E. van Donzel, W. Heinrichs, and G. Lecomte. (1997). *Encyclopedia of Islam IX: SAN-SZE* (E. J. Brill, Leiden).

Boyd, J., C. Chang, and B. Smith. (1998). "Moral Hazard under Commercial and Universal Banking," *Journal of Money, Credit and Banking*, 30(3).

Calder, N. (1980). *The Structure of Authority in Imami Shi'i Jurisprudence* (Ph.D. dissertation, School of Oriental and African Studies, University of London).

Camerer, C. (1998). "Prospect Theory in the Wild: Evidence from the Field" (Caltech SSWP #1037, Pasadena, CA).

Chapra, U. (1996). "What Is Islamic Economics," IDB Prize Winner's Lecture Series, No. 9 (Islamic Development Bank, Jeddah).

Cooter, R., and T. Ulen. (2004). *Law and Economics*, 4th Edition (Pearson Addison Wesley, Boston).

Coulson, N. (1994). *A History of Islamic Law* (Edinburgh University Press, Edinburgh).

Cummins, D., M. Weiss, and H. Zi. (1999). "Organizational Form and Efficiency: The Coexistence of Stock and Mutual Property-Liability Insurers," *Management Science*, 45(9).

Dar, H., and J. Preseley. (2000). "Lack of Profit and Loss Sharing in Islamic Banking: Management and Control Imbalances," *International Journal of Islamic Financial Services*, 2(2).

De Roover, R. (1999). *Rise and Decline of the Medici Bank, 1397–1494* (Beard Books, New York).

El-Gamal, M. (1999). "Involving Islamic Banks in Central Bank Open Market Operations," *Thunderbird International Business Review*, 41(4, 5).

El-Gamal, M. (2000). "An Economic Explication of the Prohibition of *Riba* in Classical Islamic Jurisprudence," in *Proceedings of the Third Harvard University Forum on Islamic Finance* (Center for Middle Eastern Studies, Harvard University, Cambridge, MA).

El-Gamal, M. (2001). "An Economic Explication of the Prohibition of *Gharar* in Classical Islamic Jurisprudence," *Islamic Economic Studies*, 8(2).

El-Gamal, M. (2002). "The Economics of 21st Century Islamic Financial Jurisprudence," in *Proceedings of the Fourth Harvard University Forum on Islamic Finance* (Center for Middle Eastern Studies, Harvard University, Cambridge, MA).

El-Gamal, M. (2003). "*Interest* and the Paradox of Contemporary Islamic Law and Finance," *Fordham International Law Journal*, 27(1).

El-Gamal, M. (2005). "Limits and Dangers of Shari'a Arbitrage," in S. Ali (ed.), *Islamic Finance: Current Legal and Regulatory Issues* (Islamic Finance Project, Harvard Law School, Cambridge, MA).

El-Gamal, M., and H. Inanoglu. (2004). "Islamic Banking in Turkey: Boon or Bane for the Financial Sector," in *Proceedings of the Fifth Harvard University Forum on Islamic Finance* (Center for Middle Eastern Studies, Harvard University, Cambridge, MA).

El-Gamal, M., and H. Inanoglu. (2005). "Inefficiency and Heterogeneity in Turkish Banking: 1990–2000," *Journal of Applied Econometrics*, 20(5).

Fama, E. (1980). "Agency Problems and the Theory of the Firm," *Journal of Political Economy*, 88(2).

Fama, E., and M. Jensen. (1983a). "Agency Problems and Residual Claims," *Journal of Law and Economics*, 26(2).

Fama, E., and M. Jensen. (1983b). "Separation of Ownership and Control," *Journal of Law and Economics*, 26(2).

Fox, C., B. Rogers, and A. Tversky. (1996). "Options Traders Exhibit Subadditive Decision Weights," *Journal of Risk and Uncertainty*, 13(1).

Gardner, L., and M. Grace. (1993). "X-Efficiency in the U.S. Life Insurance Industry," *Journal of Banking and Finance*, 17(2–3).

Gardner, L. and M. Grace. (1994). "Efficiency Comparisons between Mutual and Stock Life Insurance Companies" (working paper, University of Nevada, Las Vegas).

Glaeser, E., and J. Scheinkman. (1998). "Neither a Borrower nor a Lender Be: An Economic Analysis of Interest Restrictions and Usury Laws," *Journal of Law and Economics*, 41(1).

Goitien, S. (1960). "The Birth-Hour of Muslim Law," *Muslim World*, 50(1).

Greif, A. (2005). *Institutions and the Path to the Modern Economy: Lessons from Medieval Trade* (Cambridge University Press, Cambridge).

Gron, A., and D. Lucas. (1997). "External Financing and Insurance Cycles," *NBER Conference Volume on Property Casualty Insurance* (NBER, Cambridge, MA).

Hagerty, J., and J. Hallinan. (2005). "Blacks Are Much More Likely to Get Subprime Mortgages: Weaker Lender Competition in Some Low-Income Areas Is Cited as Part of the Problem," *Wall Street Journal*, April 11, p. A2.

Hallaq, W. (1984). "Was the Gate of Ijtihad Closed?" *International Journal of Middle East Studies*, 16(1).

Hallaq, W. (1993). "Was Al-Shafi'i the Master Architect of Islamic Jurisprudence?" *International Journal of Middle East Studies*, 25(4).

Hallaq, W. (1997). *A History of Islamic Legal Theories* (Cambridge University Press, Cambridge).

Hallaq, W. (2001). *Authority, Continuity and Change in Islamic Law* (Cambridge University Press, Cambridge).

Haneef, M. (1995). *Contemporary Islamic Economic Thought: A Selected Comparative Analysis* (Ikraq, Kuala Lumpur).

Hansmann, H. (1996). *Ownership of Enterprise* (Harvard University Press, Cambridge, MA).

Hart, O., and J. Moore. (1994). "A Theory of Debt Based on the Inalienability of Human Capital," *Quarterly Journal of Economics*, 109(4).

Hassan, M. K., and D. Alamgir. (2002). "Microfinancial Services and Poverty Alleviation in Bangladesh: A Comparative Analysis of Secular and Islamic NGOs," in M. Iqbal (ed.), *Islamic Economic Institutions and the Elimination of Poverty* (The Islamic Foundation, Leicester).

Hegazy, W. (2005). "*Fatwas* and the Fate of Islamic Finance: A Critique of the Practice of *Fatawa* in Contemporary Islamic Financial Markets," in S. Ali (ed.), *Islamic Finance: Current Legal and Regulatory Issues* (Islamic Finance Project, Harvard Law School, Cambridge, MA).

Hibbard, J. (2005). "The Fed Eyes Sub-prime Loans: New Disclosure Rules Aim to Flush Out Discriminatory Rates," *Business Week*, cover story, April 11.

Hodgman, D. (1961). "The Deposit Relationship and Commercial Bank Investment Behavior," *Review of Economics and Statistics*, 43(3).

Humud, S. (1976). *Tatwir Al-A'mal Al-Masrifiyya bima Yattafiqu wa Al-Shari'ah Al-Islamiyya* (Dar Al-Ittihad Al-'Arabi lil-Tiba'a, Cairo).

Ibn Manzur, J. (1992). *Lisan Al-'Arab* (Dar Sadr, Beirut).

Ibn Qayyim Al-Jawziyya, M. (n.d.) *I'lam Al-Muwaqqi'in 'an Rabb il-'Alamin* (Dar Al-Kutub Al-'Ilmiyyah, Beirut).

Ibn Rushd, M. (1997). *Bidayat Al-Mujtahid wa Nihayat Al-Muqtasid* (Dar Al-Ma'rifah, Beirut).

Ibn Taymiyya, A. (1998). *Al-Fatawa Al-Kubra* (Dar Al-Ma'rifa, Beirut).

Ibn Taymiyya, A. (2005). *Al-'Ubudiyya* (Al-Maktab Al-Islami lil-Tiba'ah w Al-Nashr, Damascus).

Iqbal, M. (2001). "Islamic and Conventional Banking in the Nineties: A Comparative Study," *Islamic Economic Studies*, 8(2).

Johnston, E., and J. McConnell. (1989). "Requiem for a Market: The Rise and Fall of a Financial Market Contract," *Review of Financial Studies*, 2(1).

Jolls, C., C. Sunstein, and R. Thaler. (2000). "A Behavioral Approach to Law and Economics," in C. Sunstein (ed.), *Behavioral Law and Economics* (Cambridge University Press, Cambridge).

Kahneman, D. and A. Tversky. (1979). "Prospect Theory: An Analysis of Decision under Risk," *Econometrica*, 47(2).

Kamali, M. H. (2000). *Islamic Commercial Law: An Analysis of Futures and Options* (Islamic Texts Society, Cambridge).

Kerridge, E. (2002). *Usury, Interest and the Reformation* (Ashgate, Hants, U.K.)

Khallaf, A. (1972). *Masadir Al-Tashri' Al-Islami fima la Nassa Fih* (Dar Al-Qalam, Kuwait).

Kuran, T. (2003). "The Islamic Commercial Crisis: Institutional Roots of Economic Underdevelopment in the Middle East," *Journal of Economic History*, 63(2).

Kuran, T. (2004a). *Islam and Mammon* (Princeton University Press, Princeton, NJ).

Kuran, T. (2004b). "Why the Middle East Is Economically Underdeveloped: Historical Mechanisms of Institutional Stagnation," *Journal of Economic Perspectives*, 18(3).

Kuran, T. (2004c). "Why the Islamic Middle East Did Not Generate an Indigenous Corporate Law" (University of Southern California Law and Economics Working Paper Series, Working Paper 16).

Kuwait Awqaf Ministry. (1995, ongoing). *Al-Mawsu'a Al-Fiqhiyya* (Ministry of Awqaf, Kuwait).

Lamm-Tennant, J., and L. Starks. (1993). "Stock versus Mutual Ownership Structures: The Risk Implications," *Journal of Business*, 66(1).

Lewis, B., V. Menage, C. Pellat, and J. Schacht. (1986). *Encyclopedia of Islam III: H-IRAM* (E. J. Brill, Leiden).

Lewis, M., and L. Algaoud. (2001). *Islamic Banking* (Edward Elgar, Cheltenham).

List, J. (2004). "Neoclassical Theory versus Prospect Theory: Evidence from the Marketplace," *Econometrica*, 72(2).

MacPherson, I. (1999). *Hands around the Globe* (World Council of Credit Unions, Madison, WI).

Makdisi. J. (1999). "The Islamic Origins of the Common Law," *North Carolina Law Review*, 77(5).

Masud, M., B. Messick, and D. Powers (eds.). (1996). *Islamic Legal Interpretation: Muftis and Their fatwas* (Harvard University Press, Cambridge, MA).

Mawdudi, A. (1986). "The Prohibition of Interest in Islam," *Al-Islam*, June.

Mayers, D., and C. Smith. (1988). "Ownership Structure across Lines of Property-Casualty Insurance," *Journal of Law and Economics*, 31(2).

Micaela, R., and K. Womack. (1999). "Conflict of Interest and the Credibility of Underwriter Analyst Recommendations," *Review of Financial Studies*, 12(4).

Nasr, S. (1991). "Islamization of Knowledge: A Critical Overview," *Islamic Studies*, 30(3).

O'Hara, M. (1981). "Property Rights and the Financial Firm," *Journal of Law and Economics*, 24(2).

Puri, M. (1996). "Commercial Banks in Investment Banking: Conflict of Interest or Certification Role?" *Journal of Financial Economics*, 40, pp. 373–401.

Posner, R. (1983). *The Economics of Justice* (Harvard University Press, Cambridge, MA).

Posner, R. (1990). *The Problems of Jurisprudence* (Harvard University Press, Cambridge, MA).

Posner, R. (1992). *Economic Analysis of the Law* (Little, Brown and Co., Boston).

Qal'a-Ji, M. (1996). *Mu'jam Lughat Al-Fuqaha'* (Dar Al-Nafa'is, Beirut).

Qutb, S. (n.d.). *Tafsir Ayat Al-Riba* (Dar Al-Buhuth Al-Islamiyya, Cairo).

Rasmusen, E. (1988). "Mutual Banks and Stock Banks," *Journal of Law and Economics*, 31(2).

Reisman, Y. (1995). *The Laws of Ribbis* (Mesorah Publications, New York).

Rida, Rashid. (1986). *Al-Riba wa Al-Mu'amalat fi Al-Islam* (Dar Ibn Zaydun, Beirut, and Maktabat Al-Kulliyat Al-Azhariyyah, Cairo).

Rosen, L. (2000). *The Justice of Islam* (Oxford University Press, Oxford).

Saeed, A. (1999). *Islamic Banking and Interest* (E. J. Brill, Leiden).

Samad, A. (1999). "Comparative Efficiency of the Islamic Bank vis-à-vis Conventional Banks in Malaysia," *IIUM Journal of Economics and Management*, 7(1).

Schleifer, A., and R. Vishny. (1997). "A Survey of Corporate Governance," *Journal of Finance*, 52(2).

Siddiqi, M. N. (1983a). *Banking without Interest* (Islamic Foundation, Leicester).

Siddiqi, M.N. (1983b). *Issues in Islamic Banking: Selected Papers* (Islamic Foundation, Leicester).

Siddiqi, M.N. (2004). *Riba, Bank Interest and the Rationale of Its Prohibition* (Islamic Development Bank [IRTI], Jeddah).

Smith, B., and M. Stutzer. (1990). "Adverse Selection, Aggregate Uncertainty, and the Role of Mutual Insurance Contracts," *Journal of Business*, 63(4).

Smith, B., and M. Stutzer. (1995). "A Theory of Mutual Formation and Moral Hazard with Evidence from the History of the Insurance Industry," *Review of Economic Studies*, 8(2).

Stern, J. (1982). "Ribit: A Halachic Anthology," *Journal of Halacha and Contemporary Society*, 46 (Fall).

Swiss Re. (1999). "Are Mutual Insurers an Endangered Species?" *Sigma*, 4.

Tantawi, M. (2001). *Mu'amalat Al-Bunuk wa Ahkamuha Al-Shar'iyya* (Nahdat Misr, Cairo).

Thomas, A. (1949). "A Note on the Origin of Uses and Trusts – Waqfs," *Southwest Law Journal*, 3.

Townsend, R. (1979). "Optimal Contracts and Competitive Markets with Costly State Verification," *Journal of Economic Theory*, 21(2).

Udovitch, A. (1970). *Partnership and Profit in Medieval Islam* (Princeton University Press, Princeton, NJ).

Udovitch, A. (1981). "Bankers without Banks: Commerce, Banking and Society in the Islamic World of the Middle Ages" (manuscript, Princeton University).

United Nations. (2004). "Who Cares Wins: Connecting Financial Markets to a Changing World," Executive Office of U.N. Secretary General: The Global Compact Project, www.unglobalcompact.org.

Useem, J. (2002). "Banking on Allah," *Fortune*, June 10, 2002.

Usmani, M. T. (1998). *An Introduction to Islamic Finance* (Idaratul Ma'arif, Karachi).

Uzair, M. (1955). *An Outline of Interestless Banking* (Idaratul Ma'arif, Karachi).

Vogel, F., and S. Hayes. (1998). *Islamic Law and Finance: Religion, Risk and Return* (Kluwer Law International, The Hague).

Warde, I. (2000). *Islamic Finance and the Global Economy* (Edinburgh University Press, Edinburgh).

Wood, J. (1970). "Two Notes on the Uniqueness of Commercial Banks," *Journal of Finance*, 25(1).

Woodbine, G. (1968). *Bracton on the Laws and Customs of England* (Harvard University Press, Cambridge, MA).

Index